SKETCHES FROM A YOUNG COUNTRY

The Canadian political and social discussion of the late nineteenth century owed a great deal to *Grip*, the satirical magazine that kept a vigilant eye on national affairs from 1873 to 1894. Illustrated and edited by an energetic, talented young reformer named John W. Bengough, *Grip* featured sketches, poetry, and political invective. Bengough's caricatures of dignitaries and his cartoons of political situations were supplemented in at least two periods by the acerbic commentary of socialist pioneer T. Phillips Thompson. Together, the two men provided a running account and critique of the era's attitudes on class, sex, race, and public policy. Bengough was part of a broad progressive alliance that linked farm and labour agitators with Christian intellectuals alarmed about the worst excesses of turn-of-the-century capitalism. *Grip* was an early, and righteous, crusader for this liberal, Protestant, reformist view.

Sketches from a Young Country is the first comprehensive study to evaluate this historically important magazine, to assess the motivations of its authors, and to set both in social and political context. The author begins by discussing the magazine's visual contribution to its time, then explores its relationship with the federal and Ontario reform parties and its anti-Tory bias. Later chapters examine *Grip*'s response to western development, its descent into 'race and creed' propaganda in the late 1880s, its anti-capitalist and anti-imperialist leanings under Thompson's influence, and its stance on such social issues as women's rights, aboriginal issues, and law and order.

Containing over a hundred of Bengough's cartoons, with captions to clarify contemporary references, and offering an assessment of *Grip* in relation to its British and American counterparts, *Sketches from a Young Country* makes an exciting contribution to popular history, Canadian politics, and the history of journalism.

CARMAN CUMMING is an adjunct professor of journalism at Carleton University and author of *Secret Craft: The Journalism of Edward Farrer*.

MR. BENGOUGH.

"GRIP'S" EDITOR AND CARTOONIST.

CARMAN CUMMING

Sketches from a Young Country: The Images of *Grip* Magazine

UNIVERSITY OF TORONTO PRESS
Toronto Buffalo London

© University of Toronto Press Incorporated 1997
Toronto Buffalo London
Printed in Canada

ISBN 0-8020-0695-7 (cloth)
ISBN 0-8020-7646-7 (paper)

Printed on acid-free paper

Canadian Cataloguing in Publication Data

Cumming, Carman
 Sketches from a young country : the images of Grip magazine

 Includes cartoons by J.W. Bengough published in Grip,
 1873–1894.
 Includes bibliographical references and index.
 ISBN 0-8020-0695-7 (bound)   ISBN 0-8020-7646-7 (pbk.)

 1. Canada – Politics and government – 1867–1896 –
 Caricatures and cartoons.   2. Ontario – Politics and
 government.   3. Grip.   4. Bengough, J.W. (John Wilson),
 1851–1923.   5. Canadian wit and humor, Pictorial –
 History.   6. Canadian wit and humor (English) – History
 and criticism.*   I. Bengough, J.W. (John Wilson), 1851–
 1923.   II. Title.

 FC173.C86 1997   971.05'02'07   C97-930168-8
 F1026.4.C86 1997

Frontispiece: John Wilson Bengough. National Archives of Canada, C100407

University of Toronto Press acknowledges the financial assistance to its publishing
program of the Canada Council for the Arts and the Ontario Arts Council.

This book has been published with the help of a grant from the Humanities and
Social Sciences Federation of Canada, using funds provided by the Social Sciences
and Humanities Research Council of Canada.

For Joey, Carmen, Katie,
and others of their generation

Contents

Illustrations

Preface

A few years ago, historian P.B. Waite remarked that *Grip* magazine was 'one of the most interesting sources for the social history of Ontario in the latter nineteenth century.' Waite was quick to add that John Bengough's magazine was biased – that while it professed to be above partisan politics and poked fun at Grit leaders, its sympathies clearly lay with the many causes that the Liberal Party espoused.[1] Both points are valid, but Waite could have gone further. *Grip* is also one of the most interesting sources of Canadian history, both social and political, and its biases provide one of the best reasons for looking at it. Its distortions are sometimes the most revealing message it gives a later age.

Through its comments and satires, and above all its cartoons, *Grip* opens a channel that allows us to scan an interesting period in Canadian history, the years from 1873 to 1894. The view through this channel is clouded by many things: by the conditioning of *Grip*'s artists and writers, by limitations in their knowledge, by their party loyalties, and by their male, WASP, Toronto sensibilities. But for all these difficulties, *Grip* remains an exceptional, perhaps a unique, opening to the two decades of its life.

Part of its value is that it exposes, mainly in Bengough's cartoons, an especially bleak time in Canadian history, a time of discontent and grievances that seemed likely to destroy the young confederation. *Grip* is also of value because of the reformist view of its artists and writers, who were inspired for one reason or another to assail the evils of the day. From what they drew and wrote, we can see both the evils (or at least some of them) and the demanded cures. Even more important is the way *Grip* unconsciously reveals the viewpoints of the time. Its pages are loaded with small and large clues about the way that at least one group of Canadians perceived women, 'lesser' races, colonial rulers, and so on. It gives us an authentic (if sometimes offensive) picture that is difficult to obtain elsewhere; and although this picture is based on an Ontario viewpoint, it is relevant to all of Canada, because Ontario's beliefs even at that time determined much of what would happen in distant corners of the country.

Grip's benefit to modern students is limited to some degree by a century of change in both language and frames of reference. Today's students might well wonder, for instance, why Bengough constantly portrayed the editor of the Toronto *Mail* as a knife-wielding 'ribstabber,' or who he meant when he spoke of the Great Tyrant of Bow Park, or what the Steel Rails Scandal was all about. To meet such problems, this book gives a sample of original *Grip* material along with explanations that set the material in context. As well, it offers a tentative interpretation of *Grip*'s significance in its day, though its chief aim is simply to bring to modern readers a taste of the magazine's distinctive art and satire.

While *Grip*'s cartoons have often been reprinted, there has been no attempt to present a wide selection and try to define the patterns they make. Bengough himself published two volumes of his early work, but they cover only the first decade of his career and miss many of the more interesting patterns. Very soon, all the *Grip* cartoons (and poems and satires) ought to be made available on compact disc, accompanied by explanation and analysis. In the meantime, this book offers some of the high and low points.

Any evaluation of Bengough's work should include not just the impact it had in his time and our own. We should remember as well that the WASP elite who ran Canada at the beginning of the twentieth century – the politicians and scholars, business leaders and journalists – were reared on *Grip*. In its images they perhaps had their first view of the political world. This view was above all a Liberal one, based on the conviction that the Tories were agents of the devil. It was also a Protestant viewpoint, certain that the Roman Catholic Church was a bastion of reaction. It was a reformist viewpoint, as pessimistic about current evils as it was optimistic about eventual earthly salvation. Finally, it was a male, central-Canadian point of view.

Yet to say that these biases damage *Grip*'s historical value would be to miss the point. It would be like saying that Dickens is valueless because he was biased against capitalists or headmasters. For our generation, *Grip* is as valuable as a hoard of ancestral letters or a family photo album. Like them, it tells us something of the way we were – and the way we were not.

Acknowledgments

Many people have helped in the preparation of this book, none more than my wife, Betty, who assisted me with the research and the proofreading, and gave constant advice and encouragement.

I am indebted as well to many archivists and scholars: Peter Rochon, Jim Burant, Rosemary Murray, and many others at the National Archives of Canada; Ken Blackwell at the Mills Library, McMaster University; Brian Winter of the Whitby, Ontario, archives; Karen Bergsteinsson of the Archives of Ontario; genealogist Larry Driffield of Toronto for information on the Bengough family; and administrator Wanda McGonigal of Bengough, Saskatchewan, for information on the town named for John Bengough.

I have built as well on scholarly work about Bengough and Phillips Thompson produced by many people, including Ramsay Cook, Russell Hann, Jay Atherton, Peter Desbarats, Terry Mosher, Dugald E. Stewart, Dennis Edward Blake, Stanley Paul Kutcher, and Greg Kealey.

At University of Toronto Press many people have been patient and helpful, including Gerald Hallowell, Karen Boersma, Rob Ferguson, and Carlotta Lemieux.

Some early work on the project was done during a sabbatical leave from Carleton University, and I acknowledge the help and encouragement of many of my former colleagues there.

SKETCHES FROM A YOUNG COUNTRY

1

The Texture of the Times

In the first few decades of Confederation, Canadians made few visual images of themselves. In compensation, they left for their grandchildren a wealth of splendid word pictures. The scenes thus passed to us show Louis Riel fighting for his life in a Regina courtroom and John A. Macdonald manoeuvring for political survival in the Commons. They show George Brown, the tyrannical Scots publisher of the Toronto *Globe*, leaning back in his editorial chair, long legs extended and eyes fixed on his oversized boots as he lectured fellow journalists about the good effects of an occasional hanging ('Eh, mon, but hangin's a *grand* thing for the criminal classes!').[1] From these descriptions, our imagination fills in the details to create an outline of the world that was. By contrast, the visual images from the times come down to us mostly in the form of posed, awkward photographs and idealized paintings, though there are some exceptions that deserve mention. Artists such as George Reid provide one treasure of insights. The photographs and sketches of the *Canadian Illustrated News* and the photos of the William Notman collection are others. But resources like these are rare.[2]

Because of this, many of the vivid impressions from those early Confederation years, especially of political life, come from the most popular satirical magazine of the time – *Grip*. The Toronto weekly lasted from 1873 to 1894, and it was drawn and edited for most of its history by a passionate, righteous, talented young reformer named John Wilson Bengough. It is no accident that so many of Bengough's cartoons show up in our history texts. His sketches of the leading figures – Macdonald, Brown, Mackenzie, Blake, Mowat, Riel – have a force that prints them on our brains, obliterating the more static images from the early days of photography. From Bengough's work we appreciate the mischievous gleam in Macdonald's eye, the ironic twist of the mouth beneath that untidy hair and bulbous nose. From his caricatures we may well have drawn our image of the bull-like features of Charles Tupper, the smooth urbanity of Wilfrid Laurier, or the lofty intellectualism of Goldwin Smith. The cartoons provide a dimension that is missing in the photographs and word pictures.

While Bengough was neither a brilliant craftsman nor an original political or social thinker, he was enormously prolific for more than fifty years and was very much in touch with his times. He was well-meaning, sincere, curious. He sketched at a furious pace, leaving likenesses and caricatures of thousands of the people of his era. At the same time, he provided some fascinating background detail. His cartoons reveal the shape and texture of life in sometimes harsh terms, from the prison whipping post and gallows to the farmyard pig-sticking frame ('Getting Ready for the Killing') and from primitive inoculation techniques to the master's switch in the one-room school. Similarly, Bengough provided many insights into social patterns and relations: the despair of the drunkard's wife and children, the awkwardness of a farmer visiting the city, the arrogance of a young sport on his new bicycle.

Moreover, *Grip* was not just a magazine of cartoons. Its columns contained – standing out in a plateau of third-rate humour and verse – some notable satire and social commentary. In alliance with T. Phillips Thompson (a much more daring journalist, who worked on and off for *Grip*), Bengough in words and pictures gave a kind of running account and critique of the era's attitudes. For instance, when Bengough (or one of his writers, but more likely Bengough) rails at prostitution and abortion in Victorian Toronto, he tells us much about both the writer and his period:

TO THE PEOPLE OF TORONTO

Oh, whited sepulchres, followers of the times,
Whose sembled indignation at foulest crimes
Is now most rampant o'er the new-made graves
Of two frail women. Had ye tried to save
Them e'er they died – Had ye banished those
Whose trade was public – Had ye even chose,
By your chaste lives, to make their living bare,
Those victims would not now be lying there ...[3]

In an instant, the verse reveals an intricate mental landscape. It shows the

GETTING READY FOR THE KILLING.

Grip, 24 Oct. 1885. *Grip*'s cartoons often unconsciously reveal aspects of nineteenth-century life – in this case, the pig-killing equipment. The intended message was part of a long-standing effort to show Macdonald's franchise reform as partisan manipulation. The 'revising power' knife refers to Tory legislation to bring enumeration under federal control.

writer's rage at the wickedness about him, his naive belief that simple reforms could remake the world, his fastidiousness (in the euphemism 'those whose trade was public'), his self-righteousness ('had ye chose by your chaste lives'), his biblical orientation ('whited sepulchres'), and his sympathetic but patronizing attitude towards women ('two frail women'). Overall, the poem is a map of both the writer's attitudes and his world.

Bengough's cartoon work is equally heavy with information about the times – and about the artist. For instance, 'The Proposed Marriage of Convenience' (5 Feb. 1887) tells us not only about the clothing styles and political attitudes of the day but about some underlying patterns – how, for instance, responsibility for the woman passed at marriage from father to husband. For the politically aware, the cartoon was a reminder that Sir

THE PROPOSED MARRIAGE OF CONVENIENCE.

Dutiful Daughter—O PAPA ! DEAR PAPA, I WOULD DO ANYTHING FOR YOU, BUT I CAN'T—I CAN'T ACCEPT THIS ODIOUS MAN !

Charles Tupper ('the ram of Cumberland') was not only a sharp operator but an inveterate philanderer.[4] This cartoon may well have helped bar him temporarily from the Tory leadership when Macdonald died four years later. Further, the cartoon encapsulates a key Liberal ploy in the election campaign that was then going on, implying that the Tories were keeping Macdonald in harness only to get themselves into office one more time before turning to a new leader.

On quite another level, the cartoon reveals Bengough's essentially romantic nature. Presenting the most stereotypical dramatic tableau of his day – the villain demanding to have his wicked way with the innocent daughter of an impoverished man – he both lightly mocks the melodrama and at the same time savours the tension it offers. With sure dramatic sense he creates suspense, an anticipation of the rescue to come. It is as though he has cast himself, or the reader, as the crucial missing character of the piece – the heroic young man who will rescue the damsel from the villain's grasp.

The way Bengough set up this dramatic tension reveals the essence of his genius; he produced an instantly recognizable parable, using symbols or myths already in the reader's mind and then intersecting them with the fresh political action. To be effective, such cartoons must command immediate understanding from the reader, producing a laugh, a nod of agreement, or at least a wry acceptance that the point is well made. The parable must also offer an underlying truth. In this case, it was the recognition of Macdonald's aging and his increasing ineffectualness combined with Tupper's greater virility – and lesser virtue.

'What Bengough lacked in technical ability he made up for with clout,' wrote the British critic William Feaver in *Masters of Caricature*.[5] Feaver may have been thinking of Bengough's ability to put himself in the minds of his readers, to know instinctively what they would recognize, what would stir them to anger or laughter. Not all modern critics have been so kind. One writer has brushed Bengough aside as a well-intentioned gentleman of 'wooden' style whose 'conception tended to obvious imagery, using situations familiar to the middle class.'[6] There is some justification for this

---

Grip, 5 Feb. 1887 (*opposite*). The essence of Bengough's skill emerges in this cartoon, which presents an instantly recognizable dramatic situation. Sir John A. Macdonald plays the role of the aging father while Sir Charles Tupper is the villain grasping for the Tory leadership. The cartoon engages the viewer in the action as the damsel's possible rescuer.

criticism, but it might also be said that Bengough's talent lay in choosing the images that readers would quickly recognize and then linking them to a political world he knew well.

Of course, in creating this magic intersection of myth and reality, Bengough often made life imitate art. The large body of caricature work coming into Canada – from *Punch, Puck, Judge,* and a dozen other British and American magazines – guided his choice to some extent. Cartoonists for all these magazines dipped into a shared pool of universal themes and symbols that were recognizable to a literate audience: the stern and hefty Grecian women who represented Britannia (or Columbia or Miss Canada; see 'How It May End'); the classical images of Trojan horses and assassinated Caesars; the well-known religious characters from the Bible or from Milton and Bunyan. There was also the rich new field of Gilbert and Sullivan operettas, with situations that would have been far more recognizable then than now. There were circus scenes that everyone knew and loved – the high-wire artist; the acrobat leaping through a hoop of flame – and puppeteers and organ-grinders and magicians. There were as well the recognized racial stereotypes: mean, slit-eyed Asians, hook-nosed Jews, rough French-Canadian habitants, and brutish Irish peasants with prognathous faces.[7]

These images were joint property, and the overlap may have extended into more subtle areas. It has often been said, for instance, that Macdonald resembled Benjamin Disraeli ('So Very Much Alike,' p. 10). Was this actually so, or was the cartoon image drawn from the poses that British artists gave to Dizzy? John Tenniel's sketch in *Punch* of Disraeli becoming premier ('Paradise and the Peri,' p. 11) seems to be re-echoed in Bengough's sketches of Macdonald. Copying, probably unconscious, may show up in other work: Bengough's caricatures of Toronto's poor (often the families of drunkards) echo the early Victorian English prints.[8] His images of Quebec are limited to shaggy peasants, domineering priests, and docile peasant women in *sabots* and winged hats ('Madame Quebec's Wild Boy,' p. 16; 'The Free and Independent Habitant,' p. 17). It is striking, too, that Bengough seems to have drawn cartoons of western Indians more frequently *before* he made an extensive tour of the plains in 1889.

Grip, 29 May 1886 (*opposite*). Bengough drew on a well-recognized bank of international symbols. (In this instance, it is notable that of the four countries represented, only Canada needs labelling.) This cartoon also invoked several conventional Ontario views: on American rapaciousness, Irish obstreperousness, and British pusillanimity in defence of Canada's interests.

HOW IT MAY END.

Britannia.—O, IF HE'S RIGHT YOU'LL HAVE TO GIVE IN ; AND IF YOU'RE RIGHT YOU'LL HAVE TO GIVE IN ; SO DON'T BOTHER ME ABOUT YOUR FISHERY TROUBLES. DON'T YOU SEE I'VE GOT MY HANDS FULL?

Miss Canada.—WELL, MAMMY, IF THAT'S HOW YOU FEEL, DON'T YOU THINK I'D BETTER JUST MARRY HIM AND GET RID OF HIM?

So Very Much Alike.

*A friendly game of Euchre at Hughenden, be-
tween the two great statesmen of modern times.*

SIR JOHN (*loq.*)—I wonder where all the
bowers are?

EARL DIZZY.—Don't know, I'm sure. I
have only three in my boot.

SIR JOHN.—And I have just one up my
sleeve!

Grip, 13 Sept. 1879 (*above*), and *Punch*, 28 Feb. 1874 (*opposite*). Bengough may not
consciously have been copying, but his styles and concepts often reflected the
work of others. These sketches raise the question of whether Macdonald and
Disraeli looked alike or whether Bengough drew on conceptions of the British
leader to frame his image of Macdonald. John Tenniel's sketch of Disraeli as an
angel flying blissfully into office could equally have been a Bengough cartoon of
Macdonald. Compare Disraeli's expression – especially the closed eyes – with
that of Macdonald in 'The Beauties of a Royal Commission' (p. 51). Although
Bengough's cartoon was drawn first, the similarity could mean that he was copying earlier Tenniel images – or that both men were drawing on other shared
models.

The observed reality may have confused his mental images, which tended
either to the 'noble savage' or 'debauched victim' pattern ('Startling Affair
in London!' p. 18).

It would be unfair, though, to accuse Bengough of lack of originality
because some of his ideas echoed British or American stereotypes. The
stock of common images was limited, and repetition was inevitable, as any
comparative study illustrates.[9] It would also be wrong to suggest that
Bengough's cartoons were entirely detached from reality. In many ways,

PARADISE AND THE PERI.

"JOY, JOY FOR EVER! MY TASK IS DONE—
THE GATES ARE PASSED, AND HEAVEN IS WON!"—*Lalla Rookh.*

⁎ The General Election had given the Conservative Leader a decided majority over Mr. Gladstone, and Mr. Disraeli entered the paradise of office as Premier for the first time.

DUAL UN-CONTROL.

SIGNOR NORTHBROOKINI, "THE STAR RIDER," IN HIS "DARING ACT" ON TWO HORSES.

⁎ Lord Northbrook, First Lord of the Admiralty, had gone as High Commissioner to enquire into the financial condition of Egypt and to report to the British Government. On his return he was faced by difficulties created by the controversy on the state of the Navy.

A RIEL UGLY POSITION.

Punch, 6 Dec. 1884 (*opposite*), and *Grip*, 29 Aug. 1885 (*above*). Bengough's classic image of Macdonald's dilemma on the hanging of Louis Riel may have been copied from Tenniel's portrayal of Lord Northbrook.

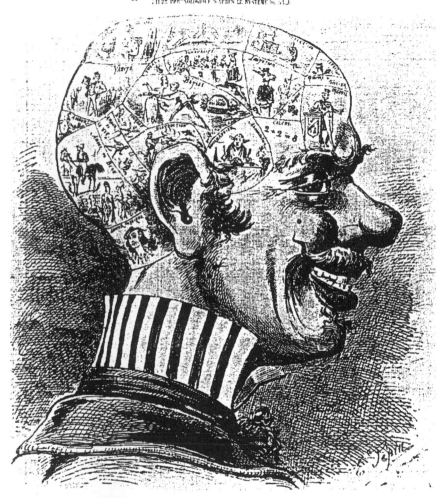

Grip, 9 Apr. 1887 (*opposite*), and Pepin, 1871 (*above*). Bengough's portrayal of Macdonald was evidently inspired by the sketch of the French artist Pepin (Edouard Guillaumin), cartoonist for *Le Grelot*. Bengough normally gave credit to such sources, but in this case he may have considered the copy too obvious to need an acknowledgment.

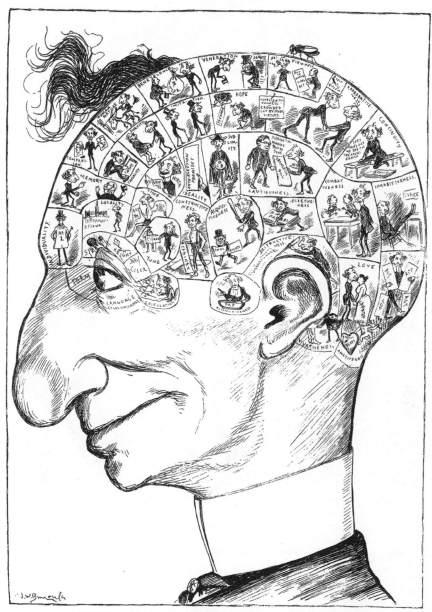

PHRENOLOGICAL CHART OF THE HEAD OF THE COUNTRY.

MADAME QUEBEC'S WILD BOY.

MME. QUEBEC.—"IT'S SO KIND OF YOU TO TAKE HIM, SIR JOHN! HE'S NEARLY BROUGHT ME TO RUIN!"

SIR JOHN.—"HAVE NO FEAR, MADAME; UNDER *MY* TUITION HE SHALL LEARN PRUDENCE, ECONOMY, INDUSTRY
AND THRIFT!"

Grip, 12 Aug. 1882. J.A. Chapleau's move to federal politics evoked Bengough's stereotypical view of Quebec's subservience to the prime minister.

THE FREE AND INDEPENDENT HABITANT

CASTING HIS BALLOT UPON THE GREAT POLITICAL QUESTIONS OF THE DAY.

Grip, 23 Oct. 1886. Here, Bengough gives classic expression to Ontario's conviction that Quebec was a backward, priest-ridden society. However, although Bengough condemned priestly interference in Quebec politics, he made no objection when Protestant clerics led Ontario's 'equal rights' battle.

STARTLING AFFAIR IN LONDON!

A PROMISING YOUNG WOMAN OFFERED FOR SALE TO THE HIGHEST BIDDER.

Grip, 11 July 1880. To personify western Canada, Bengough borrowed the American symbol of the Indian princess; and to represent land grabbers taking advantage of the government's sell-out of western lands, he used the centuries-old Jewish stereotype.

they expose a world that he took for granted – though one that we have never seen – a world of revival meetings, omnibuses, and ox carts, a world of saloons and salons. They also show us relationships that he took for granted, for his was an unhomogenized world with sharp distinctions between farmers, workers, and the bourgeoisie, a world in which officers were naturally of the upper class, clergy were elevated above their flocks, and people of British blood were naturally superior to the 'foreign element.' A world run by men.

More important, Bengough offers us, in the action of his cartoons, a rough barometer of the times, especially among the more liberal or 'progressive' elements in English Canada. Quick to catch the temper of that group, he often revealed its swings of attitude. His impatience with the aging and despotic George Brown, his disgust with Macdonald's sometimes shadowy politics, his short-lived support for tariff protection in the late 1870s, and his descent into Anglo-Protestant hysteria in the late 1880s all tell us much about the various swings in conventional thinking. This applies especially to *Grip*'s early and mature years. In its final years, the magazine was strongly influenced by Phillips Thompson's doctrinaire socialism and became less responsive to public approval. As well, Bengough himself was more caught up in specific social causes, especially prohibition and tax reform, and was less likely to follow the conventional wisdom. But over its whole lifetime, *Grip*'s policy changes tell us much about the temper of the age.

The magazine also shows us – if we look closely – some amusing sidelights on the times. Bengough's work is often criticized as cluttered, but he worked in an age when readers had much more time to savour detail. Typically, his cartoons offered a quick chuckle – and then invited more intense examination. Many of these small asides may be lost on a later generation. In the classic 'Pity the Dominie,' for instance (see p. 20), they include a dig at Prime Minister Mackenzie's tendency to take his 'lessons' from the *Globe*, a reminder of the new Liberal government's confusion on railway policy, and an unusual criticism of the low pay of Chinese 'coolie' labour. There is also an ironic reminder of the length of Macdonald's political career in the *First Book of Politics* he carries. Yet despite such small 'in' jokes, Bengough's work remains highly accessible. In the limited progression of Canadian cartoon history, it is much easier to understand and appreciate than the work of those who came even a decade or two before him – and of many who came later.[10]

In some ways, then, Bengough may be considered an innovator, especially in establishing cartoons as an adjunct of journalism. Critic Robert

PITY THE DOMINIE; OR, JOHNNY'S RETURN.

CANADA—"HERE'S OUR JOHNNY FOR YOU AGAIN, MR. MACKENZIE! YOU'LL FIND HIM APT ENOUGH, BUT FRANKLY, SIR, HE'S FULL OF MISCHIEF!"

Grip, 7 Feb. 1874. This cartoon became something of a classic, partly because it so accurately caught Canadians' ambivalence about Macdonald in the wake of the Pacific Scandal. It also displays Bengough's technique of embedding small jokes in the background of his main theme.

Fulford once observed that Canada's political cartoonists 'have met and often exceeded world standards more often than have people in any of the other journalistic arts.'[11] If this is so, Bengough perhaps pointed the way for the brilliance in our own time of such cartoonits as Duncan Macpherson, Len Norris, and Terry Mosher (Aislin). Historians Ramsay Cook and P.B. Waite, critics George Woodcock, Jack Batten, Doug Fetherling, and Peter Desbarats, as well as Terry Mosher himself, are among the many who have acknowledged Bengough's pioneering importance. Woodcock called him 'undoubtedly the first of the great Canadian cartoonists, certainly in time and perhaps also in merit,' and credited him with creating the tradition of the journalistic cartoon.[12] Scholar Dugald Stewart said that Bengough changed the nature of the journalistic cartoon by fastening onto social rather than merely political issues.[13]

Yet the overall evaluation of Bengough's career remains a mixed one. If he had an impact in his own time, it was presumably partly hidden, showing up in actions that people assumed were based on more serious influences. (Politicians or business leaders would have been slow to admit that they were influenced by a mere cartoonist.) There is also the difficult question of cause and effect – of evaluating whether Bengough was driving any particular social trend or campaign, or whether he was being driven. While he was fiercely persistent in some campaigns, especially prohibition, on others he blew with the wind. His devotion to the arcane Henry George theory of a single tax and his antagonism to the liquor interests were areas on which he would not bend, but in others he could go with the times. His attitude on imperialism is a fascinating example. At times during *Grip*'s life, Bengough was harshly critical (or allowed his writers to be harshly critical) of the British Empire. Later, in a turnaround that reflected the mood of the country, he became almost maudlin in his imperialist sentiment. The great 'race and creed' debates of his day are another, more serious, case of vacillation. He let himself be influenced by the bigotry of the times, then caught a contrary gust of public opinion and veered towards Laurier's efforts for tolerance and national unity. On the issues of settling western Canada – issues that loomed large during the *Grip* years – his outlook was consistently narrow and predictable, partisan and unrealistic.

Whether or not Bengough is seen as an originating force, there are still many reasons to study his cartoons. One is that his best work, done in the 1880s and early 1890s, came at an especially difficult time in the country's history and therefore shows us much about a period we might be tempted to ignore. In *Grip*'s early years, the mood had been more hopeful, for

Macdonald's National Policy of tariff protection had coincided with (and perhaps helped bring about) a spurt of advance in the late 1870s and early 1880s. The Canadian Pacific Railway (CPR) had been pushed through to the West Coast with remarkable persistence and had created, against a fog of scandal, a western boom and a national vision that gave reason for national pride. But the economic boom died quickly and the country's fabric was stretched to breaking by the Northwest Rebellion and the ensuing race and creed turmoil. By comparison with the later years of Laurier unity and prosperity, the late 1880s and early 1990s were not good years. The mood of pessimism drove many of the ablest young Canadians to cross the border and join a more prosperous neighbour. A significant annexation movement arose in the early 1890s, which failed not so much because of the efforts of Canadian loyalists as through the failure of American political and opinion leaders to exploit the discontent.

The combination of all these problems – the race and religion agonies combined with economic difficulties – produced what historian Frank Underhill called the deepest depression of spirit that had ever captured the Canadian mind. 'We have watched the cradle of Confederation & shouldn't like to follow the hearse,' Macdonald wrote gloomily to a colleague in 1885.[14] A few years later, Laurier wrote to Edward Blake in the same tone: 'We have come to a period in the history of this young country when premature dissolution seems to be at hand. What will be the outcome? How long can the present fabric last? Can it last at all? All these are questions which surge in my mind and to which dismal answers suggest themselves.'[15]

The social realities underlying these political difficulties were similarly bleak. While Canada trailed Britain and the United States in the rise of industrialism, its cities suffered from the full range of urban problems. Drinking was a general curse. Brutality, prostitution, and other vices were commonplace. Sanitary facilities were appalling. Courts were swift and callous. Labour unions were rising fast but were limited in their capacity to protect workers. Social safety nets were practically nonexistent. News stories of the day spoke of children found frozen in unheated tenements, of raw sewage flowing back into water pipes, of female 'shoe operatives' earning $3.50 a week – but only as long as they held onto their health.

Despite its horrors, the period had its share of vitality and ferment, and even at times a certain charm. New technology was arriving quickly – the telephone, the bicycle, the phonograph, electricity – and further wonders were constantly predicted. The West was being opened up. Hints of radical new thinking were appearing in medicine, theology, and politics. Public faith in the many possibilities for reform and progress was greater than it would be later – in almost inverse proportion, indeed, to the despair over current problems.

There was a certain vibrancy as well in the cast of characters guiding the country. Canada's politicians, journalists, railwaymen, bishops, business leaders (all males, of course) were as fine a group of rogues, saints, and manipulators as one might find in any Gilbert and Sullivan work. They were (or Bengough's pen made them seem) a colourful and bizarre lot: often grasping, often unprincipled, often tough and resourceful – yet also, in unpredictable ways, idealistic. These conditions provided splendid material for a young and reform-minded cartoonist. It is in this area, in making recognizable and fascinating characters of the political players, that Bengough made one of his greatest contributions. No other record from the time catches with such force the political ironies of the day.

Paradoxically, this is also the area that presents analysts of Bengough's work with their toughest challenge. The problem is not only that Bengough inflicted his biases on his readers but that these biases remain embedded in our history books today. It is true that through most of his career at *Grip* Bengough tried to appear politically independent, to be equally hard on Grits and Tories. But over the long term (and especially in the later years) he was decidedly more sympathetic to the Grits. He later admitted as much – adding ingenuously that it was because the Liberals tended to be more virtuous.[16]

Bengough's bias often caused him to be blindly hostile to Sir John A. Macdonald and his Tory successors, a point that is seldom noted when the cartoons are reprinted. The Tory policies certainly offered much to criticize, but there were also some things to praise, and Bengough failed to give credit where it was due. He gave almost no recognition to Macdonald's toughness in driving through the transcontinental rail line. At the time, he could see only the cost to taxpayers, the profits to manipulators, the evil of the CPR monopoly in the West, and Ottawa's procrastination and corruption in dealing with Métis and Indians. More broadly, Bengough virtually ignored Macdonald's genius in finding ground for compromise among the country's competing claims of race, religion, and region. Any such accommodations were presented in Bengough's cartoons as evidence of hypocrisy or worse.

This image problem is all the more serious because of Bengough's near monopoly of Canadian cartooning in his day. While most American cartoonists (including some of his heroes, such as Thomas Nast) were frankly partisan, later scholars can usefully match the images of rival cartoonists to provide a rough balance. But in English Canada, Bengough was almost alone in his early years.

The view of Canada through Bengough's eyes is thus a distorted one, and not just where politics is concerned. In several other areas his work is flawed by what modern eyes see as bigoted or narrow views. At the worst of the race and creed fever, his views on separate schools and bilingualism were at least as narrow as those of the Orange Order. Although he was seen in his own time as progressive on a variety of issues, which ranged from women's rights to Native and labour issues, Bengough did not escape the paternalism of his class and sex. It would be possible to draw out a selection of cartoons and satires that make him seem a racist chauvinist bigot. But this would be unfair. In the context of his times and conditioning he was very much a reformer, especially in his middle and later years. He was committed to many social causes: male and female suffrage, the breakup of monopoly, social equality. On prohibition and the single tax he went beyond devotion to become a crank. Overall, he comes through as an earnest and well-meaning Christian who believed that the world could be made better by right-thinking people who would take charge, destroy corrupt government and monopoly, curb drunkenness, and bring in fair taxation. Historian Ramsay Cook, who analysed Bengough's impact as a reformer, wrote: 'Bengough was inspired by a vision of dissenting Protestantism which looked forward to the fulfilment of God's kingdom on earth through the implementation of a few simple reforms. In religious matters he was somewhat conservative or, perhaps more accurately, evangelical; emotional rather than intellectual.'[17]

This summary is a fair one, and Bengough emerges as a classic millennialist, an apostle of the Enlightenment, a pilgrim on his way to the Shining City of the Hill. His simple optimism stands in interesting contrast to John A. Macdonald's cynical, pragmatic view of the world. The two are perhaps representative of successive eras. A clergy friend, overlooking Bengough's fits of intolerance, described him as one of the most Christlike figures he had ever known.[18] No one ever described Macdonald as Christlike, but his wry cynicism stands up as well to later analysis as the optimism of Bengough. It is ironic that Bengough, in so many ways the lesser man, showed a self-righteous tone in deploring Macdonald's weaknesses of character.

Bengough's optimism and idealism should not be seen as valueless, of course. He may reasonably be seen as a contributor to the reforming sensibility that gave birth a few decades later to the Co-operative Commonwealth Federation and other reformist groups. While he himself was never a dogmatic socialist (his views were much more moderate than those of Phillips Thompson, who gave *Grip* much of its radical tinge), he was certainly part of a broad reformist alliance, a coalition that linked farm and labour agitators with Christian intellectuals alarmed about the worst excesses of turn-of-the-century capitalism. In the end, though, he is open to the charge of naiveté.

It is all too easy, then, to review Bengough's work and find it flawed. It is (say the experts on art) derivative, cluttered, and rough. It is (say the modern reformers) tainted with bigotry. It is (say the political analysts) unfair to Tories and too kind to Grits. But still there is no question that Bengough's astonishingly large collection of work, especially his early drawing, qualifies as a national treasure.

Some of his cartoons reveal a history we would rather not know about, a history of narrowness, prejudice, and greed. But because of this, they are all the more important to us. It is notable that most of the *Grip* cartoons reprinted in history books have been of the respectable sort. They have not been the kind that showed cringing French Canadians, arrogant, sneering priests, devious Jews, thieving blacks, dissolute Irish, threatening Asians, or giddy women. This should not be surprising. When conventional views have changed, no one wants to dwell on such embarrassing reminders, especially when they represent only a small part of Bengough's work. The material thus poses an acute dilemma for those trying to capture aspects of social history. If they reprint the repulsive images, they risk hurting or offending sensitive minorities. If they do not do so, they are guilty of bad history, of bowdlerizing the past. Of these two choices, the second is the greater risk. It seems evident that we have to know as much as possible of where we have been if we are to see our present and future with any clarity.

2

Bengough, Thompson, and *Grip*

Grip was very much a product of the imagination of John Bengough. It is hardly possible to think of it as other than a reflection of his talent and beliefs. But at times it must also be seen as a blend of Bengough and T. Phillips Thompson. Thompson not only helped start the magazine, but he shaped its mature, perhaps finest, years – and helped kill it.

Unfortunately, it is often difficult to say for certain which work was Thompson's or when and how he shaped the overall tone of the magazine. There is no doubt that at times he gave *Grip* an anti-imperial and anti-capitalistic tone, but it is not always clear whether Bengough as editor guided, or was guided by, his colleague. In the absence of hard evidence, it is important to look at the personalities and background of the two men to get at least a tentative reading on their collaboration.

The patterns they shared were radicalism, satirical imagination, and perhaps a personal lack of fulfilment. Both show life patterns of increasing frustration in their mature years and the loss of that precious sense of irony that marked their early work. In both cases, missionary zeal eventually eroded their capacity for irony. The chief pattern that differentiates the two men, at least during the *Grip* years, is Bengough's mental openness, his responsiveness to the views around them. He consistently picked up the shifting waves of public opinion – indeed, at times was even too quick to take up a new idea. By contrast, Thompson, by the time of his most important collaboration with Bengough, had already closed his mind; he expended his talents by raging at the stupidity of those who failed to see the correctness of his ideas. A visionary, zealot, and true reformer – and an entirely impractical man – Thompson attacked the greed of the capitalists, the viciousness of the imperialists and militarists, and the blindness of the bourgeoisie, demanding always that the world

T. Phillips Thompson in his late years, with grandson Pierre Berton (courtesy of Pierre Berton)

conform to his vision. While Bengough also had a core of doctrinaire views, especially on tax reform and prohibition, he was much readier than his older colleague to listen and adapt, and much readier to compromise. He is thus a better reflection of his times.

It is ironic that for both men – certainly for Bengough – the creation of *Grip* may stand as their best achievement, even though they themselves probably saw it as no more than a station on the way to something greater. It is ironic, too, that their quite different, sometimes conflicting, talents and outlook combined for some time to give *Grip* a verve that neither could have achieved on his own. The heaviest irony of all is Thompson's part in driving *Grip* into the ground. Listed as associate editor in 1890, he was handed the editorship when business associates squeezed Bengough out in 1892. The new managers, and Thompson's sour outlook, combined to destroy what Bengough with his family's help had built up during two decades of exceptional effort. In the middle of 1893 *Grip* suddenly lapsed. Six months later Bengough tried to revive it with a new company, and the attempt lasted for a year, through 1894, but the old vigour never returned.

To understand *Grip*, then, it is necessary to understand something of the background and motivation of both Thompson and Bengough. Of the two, Thompson is perhaps the easier to characterize, because his radicalism dominated his life. Its roots lay at least partly in his Quaker background in industrial England, at Newcastle-on-Tyne, and partly in the injustices he saw firsthand as a reporter in Toronto courtrooms and Irish slums. Some other factor must be assumed, though, to account for his chronic discontent, his unwillingness to accept the world as he found it. This attitude showed up early in life. After coming to Ontario with his family at the age of fourteen, Thompson trained as a lawyer in St Catharines, but he declined to accept the steady prosperity of the law and switched to the uncertainties of journalism. He worked on the St Catharines *Post*, on John Ross Robertson's Toronto *Telegraph*, and later on *Grip*, the *National*, the *Globe*, the *Mail*, the *News*, and several other publications before returning to *Grip*.[1]

Described as a man of amiable temperament and caustic pen, Thompson achieved his first reputation as a humorous writer, signing his work Jimuel Briggs, D.B. (the letters stood for the degree of Dead Beat, from Coboconk University). *Grip*, probably with Bengough writing the lines, sometimes stressed Thompson's gentle and amiable qualities. This assessment (surprising for anyone who knew only his later work) was echoed by a *Saturday Night* writer, who remarked in 1890 that Thompson had 'the pen of a revolutionist and the heart of a gentle, loving woman,' adding that as Jimuel Briggs he had made all Canada laugh and that 'as a writer of pure English he is not second to Goldwin Smith.'[2] Even in 1873, when Thompson was helping to start *Grip*, he had a considerable local reputation as a satirist. But he was already moving towards more serious social reporting and analysis, especially on class and labour issues. In the late 1880s he published a major work entitled *The Politics of Labor* under the sponsorship of Henry George, chief of the American radicals attacking monopolistic capitalism.

Thompson thus travelled far, both geographically and intellectually, in the two decades between the time he helped launch *Grip* and the time he helped kill it. He was briefly co-owner and editor of the *National* newspaper. He worked in Boston as literary editor of the *Traveller* (where, according to a writer for an American magazine, 'his writings on social reforms and labor politics made him very conspicuous'). He reported for the *Globe* on Irish repression, served as chief writer for the Toronto *News* during its radical era (1883–7), and wrote for and edited such organs as the *Palladium of Labor* and the *Labor Advocate*. He became a well-known socialist, embraced theosophism (a religion combining universal brotherhood with a vision of social progress), and flirted with anarchism. For years, Toronto's intellectual circles knew Thompson as a constant iconoclast, president of the Toronto Free Thought Association and supporter of a plethora of radical causes, especially the Knights of Labor. Labour historians Greg Kealey and Bryan Palmer have described him as Canada's most significant late-nineteenth-century labour reformer.[3] In the mid-nineties he was a central figure in a local uproar when University of Toronto students went on strike after he and another labour spokesman had been denied permission to speak to the student body. A famous grandson, writer Pierre Berton, remembers him in his late years, still an inveterate radical, singing militant union songs (written by himself), and recalling the transforming impact of his Irish reporting. That experience, Thompson said, had made him regret how, as a police court humorist, he had ridiculed down-and-outers.[4]

By contrast, John Bengough was both a simpler and a more complicated personality. He was simpler in the sense that he was more open, amiable, and conventional, more ready for compromise, and more ready to pay the price for social acceptance. He was more complicated in that his amiability may have led him into opinion changes and contradictions, and this makes it harder to pin him down.

On the surface, Bengough's personal story is a conventional one of work and progress – a story that reads like a Horatio Alger tale gone slightly awry. His early life gives a picture of a high-minded, handsome young man, sure of his destiny and working with zeal and impressive success to reach it. It is only in middle life that something goes noticeably wrong, moving him away from his true but declassé calling to strive with little success in more 'elevated' arenas.

This is the flaw that gives Bengough's life an unfulfilled quality, despite a long and energetic career marked by increasing respect and status. The tragedy was that he did his best work as a young man in a type of employment that he seems to have considered second-rate. In later life he tried to produce serious literary work – and failed. He fell back on mediocre, repetitive, preachy, partisan cartoons while chasing literary dreams that produced nothing durable. His mawkish poetry and banal comic operas earned him only a slight reputation that did not last beyond his death in 1923. His efforts to write movie scripts came to nothing. His short attempt at a political career gained only small successes.

Bengough's tendency towards impatience and his reforming zeal may have been inherited from his father, who had emigrated from Scotland and who sampled several occupations while developing activist political and social views. A native of St Andrew's, Fife, John Sr was an expert stair builder and cabinet maker who opened a shop on Toronto's Victoria Street in the 1840s, married an Irish immigrant, Margaret Wilson, and started a family of seven children. John Wilson, the third child, was born on 7 April 1851. Shortly afterwards the family moved to nearby Whitby, where John Sr worked on a residence called Trafalgar Castle and later opened another shop. He was known in the town as Captain John, apparently because of his experience on a lake boat or as a marine inspector with an insurance company.[5]

In his brief memoirs, John Wilson said almost nothing of his parents – a curious omission especially since he followed his father's activist footsteps. Captain John was a prominent organizer in Reform (Liberal) politics and in the Whitby Mechanics' Institute, and was described in his obituary as an ardent crusader for a single land tax.[6] Some of the zeal for change seems to have crept into his religious views. Late in life he became a Unitarian, leaving the rest of the family in the Presbyterian Church.[7] Eventually, he moved back to Toronto, where he held a variety of minor posts, including at least one job, inspector of woodblock paving, that presumably came from his political connections.[8] A photograph taken by one of his grandchildren shows a classic Scots patriarch, with long nose and full beard.

Less is known of Bengough's mother, but it may be significant to his generally tolerant outlook that her Irish background made her something of an outsider among her husband's Scots relatives. Unlike many Canadians of the day, Bengough showed no strong tendency to attach himself to one or another of the founding races, despite his Scottish father and his British loyalties. Nor, despite his strong religious orientation, did he seem to be attached to his Presbyterian roots. He claimed to be 'equally at home in all churches,' though it is likely he meant Protestant churches.

None of this background fully explains why Bengough's interests so broadly spanned the political, social, religious, and artistic worlds. Certainly, he can be seen as a product of the Scots reform tradition as well as of Presbyterian rectitude;[9] and having been an insatiable reader during his youth in the 1850s and 1860s, it was natural that he would take Dickens as his model and combine social and artistic ambitions. As a teenager during the upheavals of the American Civil War and Canadian Confederation, Bengough must have developed some sense of the mutability of political structures. Similarly, the fact that he was brought up in an age when the railway boom made fortunes could explain why he later exhibited some ambivalence about business success, attacking those who had it while constantly seeking it for himself.

Aside from these fairly obvious factors, it is difficult to explain Bengough's mature patterns in terms of his family or his small-town Ontario background. His passionate hatred for liquor, for instance, does not seem to have come from any family or childhood trauma. Although the absence of parental images in his memoirs is intriguing, he seems to have stayed closed to his siblings. All his brothers worked with *Grip* at various times, and much later Thomas Bengough wrote some brief but generous recollections of his older brother.

Close friends and colleagues also tended to stress Bengough's kindness and congeniality – almost a kind of saintliness. At his death, a Tory who sharply criticized Bengough's work as partisan and malevolent said that Bengough himself was a charming man, 'a delightful companion, bubbling over with fun and good humor.'[10] Another tribute said he 'had a heart for fun, as his bright, cheery face always indicated.'[11] On the platform he was undoubtedly magnetic, capable of delighting and amusing a variety of audiences. But the behind-scenes personality remains opaque. Bengough left no diary revelations. The small body of his correspondence that remains to us shows him capable of real anger over social injustice but reveals little of the inner man. He had no children to write insightful memoirs. As well, it appears that no clue to his personality was left by either of his two wives: Helena Siddall, who married him in 1880 when he was twenty-nine and who died in 1902; and Annie Robertson Matteson, a friend from his school days, who married him in 1908. At the time of his second marriage, Bengough was a fifty-something Toronto alderman and Annie was a Chicago widow, deeply engaged in social service. The match may thus reflect his romantic nature and his passion for social reform.[12]

Other clues suggest that Bengough was something of a dreamer. His reminiscences show that he was first attracted to cartoons as a form of escape rather than as a reformist tool. The ability to make pictures, he wrote, 'furnishes so pleasant and convenient a method of getting rid of time which hangs heavy, or of becoming oblivious to studies which are not attractive' that it was a wonder more people did not take it up. At least one of his self-portraits shows him drifting in a fantasy world, making contact with the real world through his drawing pad ('Our Artist in the Dull Times'). This image is reinforced by a story told by Thomas about his brother's first cartoon. He made it, Thomas recalled, when confined to his home with an illness. Their older brother George usually brought home the newspaper for John, and when one day he forgot it, John cartooned him as forgetful – stepping out smartly with his cane swinging and his head left back home on the mantlepiece. The cartoon forecast the essence of Bengough's skill: the surprise twist to a familiar metaphor, making an instant and striking point.

Another significant story told by both Thomas and J.W. related to the crusty, tyrannical schoolteacher who, to everyone's surprise, came round at Christmas with a box of paints for the young artist. Thomas Bengough saw this is a defining moment: 'Simple as was this kindly act, it gave a tremendous impetus to the ambition that was surging in the young boy's brain.' Aside from this, though, Thomas did not recall his brother as exceptional: 'At school J.W. was neither a plodder nor a brilliant scholar, but he had a mind that quickly grasped the essence of things, and specially keen eyes, and a retentive memory for details, especially for human features. At the district school he got a prize for general proficiency – a book with the suggestive title, "Boyhood of Great Artists."'[13] Later on,

---

Grip, 1 July 1876 (*opposite*). Bengough's self-image combines a decisive chin and mouth with the reflective air of the aesthete. The figures in his fantasy include a flying George Brown and John A. Macdonald as the galloping nag.

OUR ARTIST IN THE DULL TIMES.

Whitby residents recalled that Bengough had made chalk sketches of some of his neighbours on their board fences.[14] There were also stories that he had run into trouble at school for drawing pictures of his teachers on the blackboard, but Bengough brushed these aside as inventions.

Whatever the childhood influences, Bengough evidently blossomed early. He was drawing prolifically in his teens, and his talent was noted and praised. His early self-portraits show a handsome, keen-eyed young man – a bit vain perhaps, if we can judge by the jutting chin and the neatly curled moustache that came and went; a bit short, if we can trust the patronizing colleague who called him a kindly little gentleman;[15] and a nonconformist (but only to a mild degree), if we can judge from the fact that he boasted of wearing an artist's smock rather than a dress suit in his first public speech. He was a teetotaller, of course, in an age of heavy drinking, especially among journalists, and he may have been a bit of a prig, judging by his story of how, when he was honoured at a dinner with New York's top cartoonists, he was disappointed that they chose to skip after-dinner speeches in favour of going off to the opening of a new restaurant.

In sum, then, Bengough seems to have been a young man of talent, drive, and character. When he left grammar school, however, he cast about for a time while looking for his niche. He worked in a photographer's shop and then in a law office before falling in love with printer's ink as a compositor, soon to be a writer, at the Whitby *Gazette*. By his own recollection, his breakthrough to the more elevated art came in an incident that gave early promise of his breadth of talent. It happened during the Franco-Prussian War, when the newspaper decided to put out a daily four-page war bulletin. This required a heavier flow of copy, and Bengough responded with a gripping serial story called 'The Murderer's Scalp, or the Shrieking Ghost of the Bloody Den.'[16] Neither John nor Thomas says much of the *Gazette*'s influence on Bengough, but it may be significant that the paper's owner-editor at that time was George Ham, a humorous, adventuring, articulate extrovert who achieved a considerable reputation as a journalist and public relations chief for the Canadian Pacific Railway. There is no certainty that Ham served as role model, but it seems likely that his striking energy and capacity for friendship would have had an effect on the young man.

Bengough himself recalled that a major formative influence was Thomas Nast's cartoon work in *Harper's Weekly*, especially the drawings that exposed the corruption of New York's 'Boss' Tweed, a central figure in the Tammany Hall Democratic gang. Bengough was just into his teens when Nast was achieving fame as a Civil War artist, and he frankly copied

Nast's approach in his early drawing. He even sent a cartoon off to *Harper's* using Nast's style to show his hero besting the Tammany villains. This incident suggests he had a good deal of self-confidence (he received a polite note in return), and the impression is reinforced by other evidence. Bengough was evidently not intimidated by the thought of taking on the tough world of Toronto journalism.

The first major advance of Bengough's career came at the beginning of the 1870s, a year or two before the birth of *Grip*, when he secured a reporting job with George Brown's Toronto *Globe*. The *Globe* was not only the leading Liberal organ but was also by far the most influential paper in the country, and although Bengough never mentioned it, his job there probably arose from his father's Scots Liberal background. Brown was attentive to the political and racial backgrounds of new employees, and a place on his paper was not easy to get.[17] But Bengough's family had paid its party dues. His father had personally supported Oliver Mowat, the man who was to dominate Ontario politics throughout the *Grip* years. He had nominated Mowat for a seat in a pre-Confederation parliament and had served as one of his 'chief stump speakers.'[18] Later, both brother Thomas and sister Mary worked for Mowat's provincial government, and the Grip Printing and Publishing Company was for some time its major printer. (This party loyalty was to extend over many decades. In their mature years, both Thomas and J.W. repeatedly asked Prime Minister Laurier for contracts and appointments, reminding him of their family's long support of the Liberal Party. Both were also close to the young William Lyon Mackenzie King.)[19]

If Bengough's political colour was fortunate, so was his timing. His move into Toronto newspapering came at a period when the city's journalistic world was in splendid ferment. While the *Globe* was still at the peak of its savage power, John A. Macdonald was making strong efforts to challenge it, plotting to buy up and merge the creaky old *Leader*, run by creaky James Beaty, and the obstreperous *Telegraph*, run by obstreperous John Ross Robertson. When these efforts failed, Macdonald and his associates in the spring of 1872 launched the *Daily Mail* as the chief Tory organ – the party champion that eventually challenged the *Globe*. Thus began one of the great competitive matches in Canadian journalism, a rivalry that was a godsend for an onlooking cartoonist. Helping even more were the murmurs of revolt in the Liberal (Reform) party against the tyranny of Brown and the *Globe*. The infighting gave *Grip* a great deal of scope for independent sniping of a kind that would guard at least for a time against too close identification with the Liberals.

Along with the various dailies, Toronto's journalistic world had a rapidly shifting stable of magazines – religious, political, radical, humorous. Some were backed by political parties or other sponsors, sometimes secretly. Both the newspapers and the magazines were served by a large body of occasional contributors and by a small number of full-time journalists (who were often able and sometimes brilliant), among them R.W. Phipps, Edward Farrer, Nicholas Flood Davin, Phillips Thompson, and E.E. Sheppard. More influential than any of them was Goldwin Smith, the noted English scholar, who had recently settled in Toronto and had set out to elevate the tone of its journalism with his erudite writing and his penchant for helping others start or maintain publications. All in all, it was an active media city, a focus for the province or even for the country. Bengough's sheet was just one more uncertain new voice at an already rowdy party.

The actual spark for the venture (by his own account) was an incident involving James Beaty. An ancient Tory warhorse, the *Leader* publisher became Bengough's most Dickensian figure: a funereal, gnarled curmudgeon in high hat and 1840s-style frock coat ('Of Comfort No Man Speak'). Beaty apparently had a habit of taking the summer air in a sidewalk armchair outside his newspaper office at the corner of King Street and Leader Lane. Bengough noticed him holding court one day and found the face and figure irresistible. He made a sketch and showed it to an acquaintance, who passed it on to Beaty's nephew Sam, the *Leader*'s business manager. Sam Beaty was much taken by it, and he strolled across the lane to Rolph Bros to have a lithographed duplicate made. Bengough in turn was impressed: 'I had not up to that time known anything of the mysteries of lithography, and the ease and accuracy with which the reproduction was done struck me with amazement; but further, it gave me an idea. Why not start a weekly comic paper with lithographed cartoons?'[20]

While Bengough makes this discovery sound rather simple, his brother Thomas suggests the process was more complicated and that Bengough for a time circulated his cartoons only by reproducing them for street sales. It is not clear exactly how he did this, but it is interesting that he started his career with the venerable eighteenth-century English pattern of street trade in satirical prints and ended it with an attempt to adjust to the twentieth-century medium of moving pictures. It is also notable that Bengough started his magazine at a time when cartoons in association with serious journalism were a rarity. Much later he mused wryly on what might have happened if, while at the *Globe*, he had had the nerve to propose cartoons to George Brown or his dour brother, Gordon. It would, he

"OF COMFORT NO MAN SPEAK;
LET'S TALK OF GRAVES, OF WORMS, AND EPITAPHS!"—Shakespeare.

Grip, 1 Nov. 1873. A sketch of James Beaty similar to this had inspired Bengough a few months earlier to start *Grip*. The scarf wrapped around the top hat was at the time a standard mark of mourning.

thought, have provoked either of those stern Scots into a state that Jimuel Briggs would have called 'a dangerous condition of aghastitude.'[21]

Illustrated humour magazines were by no means a new invention, and *Grip* was not the best of its type when it made its first appearance on 24 May 1873, ill financed (with a capital of eighteen dollars)[22] and more than a little rough in appearance. Neither Bengough nor his brother put their names on it, perhaps because of continuing ties to the *Globe*. The editor's name was listed as Charles P. Hall, apparently a pen-name or front, and within a few weeks it was announced that Phillips Thompson, 'better known as Jimuel Briggs, D.B.' would henceforth take charge of the editorial columns. Briggs continued to be listed as editor until the fall, when the pen-name Barnaby Rudge was substituted. This evidently was an attempt to reinforce the idea of vesting the magazine's personality with the character of Grip, the perky raven from Dickens's *Barnaby Rudge*.

The technique of creating this kind of persona for the sheet was of course a direct steal from *Punch*, whose jester figure had for decades politely pricked the consciences of British politicians. The style of *Grip* also was a close copy of the British magazine, with its blend of sketches, jokes, and comment. Despite Bengough's fascination for Thomas Nast, it is clear that *Punch*, and especially its great artist John (later Sir John) Tenniel, was a more important model. If Nast inspired Bengough, it was primarily with the idea that a cartoonist could have a powerful social and political influence. He had an intense admiration for Nast's cartoons, finding them 'wonderful, and their moral force in many cases great and even terrible.'[23] Along with most other North American artists, Bengough borrowed Nast's ideas and symbols – for instance, the Republican elephant, which in Canada came to represent Macdonald's National Policy.[24] But his drawing style and his approach to political satire owed more to the gentlemanly English manner than to Nast's brooding German Gothic style.

Like the English artists, Bengough favoured a light, civil tone, far removed from the savage brilliance of such Old Masters as Hogarth and Gillray or the stark, surreal work of the contemporary French artists Daumier and Gavarni.[25] He attacked almost always within tight bounds of taste, regarding himself as a gentleman of high morality. From the start, this visual style was imposed on the entire magazine, Bengough drawing not just the one or two major cartoons for each issue but also a number of smaller ones, sometimes four or five on a page. Often he did not sign them, and sometimes, to lend variety, he altered his style and signed with a pen-name. For instance, he used the name L. Côté for a style that was much leaner and less cluttered than his normal manner. (He later recalled wryly that a professor of drawing had praised Côté as a 'rare find' who should serve as a model for him.)[26]

Bengough's output is the more amazing considering that he quickly launched what amounted to a simultaneous second career as a travelling preacher-entertainer, giving 'chalk talks' – humorous lectures accompanied by rapid sketches of local or national figures. As he recalled it, he gave the first of these talks in Toronto's Music Hall at Church and Adelaide streets on a March night in 1874, when he was still in his early twenties. Armed with a ghost-written script, an easel, a supply of white newsprint paper, and a quantity of black conté crayons (and wearing his artist's smock), he proceeded to lecture on 'The Pleasantries of Public Life,' illustrating his points with about fifteen rapidly drawn sketches. The *Globe* (possibly the reviewer was friendly, given Bengough's work there) reported that the audience was repeatedly provoked to roars of laughter and that the 'facility with which the physiognomies of well known individuals were delineated' was very striking.[27]

The success of these chalk talks (again, the idea was a steal from Nast) led to wider tours, eventually taking Bengough to the United States and Britain, and even as far as Australia and New Zealand, where he was well received. Typically, he would arrive in a new town early enough to meet, study, and perhaps sketch some of its prominent citizens. Then, in the local hall that evening, he would astonish the audience by reproducing familiar faces, mingling the sketching with humorous recitations or songs and with a dash of social reform sermonizing.

Like Thompson, who also earned a significant part of his income on the platform, Bengough quickly made himself into a well-known public figure. At a time when Toronto journalism was entering one of its most interesting periods, the two men, both individually and in partnership, were producing a remarkable flow of material – in prose, poetry, sketches and lectures. Much of it was ephemeral. In *Grip*, the best of it remains.

3

Politics: The Seventies

The life of *Grip* magazine coincided roughly with the final two decades of the Macdonald era, lasting only a few years past the Old Chieftain's death in 1891. These decades were, for a later generation, the best known of Macdonald's years, extending from the Pacific Scandal to the 'Empire vs continentalism' election of March 1891. Throughout most of this period, especially the first and last parts of it, Bengough showed a persistent if often subtle hostility to the prime minister and his Tory government. While he claimed to strive for balance and to welcome openings for a clear crack at the Liberals, his protests had a defensive ring.

Over its life, *Grip* showed much more sympathy to the Grit (Liberal/Reform) cause, especially to Wilfrid Laurier and the durable Ontario premier, Oliver Mowat. Bengough also respected both Alexander Mackenzie and Edward Blake, though he had reservations about their leadership skills. The only Liberal leader he could not admire was George Brown, his former boss at the *Globe,* whose despotic control of Reform politics upset the younger and more radical wing of the party. Exactly why Bengough felt such antagonism for Brown is not clear, but it was enormously helpful to *Grip,* allowing it to seem nonpartisan in its early days.

Bengough's slant was well known (and discounted) by readers of his own times, but it may have had a subtle effect on a later generations. For as long as the country lasts, Bengough's image of Macdonald is likely to be fixed on the national consciousness. And while this image is not entirely unsympathetic (since he found Macdonald's face and personality a fascinating study), it includes a steady diet of critical cartoons, highlighted by some classic and extremely negative images that are often reprinted, including the famous 'These hands are clean' cartoon of the Pacific Scandal

('Whither Are We Drifting?') and 'How Long Is This Spree Going to Last?' Conversely, Blake, Laurier, and Mowat come down to us through Bengough's work as men of honesty and probity. They may deserve the image, but it is also possible that Bengough's view has conditioned the way we see them. It is fascinating to read in a P.B. Waite school text a remark of this kind: 'Mowat looked, and sometimes behaved, like the bright, plump little boy with glasses who was always in the front row at school under the benign eye of the teacher, while bad little Johnny Macdonald was, so to speak, with the boys at the back who got into trouble and were occasionally strapped for it.' At first glance, the images seem apt. But it may be fair to ask if they are partly the creation of Bengough, who certainly saw the leaders this way ('Gone to Tell His Dad!' p. 44; '"Oliver" at Fagin's,' p. 45). In the same text, Waite explicitly credits Bengough with shaping his image of Edward Blake: 'Blake ... was a neurotic, tense, unhappy person; *Grip* portrayed him as a Hamlet, decision trembling in the balance of his tortured mind.'[1]

If Bengough's images dominated the times, it is not surprising that the Tories made some attempt to counter them. An effort to establish a Montreal rival, the *Jester*, lasted only briefly in 1878–79.[2] Just a few issues of the *Jester* remain, and they show, in Henri Julien's able sketches, a strong, clear-sighted Sir John ('The Hen and Chicken,' p. 47), an interesting contrast to Bengough's dissolute image of the prime minister. Another attempt to set up a Tory-leaning rival in Toronto failed in the late eighties, at least partly because of Bengough's pre-eminence. An apparent attempt of the Tories to buy into *Grip* also fizzled – though it may have had a hidden and temporary measure of success.

Failing to compete with *Grip* or to subvert it, the Tories fell back on rude attacks, like this one from the Toronto *Empire*, stressing the magazine's partisanship:

> If gritty *Grip* should 'grip' a Grit,
> the Grit so gripped would growl;
> if Grit should grip *Grip* in return,
> how gritty *Grip* would howl.[3]

This kind of taunt appeared regularly and always incensed Bengough – perhaps because it was deserved.

For ease of analysis, it is useful to divide *Grip*'s political record into two

WHITHER ARE WE DRIFTING?

HOW LONG IS THIS SPREE GOING TO LAST?

Grip, 16 Aug. 1873 (*opposite*) and 5 Sept. 1885 (*above*). Two of the most destructive (and enduring) images that Bengough left of Macdonald are these cartoons, which followed, respectively, the Pacific Scandal revelations and the Northwest Rebellion.

GONE TO TELL HIS DAD!

Grip, 14 July 1883. *Grip* repeatedly painted Oliver Mowat as an honest and straight-forward youngster – in contrast to the 'bad boy' Macdonald. This cartoon marked a series of constitutional clashes between Ontario and Ottawa, in which both sides sought support from the imperial government.

"OLIVER" AT FAGIN'S.

"UPON THIS, THE YOUNG GENTLEMAN * * CAME ROUND HIM AND SHOOK HIS HANDS VERY HARD—ESPECIALLY THE ONE IN WHICH HE HELD HIS LITTLE BUNDLE. ONE YOUNG GENTLEMAN WAS VERY ANXIOUS TO HANG UP HIS HAT FOR HIM, AND ANOTHER WAS SO OBLIGING AS TO PUT HIS HANDS IN HIS POCKETS."—*Vide Oliver Twist.*

Grip, 22 Sept. 1883. Another portrayal of Mowat as an innocent child, this sketch played on a combination of audience prejudices by showing the Bleu party as Fagin (holding 'Quebec's toasting fork') and the provinces as his young thieves. (*cont.*)

contrasting decades, the first and shorter one running from the magazine's founding in 1873 to Mackenzie's resignation and George Brown's death in 1880, and the second continuing on to Bengough's departure from the magazine in 1892. In the first period, Bengough was much more inclined to be nonpartisan, especially between Macdonald and Brown, since he felt he had good reason to attack both. In the second decade, Bengough's consistent antipathy to Macdonald and his people stands in contrast to an almost constant admiration for Blake, Laurier, and Mowat – at least until the period when Phillips Thompson again became influential on the magazine.

While *Grip*'s slant was undoubtedly gritty in the early 1870s, it would be wrong to judge it by the cartoons most often reprinted in modern times, the tough Pacific Scandal sketches. It is also wrong to consider *Grip* a major player in the 1873–74 railway scandal. It may be true, as Bengough later recalled, that the scandal was a boon to the magazine, helping it stay alive,[4] but as a new and tiny sheet, deep in the shadow of the *Globe*, it had only a marginal effect. As well, the magazine's commentary on the scandal can in no way be compared with the devastating revelations and condemnations of the *Globe* as it exposed the shady connections between the Tories and the railway tycoon Sir Hugh Allan. If anything, *Grip* tended to show annoyance with the extremes of *Globe* vitriol.

In fact, the magazine's ambivalent attitude towards Brown and the *Globe* emerges as an important revelation of its political soul, reflecting the personal and ideological elements that divided the Reformers. Within the party, the *Globe*'s undoubted power begged for challenge, and *Grip* was only one of many critics who flung pebbles at the giant's ankles. Like Goldwin Smith, Bengough considered Brown a narrow, intolerant bully. 'Brown can never forgive anyone who is guilty of thinking for himself,' his magazine observed in response to a *Globe* attack on Smith. (At the same time, *Grip* was even harsher towards the 'decrepit' Tory *Leader* and its 'parasite' proprietor, James Beaty.)

Occasionally, Bengough seemed to show personal animus in his snide or gratuitous attacks on Brown, some of which were related to Brown's treatment of employees. At the time of Brown's death, though, he had qualified praise for the *Globe* editor and mentioned in passing that he had never personally met him.[5] Towards Alexander Mackenzie, by contrast,

---

(*continued*) Quebec premier Joseph-Alfred Mousseau is picking Oliver Mowat's pockets, while Manitoba's John Norquay grasps at his 'Awarded Territory' bundle. The thief trying on Mowat's hat is Ontario's Conservative leader, William Meredith.

THE HEN AND CHICKEN.

OLD HEN: — " You've cost no end of trouble in hatching, but you'll make a mighty fine bird."

YOUNG, BUT FACETIOUS, ROOSTER: — "Cardwell shall be my victory, or my *hatch*ment. — Cock-a-doodle-do."

Jester, 13 Sept. 1878. The clean-cut image of Macdonald offered by Henri Julien in the short-lived Tory magazine *Jester* provides an interesting contrast to Bengough's portrayal.

THE REFORM HOUSE SERVANTS.

PRACTICAL SANDY TO POETICAL NED.—"CAN YOU NO FIND SOMETHING ELSE TO DO IN THIS HOOSE BESIDES
POLISHING YON 'ORNAMENT' FOR EVERLASTIN'?"

Grip, 30 Aug. 1879. Despite his admiration for Alexander Mackenzie, Bengough
constantly showed him as subservient to the towering figure of George Brown.
Edward Blake was often described as an ornament to the Reform Party, but his
massive ego drew some resentment.

Bengough's personal feelings were always warmly positive. He admired Mackenzie's integrity and doggedness, even though he sometimes portrayed him as ineffectual and under the strong thumb of Brown ('The Reform House Servants').

In the early years, however, *Grip*'s political thinking was shallow, on a par with its banal and often bigoted jokes and amateurish satire. One juvenile poem, for instance, lampooned the royal commission that was looking into the Pacific Scandal:

> Three judges sit like three black crows
> Reporters sit beneath in rows ...
>
> Sir John he stepped up dapper and spry
> With a smile on his lips and a wink in his eye,
> He got cash from Sir Hugh in galore,
> The pity it was, he didn't get more.
> The Grits were bribing both left and right,
> And he bribed too, with all his might ...[6]

Bengough's visual images of the time are more powerful. Some seem even-handed, like 'Blackwash and Whitewash,' but most of his cartoons about the scandal were hostile to the government. Especially effective was the classic cartoon of Macdonald sitting as judge, witness, and advocate ('The Beauties of a Royal Commission,' p. 51) or the even more famous 'hit' in which Macdonald was portrayed saying calmly to Mackenzie, 'I admit I took the money and bribed the electors with it. Is there anything wrong about *that*?' ('We in Canada ...,' p. 52).

In its text, *Grip* was seldom so forceful, though now and then it managed to draw blood. For instance, at the beginning of 1874, after the Tories had been forced out of office and were facing a general election, one of *Grip*'s writers did a savage Miltonian treatment with Macdonald in the role of Satan:

ON THE MIGHTY FALLEN

> Erect he stands, and brazen lifts his head,
> Above the beaten rabble that he led,
> Higher in daring, scorning vain excuse:
> Master of every weapon of abuse.
> Fast from his lips the wordy torrent flows

BLACKWASH AND WHITEWASH.

ILLUSTRATING THE RECENT GREAT OPPOSITION SPEECHES, AND THE DOINGS OF THE JOLLY ROYAL COMMISSION.

Grip, 20 Sept. 1873. One of the more balanced cartoons of the Pacific Scandal era had Brown, Mackenzie, Blake, and E.B. Wood tarring one side of the prime minister while T.C. Patteson of the *Mail* and James Beaty of the *Leader* gave Macdonald the balancing whitewash.

> In foul vituperation of his foes,
> The gibe at purity, the wanton jest,
> The leer at virtue, each becomes him best.
> The baffled trickster fawning on the mob,
> Unblushing dares the hiss, defends the job.
>
> ... Shrivel the hand that blackens honest fame;
> Or lends a deeper agony to shame, –
> But when a man like this, exposed still dares
> To bawl again for trust in public ears;
> *Grip* loses pity, can no longer feel,
> And lets the vermin wriggle on his steel![7]

The publication of this poem was enough, in the codes of the day, to establish *Grip* as an unequivocally Grit sheet. In the next few issues, there-

THE BEAUTIES OF A ROYAL COMMISSION
"WHEN SHALL WE THREE MEET AGAIN?"

Grip, 23 Aug. 1873. While Macdonald did indeed shape the royal commission in the hope of containing the Pacific Scandal, this much-reprinted cartoon is curiously out of keeping with reality. It shows Macdonald confident and in charge at a time when he had just come through a period of drunken despair.

"WE IN CANADA SEEM TO HAVE LOST ALL IDEA OF JUSTICE, HONOR
AND INTEGRITY."—The Mail, 26th September.

fore, Bengough was at pains to re-establish his neutrality. He published a clumsy poem saying that while *Grip* had been 'accused of party zeal,' it actually detested political pole-cats of any stripe. Macdonald's people had for a time qualified as the foulest of polecats:

> But there's many a sinner who hides his disgrace
>   Behind the broad Aegis whose Gorgon is Brown
> *Grip* dreads not to petrefy under that face,
>   And is ready to hunt all the scalliwags down.[8]

After the Tory election defeat the magazine was somewhat easier on Macdonald, sending up both parties more or less equally. In a clever set of 'New Nursery Rhymes' it said of the Tories:

> Sing a song of scandal, a Premier fond of rye,
> With half-a-hundred Tories knocked into pie.

But at the same time it was even harsher on Brown:

> There was an old Humbug, and what do you think,
> The *Globe* which he ran gave him victuals and drink;
> Now that Government pap forms a part of his diet,
> *This raving Reformer is rather more quiet.*[9]

Similarly, in 1875, *Grip*, probably following the lead of Goldwin Smith's columns in the *Nation*, endorsed reports of a Liberal revolt against Brown and addressed this awkward and notably unhumorous poem to him (the line about Bow Park refers to Brown's huge model farm near Brantford):

> Thy time is up; thy date has fled; Canadians good and true
> Are crowding in – they'll have their way – they have no fear of you.
> They know thee foolish – know thee false; they've learnt what you're about

---

Grip, 27 Sept. 1873 (*opposite*). This devastating cartoon was published at a time when Macdonald was beginning to lose support in his own party – a slide that culminated in the government's forced resignation six weeks later. *Grip*'s use of the *Mail* quotation cleverly turned the tables on the Tories, since the remark had originally referred not to Macdonald's conduct but to the action of the Liberals in publishing his stolen correspondence.

Too long hast thou with sharp Sir John played game of 'in and out';
Get thee unto the Park of Bow; our shame, *Grip* tells thee true,
Is that too long we blindly took the lead from such as you.[10]

A satirical attack on Brown from the same period had him charged with immoderate driving and then defending himself by insisting he could drive as he liked since he had 'made this Dominion, and Province, and city what they were, and considered that, properly, everybody and everything belonged to him and must give way to his inclinations, as he was the greatest person in the land, and real King of the country.'[11] Even more striking was a savagely brilliant 1876 poem, published at a time when Brown was in trouble for criticizing a judge. Written in the style of Alexander Pope, it probably came from a pen more talented than Bengough's, perhaps the same one that had worked over the fallen Macdonald:

THE DESTINY OF A DEMAGOGUE

In prime of life, with native vigour keen,
Of stinging pen, and blatant mouth, is seen –
The people's man, just rising from the ranks ...

He uses bribes, buys, sells, the chief of all,
Yet still makes 'Purity' his party's call.
A lifetime spent in wrangling and in noise,
At length his party tastes the Treasury's joys.
Alas, they prove the ancient saying true,
Far easier to abuse than better do ...

At downright bribery we next him find,
As Justice does, and tells him all her mind.
Maddened to fury, on the courts he turns
His wrath; each column long with insults burns ...
The mask has dropped; the long deception's past.
The demagogue has done his worst – and last.[12]

Bengough's cartoons were much less harsh than this. His portrayal of Brown is not memorable – unlike his expressive Macdonald image – and in the early stages it could even be called bland. Gradually it became more critical, showing Brown as a dictator, a conservative, a purveyor of vitriolic messages, a tyrant controlling a weak but admirable Mackenzie[13] or trying to control the brilliant but rebellious Edward Blake. One satire had Brown and Mackenzie disciplining Blake for his much-discussed 1876 Aurora speech, in which he had set out a number of tentative new directions. It had Brown urging the prime minister to use on MPs the kind of toughness he himself used to control his *Globe* writers: 'Keep them doon, brak their speerit, and turn the spitefu' anger o' their subdued souls against the opposite pairty.' Another satire had Brown proposing to the *Mail* a joint effort to crush *Grip*, since every time he tried to offer a small bribe or to browbeat a judge, 'straightaway a deeabolic cairtoon sets a' folks in convulsion.'[14]

Grip's mix of views at this stage suggests not so much nonpartisanship as immaturity, a lack of the ideological direction it would later acquire. This may simply indicate that Bengough, as a young and struggling editor with few resources, was inclined to take any freelance material that looked provocative; or perhaps he was intimidated by his more experienced colleagues, Thompson and R.W. Phipps. Bengough later recalled that Phipps, a crusty and arrogant writer, produced a great proportion of *Grip*'s best prose and verse for several years.[15] He also named a number of other freelance contributors but claimed that he himself wrote a great deal of the magazine during the early years. It seems certain that *Grip*'s strong antagonism for both Macdonald and Brown, as well as its disgust with an old style of corrupt politics, represented the editor's core views. Phillips Thompson, in the periods when he was editing *Grip* or writing for it, would have sharpened these views. The antagonism for Brown may also have been inspired by the campaign Goldwin Smith was running in a number of Toronto publications.

If there was a consistent thread to the magazine's views in this period, it was the regular support for the amorphous ginger group at the edges of the Liberal Party, a group that was pressing for 'true reform' and, on its most critical days, talking of a possible third party, one that would be more pure and high-minded than the two 'old' parties. As part of this group, *Grip* encouraged any signs of revolt against Brown that occurred in Grit papers and sometimes took sides in the internal wrangles of the ginger group.[16]

The magazine went through odd contortions, for instance, on Canada First, the movement that emerged partly to reflect these reformist views. In December 1873 *Grip* seemed to welcome Canada First, portraying it as a small, serious, sword-wielding 'giant-killer,' a cross between David and Saint George, with feet planted firmly on the heads of both Tory and Grit leaders.[17] A week later an E.D. Thomson poem saluted the 'Canadian

Party': 'Well done! for the time is close by you / When your motto shall sound through the land.'[18] Another effusive poem lauded the Aryan or nordic mysticism that was part of Canada First's vague nationalism:

GRIP TO CANADA

Arise, fair land! My countrymen arise!
Be strong in sense and bold in enterprise.
Lay by small feuds; crush down mistaken spleen;
And let the Orange mingle with the Green.
Let Celt and Saxon know each draws his fires
From far off Aryan dames and Aryan sires,
And stand up worthy of the future nigh ...[19]

However, *Grip* soon turned against Canada First, possibly because of Thompson's influence. At the beginning of 1874, in the midst of the election campaign that confirmed the Liberals in power, Thompson and a partner launched a paper called the *National*, which they hoped would become the voice of Canada First and tariff protection. But they were snubbed, on the eve of their first issue, by Goldwin Smith and the Canadian National Association, which claimed to be the hard core of the movement. This group (described by the *National* as '*dillitanti* [*sic*] with a penchant for amateur journalism') was setting up its own weekly of political comment, the *Nation*, and wanted no competition.[20]

Thompson stayed with the *National* for more than a year, but he probably continued to write for *Grip*. His views seem to have coincided with those of 'Demos Mudge,' who wrote occasional *Grip* columns in this period and also edited some of its issues. The magazine consequently dropped its normal admiration for Goldwin Smith, brushing aside Canada First as 'Goldwin's Myth' or 'a party by the name of Smith.'[21] Its antagonism was ill focused, though the same could be said for the movement itself, which under the influence of Smith and W.H. Howland was considering party status and proposing independence from Britain. *Grip* seemed opposed to this development as it had been to the pro-Empire stance of the Canada First founders (including imperialist George Taylor Denison), but its voice was uncertain.[22] In early 1874 Demos Mudge observed that Canada First was innocuous – almost as harmless as the *Nation*. 'But the Independence Men mean something. Their object is very definite.'[23] Later that year a satire criticized the *Nation* for failing to come out flatly for independence,[24] yet a Bengough cartoon of the same period clearly joined George Brown in attacking Smith's 'anti-British' ideas and promising that Canada would pay no attention to them.[25] It seems clear that Bengough's support for the British connection clashed with Thompson's independence views. The result was a negative but studiously vague attitude towards Canada First. Late in 1874, *Grip* reported that the movement had died and suggested an appropriate epitaph:

> Sacred to the Memory
> of
> CANADA FIRST
> Man's life is short but mine was shorter
> I died for want of a supporter[26]

In the spring of 1875, *Grip* spoke of a scholar's post-mortem on the movement and said that the public verdict would 'no doubt be that the unlamented deceased committed suicide.' A statement of *Grip*'s reservations on Canada First, still somewhat vague, emerged in an 1876 comment on the death of the *Nation*. The movement, it said, had arrived as an infant of promise, with the mission of proclaiming colonial independence of thought and speech. But as soon as it was able to speak, it 'squeaked unmistakable London snobbery.'[27] This phrasing, stressing the independence of colonial thought and speech but stopping short of political independence, was probably no accident. Bengough would always resist the efforts of Thompson and Smith to break the British connection, and he especially opposed Smith's dreams of a continental union. He continued to admire Smith's talent, however. On the *Nation*'s death, the magazine published a poem entitled 'Grip to Goldwin,' which stated, 'The *Nation* rose when your keen pen / Was given; that lost, it fell again.'[28]

Canada First was never more than a sideshow attraction to Canada's main Tory-Grit bout, and in that arena *Grip* managed for the most part to maintain its image of neutrality throughout the mid-seventies. During the life of the Mackenzie government (1873–78), the magazine often returned to the theme of Brown's ominous and reactionary influence on the government and Blake's reluctance to accept it. *Grip* also published relatively mild jabs at Mackenzie, like this 1875 poem:

A WORD TO THE PREMIER

> Sworn in full fourteen months ago,
> You've precious little done, you know;

THE STEEL RAILS "DIFFICULTY."

> *Grip* thinks you're most confounded slow
> Mackenzie.[29]

But on the major issues of the day, especially on the never-ending list of railway problems, its slant was clear. On the so-called Steel Rails Scandal, when the Montreal *Gazette* charged that Mackenzie's brother had profited from a government contract, Bengough depicted the prime minister as being completely vindicated ('The Steel Rails "Difficulty"'), and on an investigation into the Tories' handling of the Northern Railway, Mackenzie became the honest cop, exposing a nest of 'boodling' Tories ('What Investigation Revealed,' p. 60).

At the same time, *Grip* did not let up on the Tory *Daily Mail*, whose legendary mission was to 'stab the Grits under the fifth rib every lawful day of the week.' The *Mail*'s efforts were lampooned in poems such as this:

BY THE MANAGER OF THE 'MAIL'

> Knife-grinder, hither! come and grind my stabber!
> Last week's fifth ribs have dulled the edge like thunder,
> Come, start your wheel, I've got more victims waiting
> To feel its mettle.[30]

After a court ordered the paper's editor, T.C. Patteson, to pay twenty cents to Grit politician Adam Crooks, one of his victims, *Grip* portrayed Patteson as offering to pay an extra shilling to cover his next 'stabbing' ('A Hint for the "Mail" Manager').

Bengough also showed his political leanings by working with other Grit

---

Grip, 30 Oct. 1875 (*opposite*). When Mackenzie's government was accused of giving a contract to a firm linked to his brother, Bengough was happy to accept the prime minister's rebuttal. The man crushed under the train is Thomas White of the Tory *Gazette* of Montreal. The heart-broken man in the background is T.C. Patteson, manager of the *Mail*, who is saying, 'Another slander crushed! What will become of us?'

Grip, 7 Apr. 1877 (What Investigation Revealed, p. 60). This cartoon is a send-up of the parliamentary committee that was investigating Tory corruption related to campaign contributions from the heavily subsidized Northern Railway. Bengough accepted the validity of the charges – unlike his reaction to the Steel Rails Scandal.

WHAT INVESTIGATION REVEALED.

A HINT FOR THE "MAIL" MANAGER;
OR, "STABBING UNDER THE FIFTH RIB" SYSTEMATISED.

Grip, 24 Apr. 1875. This sketch lampooned the *Mail*'s legendary mission 'to stab the Grits under the fifth rib every lawful day of the week.' After a victim claims a twenty-cent libel award, manager T.C. Patteson pays up another shilling to cover his next stabbing. Ironically, Patteson had hoped that his paper would elevate the tone of political journalism, but he found himself bound by Macdonald's journalistic rule that 'scalps must be taken.'

editors to keep the Pacific Scandal alive. (Tory journalists were busily brushing it aside as the 'Pacific Slander,' insisting it should be seen as a minor fuss, no more serious than various Liberal scams.) When Sir John A. was driven to defend his actions, *Grip* showed him forcing his claims on more principled followers ('The Political Mrs. Squeers'). The magazine did not ignore Liberal scandals, but it is interesting that in an 1876 episode when Speaker Timothy Warren Anglin was accused of corrupt practices related to government printing, *Grip* used the scandal to get at the *Globe* rather than the government. Its satirical poem had Brown singing this song:

> What if Speaker Anglin got
> Certain money he should not?
> Clear eight thousand – was it not
> Just an inadvertence? ...[31]

In a later comment, Bengough seemed to admit that he had been reluctant to dwell on Liberal scandals during this period. 'The Mackenzie government was assailed from time to time with charges of wrong doing,' he recalled, 'but the facts were in every case found to favor the Ministry.'[32]

Grip, 5 Aug. 1876 (*opposite*). As the Conservative press played up the idea that the Pacific Scandal was only a slander, Bengough portrayed Macdonald as Mrs Squeers, the abominable schoolmistress of *Nicholas Nickleby*, forcing that unpalatable doctrine down the throats of more principled followers. The immediate victim is M.C. Cameron, Tory leader in the Ontario legislature. In the foreground, Patteson of the *Mail* is saying, 'She can't sicken me! I can swallow anything!'

Grip, 19 Aug. 1876 (The Only Satisfying Picnic, After All! p. 64). The political picnic reached its zenith in the 1870s, as shown by the list of picnics Sir John has already attended. While Blake, Sir Richard Cartwright, and Mackenzie are closest to the Treasury pie, the chief targets of the cartoon are Joseph Cauchon and George Brown, the giver and receiver of pap (patronage). The irony is that Brown had accused Cauchon of speculating at the expense of asylum inmates, an offence that was 'rank and smelled to heaven' – but had been obliged to hold his tongue when Mackenzie took Cauchon into the cabinet. The small figure behind Macdonald is J.C. Rykert, an unsavoury politician who sometimes represented Lincoln riding.

THE POLITICAL MRS. SQUEERS AND HER NAUSEOUS DOSE.

THE ONLY SATISFYING PICNIC, AFTER ALL!

He seemed even-handed, though, in a much-reprinted cartoon that showed Blake, Mackenzie, and Sir Richard Cartwright gathered around the Treasury pie ('The Only Satisfying Picnic, After All!').

Grip's efforts to seem nonpartisan may have been helped by the fact that, for a time, the magazine and the Tory party were on converging paths in support of tariff protection. When the topic first emerged from limited to general discussion in the depression doldrums of 1876, Bengough (in contrast to his later strong support for free trade) was sympathetic to the idea. He pushed tariff protection on the Grits, implying that George Brown was preventing Mackenzie from taking it up ('Wanted – Protection!!' p. 66), and he accused the Tories of flirting with it only as a way of getting back into office.[33] Through much of 1876, the magazine sporadically promoted the idea, its enthusiasm showing less in the cartoons than in the text. The latter was probably influenced by Thompson, who was pushing the idea at the *National*, and by Phipps, who claimed to be the creator of the policy. (After the 1878 election, he was irrationally bitter at Macdonald for failing to reward him with a high post.)[34] A typical *Grip* poem of the period told Canadians they were the laughing-stock of the world because they chose to remain a farming nation, bringing in manufactured goods from abroad:

> ... You toil unceasing for a pittance bare.
> The profit goes to him, who fat and fair
> In other and more cunning regions dwells
> And manufactures, and complacent sells
> The fruits of twenty minutes work to you
> For that which took you two full days to do.[35]

Another poem reported the chant of the free trader:

> Hurrah for Free Trade that shuts up all our shops!
> Hurrah for Free Trade that makes cheap all our crops!
> Hurrah for Free Trade that makes prices all small!
> And leaves us no money to buy with at all.[36]

For a time, as the Tories moved towards a protectionist platform, it looked as though the magazine might be switching its political colours, especially when it boasted of its independence from the Grits. On one occasion it said that the *Globe* never mentioned *Grip* 'because *Grip* will

WANTED—PROTECTION!!

not have his wings clipped and live in the old rickety cage of Gritism.'
On another occasion it said that the *Globe* had switched to 'thorough
Conservatism' and was preventing Blake from launching any reforms.
Another satire, early in 1878, had *Grip* lecturing Mackenzie for not
adopting protection, and the prime minister replying, 'If we gie Protec-
tion, the *Globe* wad turn on us like a fleeing dragon an' oot we gang.'[37]
However, as the Tories came closer to consensus on their protective
National Policy, *Grip* seemed to back off, and it returned to hints about a
nebulous third party:

> Cry the Tories, 'You're doing things utterly wrong,'
> Cry the Grits, 'So in your day did you' ...
> Our two parties are parties of knaves, it is plain,
> 'What a pity,' says *Grip*, 'there's no third.'[38]

In the run-up to the 1878 election, *Grip*'s cartoons reflected this kind of
balance. 'The Mysterious Handwriting on the Wall' (23 Feb. 1878)
painted the Grits as plump and overconfident, while Blake's departure
from the cabinet was seen as removal of the government's moral weight.[39]
'On Their Trial' (1 June 1878) showed a remarkably spry and fresh-faced
Macdonald presenting a jury with a bill of Liberal sins. Bengough's summary noted that the indictment included many sins of commission and
'one overwhelming sin of omission in the matter of tariff reform.'[40] Gradually, however, Bengough's enthusiasm for the protective tariff waned.
He took the curve carefully, portraying the National Policy at one point
during the summer of 1878 as a Trojan Horse by which the Tories hoped
to gain office ('Ancient Tory Tactics,' p. 70).[41] During the actual campaign, while not opposing protection in principle, he accused the Tories
of a two-faced approach, delivering one message in Ontario and another
in the Maritimes.

In general, the magazine was remarkably neutral throughout the campaign, especially in comparison with its earlier and later attacks on the

---

Grip, 26 Feb. 1876 (*opposite*). This is one of the cartoons that Bengough left out
when, after he had changed his views on tariff protection, he published a
collection of his work. It is notable that Uncle Sam looks very much like George
Brown, who, in Bengough's view, was preventing Mackenzie from endorsing
protection.

THE MYSTERIOUS HANDWRITING ON THE WALL.

Grip, 23 Feb. 1878. Bengough assumed a high level of biblical knowledge on the part of his readers. In this sketch, he combined the New Testament loaves-and-fishes miracle with the Old Testament incident in which Daniel interpreted the mysterious writing on the wall that predicted the downfall of Babylonian King Belshazzar ('Mene, mene, tekel, upharsin'). While Macdonald writes on the wall, Tupper says, 'Hurry up with "upharsin" – I'm hungry for the loaves and fishes.'

ON THEIR TRIAL.

Grip, 1 June 1878. Bengough's even-handedness before the 1878 election is shown not only in the indictment list (which details a number of scandals in which the Grits were accused, including printing contracts to Speaker T.W. Anglin and the Steel Rails Issue) but in Macdonald's youthful vigour and the Grits' nervousness.

Tories. But just before the vote, a renewed faith in the Grits emerged. 'Renewing the Lease' predicted Mackenzie's re-election and said he deserved it, since he had been a faithful tenant, in contrast to Macdonald's sloppiness and irresponsibility. When Mackenzie lost, Bengough produced a 'mea culpa' cartoon entitled 'O, Our Prophetic Soul' (p. 72). (Interestingly, he portrayed himself almost as a teenager, as if this might excuse his faulty judgment.)

In the wake of the election, *Grip* seemed to accept the National Policy with equanimity. It stated that it had made fun of it because the policy's variations appeared to have 'more of the ludicrous than the serious in them,' but the sovereign public had taken a different view and might in the long run prove wiser than *Grip*. This comment led some people to think *Grip* was edging towards the Tories. The following week the magazine took

ANCIENT ~~TROY~~ TACTICS
OR

Grip, 6 July 1878 (*above*). Bengough gradually dropped his support for tariff protection and portrayed it as a Tory ploy to gain office. The Tories already aboard the Trojan Horse include Nicholas Flood Davin, James Beaty, and Sir David Macpherson, as well as Tupper and Macdonald. J. Burr Plumb is climbing the ladder.

Grip, 14 Sept. 1878 (*opposite*). On the eve of the 1878 election, Bengough's Grit sympathies re-emerged, as seen in this portrayal of Macdonald as a ne'er-do-well accompanied by several curs representing his past sins. Macdonald is saying, 'Turn that tenant out and give me the farm again. I have a grand new Plan for running it!' Mackenzie replies, 'The cheek of the Fellow! Just when I have reclaimed it from the state he left it in!!!'

---

issue with one such report, saying that it would be happy if the new policy brought the blessings its sponsors promised but '*Grip* has not changed his opinion, which is that the National Policy as variously propositioned by the Conservative leaders in the various provinces is impracticable.'[42] Nowhere did the magazine admit that it had been assiduously plugging protection

RENEWING THE LEASE.

MISS CANADA (TO JOHN A.)—"YOU WANT THE FARM AGAIN: YOU LEFT IT IN A SHOCKING CONDITION FIVE YEARS AGO, AND THE PRESENT TENANT HAS ALMOST RESTORED IT BY HIS INDUSTRY. YOUR 'PLAN' LOOKS BOGUS. I WILL RENEW MACKENZIE'S LEASE."

O, OUR PROPHETIC SOUL!

(See last week's Cartoon.)

JOHN A.—"I DON'T KNOW, BUT IT SEEMS TO ME THIS PICTURE OF YOURS, MY PROPHETIC FRIEND, NEEDS A LITTLE 'RE-ADJUSTMENT,' DON'T IT, HEY?"

only a year or so earlier. Similarly, when Bengough published his major collection of cartoons eight years later, he carefully excluded those that had supported protection and used instead a number that showed the Tories as inconsistent or as having taken up the policy for cynical reasons.[43] A judicious editing of the past also showed in Bengough's later comment that he had portrayed the National Policy as a white elephant because he believed it would prove to be an embarrassment to the Tories. But at the time of the election, he had portrayed it as a very powerful elephant indeed, crushing the Grit foes ('Riding into Power').[44]

While distancing itself from the National Policy after the 1878 election, *Grip* seemed happy to emphasize the defeat of George Brown and the *Globe,* and to back the efforts of those Grits who wanted to see Blake replace the Brown and Mackenzie leadership ('Clamoring for the Fancy Doll'). With unrestrained amusement, it printed a letter 'To the Globe' that began:

> And art thou quite broke down, turned out to grass,
> Old warhorse of the past, whose sturdy charge
> Bore down Conservatives full oft en masse?
> What, art thou quite worn out, and set at large?[45]

Also in the post-election period, *Grip* took a turn towards respectability. In the spring of 1879, about the time the *Jester* was folding, the magazine expanded from four to eight pages and introduced a much more professional and sedate format.[46] It printed its main cartoon directly in the magazine (rather than folding it into the four-page issue) and added many more small cartoons, along with much more freelance material. It also inaugurated some short-lived columns on theatre and music in a clear bid to go upscale. Circulation increased, from a claimed total of three thousand in its first year to seven thousand or more in the early 1880s.[47] For the first time, Bengough listed his name as editor.

The effect of these changes was to de-emphasize politics to a degree. On occasion, the magazine still tormented the Tories, warning them not to repeat the sins of the past, criticizing their confusion in implementing the National Policy, or condemning their 'spoils' approach in dismissing Grit

---

Grip, 21 Sept. 1878 (*opposite*). After Macdonald's return to power, Bengough portrayed him much more sympathetically – and showed the Grip raven (upper left) vowing to get out of the prophecy business.

RIDING INTO POWER.

Grip, 28 Sept. 1878. This cartoon is a dig at R.W. Phipps, a frequent *Grip* writer, who claimed to have devised the National Policy and resented Macdonald's refusal to bring him into the new government. Macdonald is saying, 'This elephant belongs to Phipps. He imported it and no one else knows how to manage it.' Phipps, at the front of the elephant, is saying, 'I can pitch them all off if I like.'

CLAMORING FOR THE FANCY DOLL.

Grip, 7 Dec. 1878. In his treatment of the Liberal leaders, Bengough drew as an insider, reflecting the party's ambivalence about replacing Mackenzie with Blake. Again, Brown is the controller, manipulating both the party and the leaders. He is saying, 'Hoot-toot! ye hizzie! Be content wi' this one! Yon's only for ornament!'

SIR JOHN'S CROWNING VICTORY.

Grip, 23 Aug. 1879. Here, Bengough has George Brown crying 'He needs an unco' dip o this, Your Majesty!' as he tries to pour whitewash on Macdonald. Despite his political leanings, Bengough had a grudging admiration for Macdonald's wit and mischievousness, and a corresponding dislike of Brown's humourless tyranny. These personal feelings helped maintain a balance in his cartooning – but the advantage disappeared with Brown's death a few months after this cartoon.

civil servants.[48] More rarely, the old acid reappeared, as in a cruel satire late in 1878 that pictured Sir John bragging in a drunken stupor about his total control of his party. (The Commons would keep on backing him, he claimed, even if he brought in a bill forcing all Canadians to get their back teeth drawn.)[49] But when Sir John the following year was admitted to the Imperial Privy Council – an honour that overcame much of the shame of the Pacific Scandal – Bengough seemed to take pleasure in the prime minister's triumph over Brown ('Sir John's Crowning Victory').

Where the Grits were concerned, *Grip* more often spoke as an insider, taking part in internal squabbles. In the spring of 1880, when the party after much agony resolved to remove Mackenzie from the leadership, *Grip* reflected its ambivalence, accusing party members of betrayal while at the same time pressing for Mackenzie to go. At the end of March it ran a poetic tribute that began:

> Mackenzie, while you stand alone,
> Stout foes before, false friends behind,
> Deserted, soon to be o'erthrown,
> Feeling how thankless is mankind,
> Let one impartial voice proclaim ...
> Honored shall be thy stainless name![50]

Yet only two weeks later, just before Mackenzie's departure, Bengough querulously portrayed him hanging onto his hobby-horse, refusing to give it up to aid the party and 'give the brilliant Ned a chance.'[51]

While the Grits were coping with this problem in the nominal leadership, even more profound change was signalled when a disgruntled printer shot and wounded George Brown. *Grip*'s first reaction (at a time when Brown's wound seemed minor) was unsympathetic. It ran a cartoon in rather bad taste showing Macdonald lecturing the assassin, telling him that Brown's disappearance would help the Grits and hurt the Tories. This was balanced by a courteous tribute, however, and at Brown's unexpected death, *Grip* saluted him as an honest man and true patriot.[52] Bengough wrote one of his soon-to-be-famous poetic elegies, constrained by his need to mention Brown's faults and errors:

> ... he bore a manly front,
> Lending his pen to freedom's sacred cause,
> Counselling wisely for the nation's weal,
> And smiting down the ills that menaced her ...
>
> He hated falsehood with a burning scorn,
> But may have erred, mistaking true for false;
> His nature was a rushing mountain stream,
> His faults but eddies which its swiftness bred.[53]

At the same time, *Grip* seemed euphoric about the prospects for a 'new spirit' in politics – a new spirit presumably made possible by the disappearance of Mackenzie and Brown. 'The new leader of the Liberal party proves to be a statesman in the highest and best sense – pure in language – lofty in aims – high-minded in method – successful in carrying out every good project.'[54] Clearly, Bengough realized that Brown's death and Mackenzie's departure had ended an era, transforming the political map for Liberal leaders and supporters. But it is not so apparent that he fully appreciated how this would change *Grip*'s position.

4

Politics: The Eighties

In its second decade, *Grip* earned its enduring reputation as a Grit-leaning organ. It moved perceptibly from a position of moderate party support in the election of 1882 (when Tory hopes of its neutrality were dashed) to a clear backing of the Grits in the election of 1887 and outspoken advocacy in the 'loyalty' election of 1891. In that last campaign (the Liberals' fourth loss in a row), the extent of the magazine's commitment showed vividly in commentary and poems that ridiculed Macdonald's 'Old Flag, Old Policy' campaign and his warnings that the Liberals' free trade platform amounted to annexationism:

> And now we go in for everything old,
>   Since Sir John has set the fashion,
> Old Leader, Old Policy, Old Red Flag,
>   To stir each patriot's passion;
> Old chestnuts, old tricks and old promises too,
>   And the same old scale of wages,
> Old prices, old clothes, old heelers, old bribes,
>   The old, old campaign rages![1]

Clearly, much had changed since *Grip*'s neutral stance of 1878. As Macdonald fought his final campaign, painting the Grits as secret traitors, the magazine reacted with outright contempt: 'The nonsensical ravings of the Tory leaders and organs just now in denunciation of "traitors" and "treason" are calculated to make us rub our eyes and wonder whether we are really living near the close of the nineteenth century or in the Middle Ages.' An elaborate satire accused the Tories of planning to bring back the institutions and ideals of the Dark Ages: the Inquisition, the burning of witches, the drawing and quartering of criminals.[2]

Grip tried to give the appearance of detachment by criticizing small aspects of Liberal policy, but its heart was not in it. The overall tone recalled the early days when *Grip* had tormented John A. in the Pacific Scandal. It was as though the magazine, nearing the end of its life, was giving up the pretence of nonpartisanship and returning to the old faith.

One sign of this was a lack of restraint in the long-running fight over its political bias. When, after the 1891 election, the Tory Halifax *Herald* remarked that *Grip* had always been a 'dirty, disreputable and disloyal sheet,' the magazine snarled back in a way that was typical of election-time exchanges between political editors but was not in *Grip*'s once-moderate style. Considering the source of this comment, it said, the charge amounted to a compliment: 'We are "dirty" because we have not wallowed in the mire of the Pacific Scandal, and defended every government job from that day to the present; "disreputable" because we have not fawned upon every boodler and rascal in public life; and "disloyal" because we have not helped to hold up the old flag as a screen behind which the toilers of this country might be robbed.'[3] The toughness of this language reflects not so much a momentary removal of the mask as a maturing of the magazine – a willingness to speak its mind and an unwillingness to make the effort to please every reader.

The distinctly partisan attitude was evident throughout the eighties. It showed early in the decade when *Grip*'s attacks on CPR financing and other issues led to a slanging match with prominent Tories. It was more evident in the 1882 election, when its assault on the gerrymander bill killed Tory hopes that the magazine would remain even-handed.[4] It was even more pronounced, especially in relation to Oliver Mowat's provincial government, after the Grip Printing and Publishing Company in mid-decade became a major printer of that government's material and the Tories tried unsuccessfully to set up a rival sheet. It showed up in the great issues of the late 1880s – in criticism of Macdonald's handling of the Northwest Rebellion and in support of the Liberals' free trade campaign – and it showed in the great race and creed wars, when *Grip* backed Anglo-Protestant supremacy against the government's efforts to conciliate Catholicism and French Canada. It showed up even more forcefully when Wilfrid Laurier in 1887 succeeded Blake as leader of the federal Liberals, soon gaining Bengough's warm personal backing.

For the politically aware, *Grip*'s shift to a more partisan stance may have been signalled in the spring of 1881 by a short satirical poem that broke the magazine's pattern of mild neutrality. The poem was a savage personal attack on J. Burr Plumb, a prominent Tory from Niagara Falls who had once been a favourite of *Grip*. Plumb, who was an amateur poet, took a special interest in Toronto journalism, writing occasionally for the *Mail*, and he seems to have engaged in an effort to neutralize *Grip*. At some point, possibly around the time of the 1878 election, he and other Tories bought an interest in the *Grip* publishing company. Around the same time, he brought Bengough to the prime minister for an amiable chat in a room just off the Commons, and he may have been partially responsible when *Grip*, after the 1878 election, was added to the government's patronage list.[5] Shortly before the election the magazine spoke of its genuine respect for Plumb, remarking that he was 'about the only politician in Canada who can make a long speech without descending to personalities.'[6] But in 1881, for unknown reasons, *Grip* turned on its former friend, running a clever poem signed by 'Garde' that went beyond political satire and subjected Plumb to vicious humiliation:

TO YE MEMBER FOR NI-G-RA

When nature works, dear Plumb, she has in view
From first to last a purpose – therefore you
Were made for something. What? Ah! That's the rub.

The poem went on to say that Plumb, on the available evidence, was obviously not made to be a poet, orator, or statesman, and concluded:

What were you made for then?
To do the dirty work of other men?
To be a vain and garrulous M.P.?
Mistaking sound and incivility
For argument and wit? To be the pest
Of other men with souls above a silly jest?
If made for these – then nature, artist true,
Outdid herself, dear Plumb, when making you.[7]

This poem set off a rattling exchange that pitted Bengough against Plumb and two other senior Tories who had at times taken hits from *Grip*: Sir David Macpherson of Toronto and Thomas White of Montreal, publisher of the Tory *Gazette*. The affray began in June, when the *Mail* published an anonymous attack on Blake, and *Grip* claimed that it had been written by 'ribstabber' Plumb.[8] Plumb replied in the *Mail*, disclaiming authorship and denouncing *Grip*'s partisanship: 'Although he [*Grip*] loudly repeats that he has no political bias, it is well known that his croak is for the most part in harmony with the Grits.' Bengough then wrote to the *Mail* denying that his magazine was a Grit organ and challenging Plumb to name any occasion on which it had attacked the Tories unjustly or had ever 'let slip a fair opportunity of attacking and exposing the Grits.' He also, imprudently, defended his decision to pin the attack on Plumb, saying that the MP belonged to the extreme section of the Tory party, so that when 'ribstabbing' came up for caricature, it was not unjust to use him as a representative figure.[9]

This led to a series of sneering lectures on Bengough's ethics by the *Gazette*, which brushed *Grip* aside as just another of those Liberal journals that thought Blake should be above criticism.[10] Bengough in turn published a cartoon ('Who Killed Cock Robin?') showing Plumb and White competing for the honour of killing the *Grip* raven. The *Mail* then ran an editorial listing many occasions when *Grip* could have portrayed Blake as a ribstabber, and concluding with the statement that *Grip* had indeed become a Grit organ.[11]

One irony of the situation was that both this editorial and the original attack on Blake had in fact been written by Macpherson, who had his own reasons to stab at *Grip*'s lower ribs. More than two years earlier (a short time, as political vengeance is measured) Macpherson had been the victim of a *Grip* attack that was exceptional for its personal cruelty. Written in Scottish dialect, it was entitled 'Ta Phairson' and included the lines:

> When measured wi' a tailor's tape around his saucy person,
> There's few in a' the kintra side so great as is Ta Phairson;
> But if ye measure *manhood* by fairness, truth and candor,
> Ye'll scarce find ony *smaller* man however far ye wander.[12]

This poem, like the one on Plumb, may in fact may have been written by R.W. Phipps in his period of resentment over Macdonald's neglect of him.[13] But in the 1881 episode all the public heat was directed at Bengough.

When the shooting died down, both Plumb and Macpherson wrote to Macdonald giving their side of the story. 'The Grit press tried to fasten on me the authorship of Macpherson's stinging attack on Blake,' Plumb wrote. '*Grip* cartooned me as a ribstabber and gave me an opportunity of

WHO KILLED COCK ROBIN?

| 'Twas I, says Burr Plumb,
 I knocked him dumb! | Oh, no, not quite!
 'Twas I, says Tom White. |

Grip, 2 July 1881. Sharp exchanges between *Grip* and J. Burr Plumb (right, despite the caption placing) signalled the start of a more partisan, anti-Tory attitude by the magazine. The figure on the left is Thomas White of the Montreal *Gazette*.

showing up his partisanship. He replied through the *Mail* challenging me to show that he had ever shown a partisan leaning, upon which I gave him a lesson which I think may do him good.'[14] Macpherson took credit for the second *Mail* editorial, saying he had written it because Plumb's attack seemed to have missed the mark and he wanted to knock together *Grip*'s and Blake's heads.[15]

Despite the 1881 episode, or possibly because of it, Macdonald the next year followed Plumb's lead and bought shares in the newly reorganized Grip Printing and Publishing Company. This action seems odd in the light of *Grip*'s Grit tendencies, but it is not inconsistent with the patterns of press manipulation of the day. Efforts by the parties to infiltrate opposition media, to influence them, or keep a listening post in them were commonplace. As a *Nation* writer (presumably Goldwin Smith) had observed a few years earlier, it was not uncommon in Canadian journalism to find that shares and stocks were 'transferred for an inky consideration.'[16] While *Grip* was by no means the most influential of Toronto publications, the Tories would have been happy to spend money to check its partisanship.[17] It may be significant that Macdonald's *Grip* shares were eventually transferred to Senator W.E. Sanford, a Hamilton Tory who was quite capable of this kind of manipulation. A few years after the *Grip* episode, Sanford proposed that the Tories try to buy the *Globe* so that they could pull its fangs while continuing to operate it as an ostensibly Liberal sheet.[18]

Macdonald's personal papers contain several reference to his holding in the Grip company, which consisted of a small block of fifty shares worth about five hundred dollars, held in trust for him from 1882 to 1888 by the Toronto lawyer William P. Atkinson.[19] The motivation for buying the shares is not spelled out, but it could hardly have been nonpolitical – and indeed there are indications that Macdonald was disappointed in his hopes of neutralizing *Grip*. For example, in the wake of the 1882 election, he received a letter from Plumb saying that the group of Tory shareholders planned to insist that Bengough take the *Grip* stock off their hands, and that there was no public market for it. A more specific indication of Macdonald's attempt to influence *Grip* can be found in an 1888 letter from Plumb that bitterly criticized Bengough and implied that he had broken faith with the party:

All the subscriptions for that scoundrel Bengough were made in the name of W.P. Atkinson of Toronto, and the stock is held by him in trust ...

If you wish he [Atkinson] will transfer the shares to whomever you may designate. There are some dividends. I don't know how many or how much, for being hard up after the N Wellington election and scrutiny [in 1882], I sold out at a heavy loss.

I shall never forgive myself for being taken in by that snivelling little [unclear] who never meant to keep faith with us.[20]

It seems, then, that Bengough at some point promised neutrality to Tory backers – an easy promise to make, since he had repeatedly insisted in *Grip*'s columns that he meant to be nonpartisan. If he had indeed made such a promise, that would account for the rather grudging personal endorsement that *Grip* gave Plumb in the 1882 campaign. It observed that while Plumb was merely human and thus apt to make mistakes, he was 'certainly one of the most intelligent and scholarly men in Canadian public life.'[21]

In his memoirs, written when both Plumb and Macdonald were dead, Bengough was less than frank about the episode. He recalled how Plumb had introduced him to the prime minister – the only occasion that Bengough actually met Macdonald – but he said nothing about Tory ownership of *Grip* shares or about accusations of betrayal. He had simply 'happened to be in the House' when Plumb offered to introduce him to the prime minister and brought Macdonald to a side room for a friendly encounter: 'I was indeed much affected at the air of humility and even bashfulness which the great leader displayed, though he assured me that they all enjoyed the hits I made at them.'[22] This encounter was presumably in the late seventies or early eighties, since Macdonald would hardly have enjoyed the 'hits' of the mid- or late eighties, and Plumb would certainly not have been so hospitable after the 1881 poem.

In any event, if the Tories hoped to keep Bengough in check for the 1882 campaign, they did not succeed. The magazine was notably more critical than it had been in 1878, especially on railway policy and the so-called Gerrymander Act, Macdonald's legendary attempt to 'hive the Grits' by herding them together in as few ridings as possible. In his memoirs, Bengough recalled an attack from Plumb over *Grip*'s handling of this issue; he cited it, though, only as part of an unconvincing argument that he had been equally attacked by both sides, giving no indication that he had been accused of bad faith.

Grip's slide into the Liberal camp was accentuated in 1884 when it became known that the Grip Printing and Publishing Company had won a major contract to handle all the printing for Oliver Mowat's provincial government. While some attempt was made to dissociate the magazine

from the expanding printing operation, the news created an embarrassment in view of the righteous tone of *Grip*'s many attacks on patronage
printing. Along with other Grit-leaning organs, *Grip* had for years tormented the *Mail* for its federal printing contracts, so the Tory organ was
delighted to be able to charge that *Grip* – 'that virtuous opponent of
high-priced typography' – had its claws deep in the bleeding treasury of
Ontario's Liberal government and was getting $37,000 per annum for its
'smirking Gritism.'[23]

Grip did not deny the connection, but it insisted that all its printing was
obtained by tender and was 'awarded, according to law, to the lowest ten-
derer.' This claim was questionable, given a later admission by Thomas
Bengough that $5,000 was paid to a competitor to secure the contract.[24]
The magazine also went to some lengths to prove that its editorial content was not affected by the printing work. On one occasion it attacked
the 'miserable meanness' of the Mowat government and added gratuitously that the attack 'might sound queer' to people who had read in the
Tory scandal press about how *Grip* was fattening on the provincial treasury to the tune of $35,000 a year.[25]

This close connection with the Liberals, along with Bengough's harsh
treatment of Macdonald's government after the Northwest Rebellion of
1885, makes it understandable why Tory insiders later that year attempted
to create a rival to *Grip*. Their attempt has been described by Dugald E.
Stewart, who tells how a former public servant named Charles William
Allen proposed to set up the *Mirror* to carry, among other things, occasional political cartoons that would be 'effective counter-attacks ... against
the constant assaults of "Grip,"' which had 'enjoyed unopposed posses-
sion of its own peculiar field for twelve years.' Allen cautioned that the
Mirror's stock should be held 'exclusively by friends on our own side' but
said the endeavour would be a sound business venture. Christopher
Bunting of the *Mail* had reviewed the project with him, he wrote, and felt
it could 'run on its own legs, if once fairly started.'[26]

However, the *Mirror* failed to rise above a crawl. Stewart says that it was
poorly organized and appeared only three times, although it drew financial support from at least two cabinet ministers, Edgar Dewdney and C.H.
Tupper, the son of Sir Charles Tupper. Stewart also notes several curious
aspects of the project: first, that the only issue extant contains no political
cartoons, even though several artists were associated with it; second, that
Bengough's younger brother William worked on it. William, an able artist
who would later do occasional work for *Grip* before moving to New
York,[27] was then a young engraver and lithographer with the Toronto

Lithographing Company, which put out the *Mirror*. Stewart says that William Bengough seems to have exercised control over the *Mirror* and published it without cartoons even though there were two artists among its directors. He adds that William's association with a Tory project is curious but that it 'remains speculation' to suggest that he changed the *Mirror* in order to protect *Grip* from competition.[28]

Whatever the full story, it seems clear that backroom politics, especially the provincial contract, lay behind Bengough's eventual expulsion from *Grip* and also led to the magazine's suspension a year later. The evidence for this can be found in a 1939 memorandum by Thomas Bengough which, while frustratingly incomplete, blames *Grip*'s downfall on a long series of internal manoeuvres related to the printing contract:

It cost the Company about $5,000. to secure this contract by paying off a party who had made a lower tender, the result being that Grip had to take the work at $5,000 less than their own figure. This looked like a paying proposition, however, for a former contractor had cleared about $80,000. from the contract – at least this was reported, and the story was pretty well verified by the fact that that contractor became a Bank Director. However, the contract resulted in a *loss* to the Grip Company – a mysterious result that was never explained.

Thomas went on to blame the bindery foreman T.G. Wilson – who later became general manager – and a printing foreman named Murray, two men who 'called themselves the "honey-bees"' (presumably implying that they were procurers of political patronage) who had 'arranged matters so that, by boring from the inside, they removed the members of the Grip board, and Wilson came to the fore as the big boss.' Losses from the government contract and general mismanagement forced the selling off of some assets, Thomas said, 'and the Grip company went out of business, with a total loss to J.W.B. and his brother of their total investment.'[29] Although Thomas did not mention it, the manoeuvring also led to a falling out with the Mowat government. After the first two years of the printing contract, the Grip company complained that the government was not living up to its promise of exclusivity. The company hired the noted Liberal lawyer-politician J.D. Edgar to press the claim, but he could get no satisfaction and the dispute dragged on for years.[30]

While this sequence suggests a break in what had been close relations between *Grip* and Mowat, it is not clear to what extent Bengough was able (or wanted) to hold the magazine aloof from the printing company's business connections with the government. In later years, when he worked openly for the Liberals, Bengough was willing enough to admit a lifelong bias in favour of the party. He stated that he had made a real effort to live up to his professions of independence but that 'it is possible – indeed I suppose it is inevitable – that some bias in favor of Liberal principles must have been manifest.' At the same time, he insisted that he was not blind to Liberal shortcomings, adding lamely that the provincial ministers were too upright to be good subjects for attack, while the federal ministers were better material for cartooning, with faces that 'lent themselves readily to portrayal.'[31]

One of the most interesting aspects of *Grip*'s support of Mowat emerges in its subtle attempt in the mid-eighties – about a year after the printing contract was signed – to promote him as the leader of the federal party, replacing Blake. Bengough had always admired Blake, often describing him as a man of high honour, 'the best legal intellect in Canada,'[32] and a strong candidate to lead a third party built on Reform's left wing ('The Dangerous "Third Party"'). But periodically, especially after the Liberal failures in the 1882 and 1887 elections, *Grip* showed him as an abstruse or vacillating scholar, a man of doubtful leadership abilities. At one point in 1885, wielding the knife with care, it openly suggested that it was time for Blake to go. It said that all Canadians had the most profound respect for him, but it was also universally felt that he was not Mowat's equal as a leader: 'Mr. Blake is doing just as well as a man of his temperament could do – he is casting pearls of learning before the most swinish herd that ever sat in the House of Commons, and he is doubtless working hard in his own way. But he is not a fighter, and what the Grits need now is a political bull-dog to lead them, and the general belief is that the plucky Oliver Mowat is just the man to fill the bill.'[33]

When this produced no discernible reaction, the magazine grew rougher. It attacked Blake for supporting a pay increase for MPs (a '$500 salary grab') and followed up with an editorial attacking the leader personally ('The Salary Grab,' p. 90). The occasion was a convention of young Liberals, and *Grip* urged them to break away from the old parties: 'Both these rotten organizations of the past must go – these parties of small-soulled salary grabbers – the one led by a corruptionist, the other by a coward, and both past all useful purpose in our day and generation. Away with them, and give us *men!* Let the young Liberals cut their connections, if such exists, with effete Gritism, and hoist the banner of the Third Party.'[34] This outburst must have provoked a strong reaction from Grit 'friends,' for *Grip* pulled back stiffly the following week, stating that Mr Blake was understood to be 'painfully affected' by the attacks, that he had

THE DANGEROUS "THIRD PARTY."

MISS GRIT.—"OH, EDWARD, SWEAR YOU'LL BE TRUE TO ME."
EDWARD.—"I'LL BE TRUE—COMPARATIVELY—BUT I NEVER SWEAR."

Grip, 3 Dec. 1881. Throughout the 1880s, *Grip*'s support for the Reform/Liberal
Party was qualified only by sporadic interest in the creation of a radical third party
on the progressive edge of the old party.

THE SALARY GRAB.

CONSTANCE—(*Miss Canada*):

Hast thou not spoke like thunder on my side? Been sworn my soldier? Bidding me depend upon thy stars, thy fortune, and thy strength? And dost thou now fall over to my foes? Thou wear a lion's hide! Doff it for shame, and hang a calf's skin on those recreant limbs!

—*Shakespeare.*

cancelled his *Grip* subscription and had indicated, quite wrongly, that he saw the strictures as 'personal to himself.' (How Bengough could have considered the 'coward' label as other than personal was not explained, and it is safe to say that he must have suffered for the remark. A quarter-century later he was still defending its fairness.)[35]

Over the next few years the magazine continued to blow hot and cold on Blake. Early in 1886 it had strong praise for the leader as a moral Christian statesman, a man of conscience who refused to make capital of race and sectional feeling, a man whose qualities provided 'the ground-work of hope for this dominion.' But later in the year it said that Blake was afraid to seize on the 'living issues of the day.' When Grit newspapers defended their leader, *Grip* observed that if Blake really was a better fighting man than Mowat, he should not so carefully conceal the proof.[36]

On another occasion *Grip* declared ('at the risk of being denounced as a Tory hireling by the *Globe*') that Blake had failed to put forward a clear and plain program: 'Has he any radical cure to offer for the demonstrated rottenness of our system of Government? Is he for or against the saloon? Does he declare specifically and emphatically for manhood suffrage? Is he for or against the present emigration system?' More hurtfully, *Grip* repeated the charge of cowardice in a cartoon accusing Blake of failing to lead his party on the prohibition issue.[37] At the same time, it reiterated a third-party refrain that was now becoming typical, to the effect that thousands of decent people in both parties were waking up to protest Canada's machine politics and that the 'cleanly element were about to break away from the corruptionists and deal-makers.'[38] In effect, *Grip* was again giving voice to the ginger group in the party, which had supported Blake against Brown but which now found Blake too conservative.

However, the critical tone disappeared in the run-up to the federal election of early 1887. Like many party journalists, *Grip* tended to put aside independent ideas under the pressure of campaign exigencies. It kept up a barrage of criticism against the Tories ('Another Fervent

---

Grip, 25 July 1885 (*opposite*). In the 1880s, *Grip* was increasingly seen as an organ of Premier Oliver Mowat, especially when it began a campaign to put Mowat into the federal Liberal leadership as a replacement for Blake. When Blake voted for a pay increase for MPs, Bengough showed him as a 'salary grabber' – and provoked fury within the party. The cartoon is based on Shakespeare's *King John*, act 3, where Constance, mother of Prince Arthur, condemns the faithlessness of the archduke of Austria.

ANOTHER FERVENT APPEAL TO THE BREECHES POCKETS!

SHOCKING ACCIDENT TO THE PAY-CAR "JAMAICA"

(For particulars see papers of Dec. 29th.)

A MEETING OF THE CABINET.

Sir John—NOW, GENTLEMEN, THE FIRST IMPORTANT BUSINESS IS—HOW CAN WE FIX THINGS FOR OUR PARTY?

Appeal ...,' p. 92) while judiciously boosting Blake and at the same time reassuring Toronto manufacturers by lightly criticizing Blake's moderate attitude on protection.[39] When the Tories lost an Ontario provincial election, Bengough blamed interference by Macdonald ('Shocking Accident to the Pay-Car "Jamaica,"' p. 93). When they won their third federal victory in a row, he dropped all pretence of neutrality and portrayed the reassembled cabinet as a gang of brawlers, boodlers, and boozers ('A Meeting of the Cabinet,' pp. 94–5).

Grip's later assessment of Blake continued to be mixed. It was kindly in its comments both when Blake stepped down from the leadership in 1887 and when he left Canada in 1892 to stand for an Irish seat in the British Parliament. Yet an 1891 throwaway comment (probably from Phillips Thompson) was gratuitously harsh: 'It is commonly said that Hon. Edward Blake failed as a party leader. This is a mistake. He did not fail as a party leader because he never led.'[40]

When Wilfrid Laurier succeeded Blake in 1887, Bengough at first showed doubts of the same kind ('Whither Are We Drifting?').[41] But he quickly developed an almost passionate personal admiration for the new

---

Grip, 20 Nov. 1886 (Another Fervent Appeal ..., p. 92). Between elections, Bengough sometimes engaged in the squabbling within the Liberal Party, but when elections were called he returned to his first loyalty. The trousers labelled 'boy' (far right) refer to the well-known cry of the patronage seeker, 'Something for the boy!'

Grip, 8 Jan. 1887 (Shocking Accident ..., p. 93). In the midst of overlapping Ontario and federal election campaigns, *Grip* derided Macdonald's failed attempt on behalf of the provincial Tory leader, W.R. Meredith (foreground). John Carling peers out of the window (his occupation as brewer signalled by the bottle). Another member of the Macdonald cabinet, George Foster, sits on the ground in front of the train. The word 'pay-car' in the caption is a suggestion that Macdonald's private railway car had been used for dispensing boodle. The 'Ross Bibles' scattered in the wreckage symbolize a furious controversy over the nondenominational school scriptures that were issued by Mowat's education minister, G.W. Ross.

Grip, 19 March 1887 (A Meeting of the Cabinet, pp. 94–5). With the Tories victorious for the third time in a row, a frustrated Bengough abandoned caution and portrayed the cabinet as a band of brawlers and boodlers. The harshest image is that of Tupper, at the end of the table, dressed as a hustler. Alexander Campbell, behind Macdonald, is shown in his new finery as Ontario's lieutenant-governor. The only minister unidentified is Adolphe Caron, who is clutched by Chapleau's right hand.

WHITHER ARE WE DRIFTING?

Grip, 13 Aug. 1887. When Wilfrid Laurier took over the Liberal leadership from
Blake in 1887, Bengough was at first uncertain about him. But very soon the
image, both in the cartoons and in *Grip*'s written comment, became strongly
positive.

chief, even though he still flirted with the idea of a third party and could
not bring himself to agree with Laurier on the major race and creed
issues of the day. At the end of Laurier's first full session as leader, *Grip*
praised his potential in language that it had never before brought out for
any politician: 'At first there was some doubt felt as to whether, with all
his classic eloquence, Mr. Laurier would be a successful leader. That he
was a pure-hearted gentleman, profoundly esteemed by all who knew him
regardless of party, did not necessarily prove that he had the unique gift
of leadership. But the record of the session shows that he does possess
this gift, and new hope has run through the party ranks.' Two years later,
Grip was even more effusive: 'There is no more able, pure and popular
man to be found in the party, and it would be impossible for Liberals in

SHEEP'S EYES.

BLAKE—" No, madam : we've been regularly divorced and I'm no more desirous to resume than I was to assume or to retain you. My only hope is that you will fix your confidence and affection upon the man you have."

CARTWRIGHT *(sotto voce)*—" Or, ahem ! on me ! "

Grip, 19 July 1890. Ontario Liberals who were unhappy about serving under a French-Canadian leader talked of bringing back Blake or of giving the leadership to Ontario's pompous Sir Richard Cartwright, but Bengough advised the flighty party to stick with Laurier.

Grip, 23 May 1891 (*opposite*). The positive image of the Liberal leaders in this cartoon contrasts vividly with the shady Tory leaders depicted in 'A Meeting of the Cabinet.' The 'pet' is J. Israel Tarte, the Quebec journalist-politician who had

THE PET OF THE OPPOSITION.

(*continued*) crossed to the Liberals the previous year, bearing devastating evidence of Tory malfeasance in the McGreevy affair.

A NICE MAN, BUT OUT OF A JOB.

LAURIER: "It's most gratifying, I assure you, madam, to hear you speak of me as a scholar, a gentleman, a statesman, a clean handed leader, a large hearted patriot, etc., etc.. but if these are your sentiments, isn't it remarkable that you do not avail yourself of my services?"

Grip, no. 1051, 20 Jan. 1894. In its final year, *Grip* more or less openly supported Laurier. It may be significant that in this instance Bengough used his L. Côté pen-name rather than taking responsibility for the adulation.

---

general to give any leader more confidence and affection than they give Mr. Laurier.'[42] When Ontario Liberals, unhappy at serving a French-Canadian leader, talked of bringing back Blake or replacing Laurier with Sir Richard Cartwright, Bengough ridiculed them ('Sheep's Eyes'), and in 1891 he was openly worshipful in a cartoon that portrayed the Liberal leaders admiring Laurier ('The Pet of the Opposition').

Similarly, when Bengough revived *Grip* for its final chapter in 1894, he openly favoured Laurier. Cartoons such as 'A Nice Man, but Out of a Job' went well over the edge of propaganda, and it is understandable that Bengough signed it with his Côté pen-name. Some poems and satires were equally blatant:

THE PRAIRIE FIRE

See, along the western sky
  The smoke cloud rolling dark,
The heather is ablaze – some hand
  Has thrown a kindling spark.

Yes! Laurier's hand has done the work,
  Or, rather, Laurier's tongue –
For he's been on a 'sparking' tour,
  And Free Trade he has sung.

The West, parched dry for many a year
  Of blighting tariff drouth,
Has blazed responsive to the touch
  Of economic truth ...[43]

Grip had never been this kind to Oliver Mowat, though its coverage of him throughout the 1880s had nearly always been positive. Occasionally the magazine had suggested that the 'little premier' had been too agreeable to Archbishop Lynch ('The Popular Idea'; 'The Double Personality') or that he had failed to support 'progressive' social measures. But in general the worst *Grip* could do was accuse the premier of sins that would have been virtues in the eyes of many Ontario voters – that he had failed to support prohibition and women's suffrage, for instance, or had been parsimonious with public money. While Bengough sometimes poked fun at Mowat, he cartooned him as dogged, serious, honest, judicious, and purposeful ('Then They Rode Back ...,' p. 105). A typically kind comment, after an election victory, stated that the premier hoped to retain the favour of Ontario voters 'by adhering to his past practice of square dealing, and by strict adherence to business.'[44] A typically kind cartoon had him defending Ontario's pocketbook from Quebec's demand for 'better terms' ('On Guard,' p. 106).

On some of the occasions when *Grip* did criticize the provincial government, its comments had a forced quality. Early in 1886, miffed by a Halifax *Herald* comment that *Grip* was a supporter of Mowat, the magazine claimed that its policy was to give praise and blame where merited, and it went on to condemn the government's 'small-soulled niggardliness' and 'miserable meanness.' But it was notably restrained in, for instance, criticizing Mowat's 'political mistake' in appointing his son as sheriff of Toronto.[45]

THE POPULAR IDEA

OF THE RELATION WHICH EXISTS BETWEEN THE PREMIER AND THE
ARCHBISHOP.

Grip, 26 June 1886 (*above*) and 9 Feb. 1889 (*opposite*). In an age when religion and politics were never far apart, Oliver Mowat was criticized even by his friends for his conciliatory relations with the Roman Catholic Church, especially with the forceful archbishop of Toronto, John Joseph Lynch. In 'The Double Personality,'

THE DOUBLE PERSONALITY.

Dr Protestant Jekyll would have been a most acceptable President for the
New Alliance if it had not been for Mr. Politician Hyde.

(*continued*) Bengough implies that Mowat has delayed supporting prohibition in
order to retain Catholic votes. The 'New Alliance' refers to an effort by Bengough
and others to combine the short-lived equal rights movement with supporters of
prohibition and other social reforms.

In 1890, with Phillips Thompson again writing at *Grip* while its business managers were suing the government over the printing contract, the magazine became more critical of Mowat. In one instance it even lumped him with Macdonald and Quebec's Honoré Mercier. 'We have no statesmen in our politics,' it complained. 'The methods by which Sir John, Mr. Mowat and Mr. Mercier sustain themselves in power are simply the methods of the ward politician practiced on a larger scale.' The following year, *Grip* was even harsher: 'For many years the right of the Provincial administration to call itself a "Reform" one has been a standing joke ... Progressive legislation came from it as one extracts juice from a lemon – by the squeezing process.'

After Bengough's departure from *Grip* in mid-1892, any lingering respect for Mowat disappeared. On one occasion the magazine reported sarcastically on an effort to raise money for a statue to Mowat. If anyone thought it wrong to do so while the premier was still alive, it said, a good reply was available, since 'it must be remembered that after all Mowat is not so very much alive.' A few weeks later, it remarked (in language Bengough never would have permitted) that Mowat had been made a knight 'to tickle his senile vanity' and that he had become a 'vain, conceited old man who ought to be thinking of other things than strutting about in antiquated finery to receive the servile homage of snobs.' In a sense, this writing shows how kind Bengough had been to the provincial leader, especially in the mid-eighties when *Grip* had been boosting him for the national leadership.[46]

Grip's sympathy for Mowat and Laurier in the late eighties contrasted with its increasing nastiness towards the Tories, symbolized by the cartoon 'A Meeting of the Cabinet' or by the editorial howls about the 'bribery, boodling, and betrayal of trust' that were running riot in the capital.[47] An 1886 poem by Alexander M'Lachlan, the well-known 'proletarian' poet who often wrote for *Grip*, is typical of this attitude:

THE BIG BANDITTI

Our Canada has in her day
Had swarms of dirty jobbers;

Grip, 3 Mar. 1883 (*opposite*). Bengough usually showed Mowat as plucky and determined, as on this occasion, when the premier had lost some of his majority in recent elections. The references to the boundary award and the streams bill recall how Mowat had upheld provincial rights against Ottawa, expanding Ontario's boundaries as he did so.

"THEN THEY RODE BACK, BUT *NOT* THE SIX HUNDRED!"

ON GUARD.

Mr. Mowat Defended our Territory, let Him now Defend our Pocket-Book!

> But ne'er till now such an array
>   Of Ministerial robbers ...
>
> With greedy hands they've seized the lands
>   God meant for toiling men;
> Why in His might did he not smite
>   The swindlers in their day? ...[48]

Conscious of the widespread respect for Macdonald, Bengough was inclined to direct his sharpest barbs at his aides, especially Tupper and some of the French-Canadian ministers. Occasionally his cartoons hinted at personal sympathy for Macdonald, as in 'Orpheus' (3 April 1886; p. 109), which showed the prime minister peacefully uniting the Orange lion and the Bleu lamb, or in '"Dying!" Your Grandmother!' (18 Dec. 1886; p. 110), which paid tribute to the prime minister's amiable and mischievous qualities – as well as his durability. The most consistent image of Macdonald, however, was that of manipulator. The Old Chieftain's skill in holding together the country's diverse elements constantly emerged in Bengough's cartoons as corruption and exploitation. In various ways his images backed up the refrain of the Liberals that the Tory ministry could not possibly last after Macdonald and that the leader was about to retire ('Depending on One Man,' p. 111). Indeed, Bengough's cartoons predicting Macdonald's imminent retirement appeared for more than a decade.[49]

In the final months of Macdonald's life, *Grip*'s contempt for the government deepened. It said the McGreevy scandal, which revealed contract paybacks to Tory ministers, showed that the country was in the last stages of rottenness and that 'if a thorough and radical reform' was not at once inaugurated, 'disaster is surely coming to this country.'[50] The same warning of dissolution appears in the spine-tingling, almost supernatural, cartoon that turned out to be the last one Bengough drew of the prime minister during his lifetime ('A Private View,' p. 112). In it, Sir John was portrayed as an ancient, decrepit, stooped man – far more ancient than he had seemed in cartoons even a few weeks earlier. More strikingly, he

---

Grip, 2 Aug. 1890 (*opposite*). As Ontario moved ahead in the late nineteenth century, it developed the conviction that the rest of the country, with Macdonald's connivance, was trying to make off with its wealth. Bengough nourished this belief and portrayed Mowat as the province's defender. The small figure in the background leading Quebec's demand for better terms is Premier Honoré Mercier.

was shown staring into a black void. He and his companion seem to be dressed for a funeral, and the eerie quality is enhanced by a vague female figure who seems to be rising from a shroud. The ostensible point of the cartoon was that the 'artist' Cartwright was showing off his gloomy Grit view of the future of Canada – a solid black prospect. But the deathlike quality was at the least startling, considering that this cartoon entered Canadian homes on almost the same day as word of Macdonald's fatal stroke.

A few days later, as news of Macdonald's death dominated the front pages, Bengough reacted with nostalgia but also with a clear feeling that things might now be better. *Grip*'s oft-reprinted main cartoon on the death was suitably sentimental – a dolorous depiction of an old horse standing against the sunset ('The Empty Saddle,' p.113). But its editorial note was cold. It said that Macdonald, with only a single break since Confederation, had been 'the absolute autocrat of our destiny,' and it added, 'Never more shall we see one-man government in this land, and the prospect is not an unpleasant one.'[51] The following week this note was accentuated by another famous cartoon, which showed the mourning female

---

Grip, 3 Apr. 1886 (*opposite*). Macdonald's remarkable skill in holding together a party of all races, religions, classes, and regions generally emerged in Bengough's cartoons as a matter of manipulation, corruption, and exploitation. This cartoon was a notable (if ironic) exception, showing Macdonald, just a few tense months after the hanging of Riel, leading the Orange lion and the *Bleu* lamb.

Grip, 18 Dec. 1886 ('Dying!' Your Grandmother! p. 110). Rumours that Macdonald had died or was on the verge of retirement cropped up constantly in the last two decades of his career. Bengough wryly conceded in this cartoon that the Old Chieftain always had the last chuckle.

Grip, 1 May 1886 (Depending on One Man, p. 111). Recognizing Sir John's personal popularity in his last years, Bengough directed his severest attacks not on him but on his party, showing it as weak and corrupt. The 'G. Washington's Farewell Address' in Macdonald's pocket recalls a hoax in which the Toronto *News* published a Macdonald 'farewell address' that turned out to be George Washington's.

Grip, 30 May 1891 (A Private View, p. 112). Bengough's last cartoon of the prime minister during his lifetime was a curiously prescient one of an aged Macdonald peering into a black void. Drawn in the very week that Macdonald suffered his crippling stroke, it showed the prime minister looking at the bleak picture of Canada's future painted by Liberal Sir Richard Cartwright.

ORPHEUS;

OR, THE LION AND THE LAMB.

"DYING!" YOUR GRANDMOTHER!

" You all remember how poorly the wolf made out to be when he was luring innocent Red Riding Hood to her doom.   But his appetite was good, as she found to her cost ;   and as you will find to yours if you allow yourselves to be lured in like fashion."—*Vide Blake's speech at Wingham.*

DEPENDING ON ONE MAN.

The Party.--O, PRAY DON'T TALK OF GETTING OLD AND GIVING OUT! I CAN'T ABEAR THE IDEA!

A PRIVATE VIEW

Of Cartwright's Remarkable Picture, a Nocturne in Black, Entitled "The Future of Canada."

THE EMPTY SADDLE.

NOW LET HIS ERRORS BE BURIED AND FORGOTTEN!

Grip, 13 June 1891 (The Empty Saddle, p. 113), and 20 June 1891 (Now Let His Errors ..., *above*). When word came of Macdonald's death, Bengough captured some of the poignancy with his sketch of the empty saddle. But the following week he rendered a harsh verdict on the prime minister's career. The 'red parlor' refers to the legendary room at Toronto's Queen's Hotel where Macdonald dispensed patronage.

figure of Canada dropping into a grave some of Sir John's less admirable measures, over the caption 'Now Let His Errors Be Buried and Forgotten!' Many Tories, caught up in the great emotion of Macdonald's departure, found the cartoon hard to forgive, despite a memorable Bengough poem that acknowledged Sir John's supreme role in Canadian politics:

> And he is dead, they say!
> The words confuse and mock the general ear –
> What! Can there be a House and members here
> And no John A?[52]

Macdonald's death was a critical moment in Bengough's career, just as George Brown's had been. For almost twenty years his drawings of Sir John's craggy features had delighted everyone, even (at times) Tories, and had been part of the ebb and flow of political fortunes. As at Brown's death, Bengough greeted Macdonald's end as the beginning of a new age. But again, he may not have realized what kind of impact it would have on his own career.

5

Grip and the Press Wars

Throughout the 1880s, *Grip*'s political slant emerged most clearly in its handling of a kind of politics that has long since disappeared: the surrogate battles among party journalists. In this arena the magazine had a unique place, both in defining the quirks and slants of various publications and in making their publishers and editors into public figures.

This role has proved especially helpful to a later generation in view of the tradition of so-called impersonal journalism that was still more or less in operation at the time. The tradition decreed that journalists should write anonymously the message of their publishers or parties. The listing of editors' names on a masthead was rare, and some even saw it as bad form for an attacking editor to name a rival. It was acceptable to attack publishers, especially those like Brown or Beaty who were political figures as well, but their hired editors and writers were more or less immune. In the eighties, as newspapers grew larger and the publishers' direct control waned, the journalists became more significant figures. *Grip* accentuated this trend. The magazine was itself a soldier in the political battles, of course, but it made a more important contribution by undermining the impersonal style and showing, as recognizable characters, the interesting band of warriors engaged in the fight. Thus, through *Grip*, the reading public came to know the glowering figure of John Ross Robertson (*Telegram*), the shifty glance of Billy Maclean (*World*), and the bearded, Bohemian sneer of E.E. Sheppard (*News/Saturday Night*). Particularly important in this process were the great rivals, the Grit *Globe* and the Tory *Mail*, whose changes in editorship affected *Grip*'s attitudes in a way that almost seemed to change its politics.

In the early 1880s, while the brilliant Irishman, Edward (Ned) Farrer, was editing the *Mail*, *Grip* had many kind words for the paper and said

THE EDITOR OF THE "MAIL" AS "DR· PANGLOSS, LL·D ♣ A.S·S."

"I AM NOTHING IF NOT QUOTICAL"—IAGO—AHEM!—"THE PEN IS MIGHTIER THAN THE SWORD"—BULWER—AHEM!—TO "WRITE ME DOWN AN"—AH!—AHEM!—SHAKESPEARE!"

Grip, 24 Mar. 1883. Some of the sharpest political battles of *Grip*'s era were conducted by surrogate warriors – the editors of the party newspapers, who emerged as public figures through Bengough's sketches. One of his favourite targets was Martin J. Griffin, the partisan editor of the *Mail*, who inspired Bengough to coin the term Griffinism.

that it clearly passed the *Globe* in quality. But *Grip* had nothing but contempt for the *Mail*'s manager, Christopher (Boss) Bunting, who, it said, wanted to make himself into a Tory George Brown, even though he matched Brown only in a few of his weaknesses.[1] When Farrer left the editorship and was replaced by Martin J. Griffin, a doctrinaire Tory who was pleased to stab his opponents under the fifth rib every lawful morning, *Grip*'s dislike widened into pathological contempt for the Tory paper. The *Mail* responded in kind, setting up what appeared to be a traditional knife fight between the party organs.

Griffin called *Grip* 'Mr. Blake's illustrated organ,' while *Grip* jeered at

WILL SHE DROWN THEM?

the *Mail*'s 'dyspeptic little Editor' – a man nervous, sour, and cantankerous – and said that Bunting 'owns an editor who will write anything he is asked to.' When Griffin penned a famous description of Grit convention delegates as a 'semi-civilized crowd of dull-witted partizans,' Bengough said that Griffin himself was a 'semi-civilized partizan' who allowed 'his crazy zeal to run away with his judgment.' He called Griffin talented but ludicrous, frequently portrayed him as a rodent or cur, and brushed off the *Mail* as an organ of aesthetic muck ('The Editor of the "Mail,"' p. 117).[2]

In time, Bengough came to portray Griffin as a symbol of the depravity of the party press, coining the word Griffinism to express his contempt. When Macdonald in 1883 said that no newspaper could afford to be simply a servile tool of government, Bengough stretched a point to interpret the remark as a slap at the *Mail*'s sycophancy and cartooned the paper as a snivelling cur being kicked by its master. When Bunting early in 1884 was caught up in a major scandal over subverting Liberal politicians with cash payments, and when Griffin defended his chief, Bengough's language and imagery became almost as nasty as the journalism he was condemning. Without waiting for the court verdict, he cartooned Bunting and his allies week after week as rats caught in a trap; when they were eventually cleared, they became rats escaping a trap ('Will She Drown Them?').[3]

This hostility towards the *Mail* naturally left *Grip* looking like a Grit organ. Bengough sought to maintain the old balance by occasionally sniping at the *Globe*, but with George Brown gone and less arrogant successors in command there, his heart was not in it. Like most Toronto journalists, Bengough admired the craftsmanship of Gordon Brown, who had taken over from his brother. This admiration caused him to resist the Blake wing when it sought, after the 1882 election, to eject Brown and take full control of the party paper ('Cutting the Apron String'). Instead of backing the Blake people, *Grip* praised Gordon Brown's unflinching convictions, especially on free trade, a matter on which Blake had been

---

Grip, 29 Mar. 1884 (Will She Drown Them? pp. 118–19). The *Mail*'s manager, Christopher Bunting, a sometime Tory MP and local party boss, was a favourite Bengough target. When Bunting was charged with trying to bribe Grit politicians, Bengough portrayed him and his associates as rats caught in a trap . The *Mail*'s editor, Martin Griffin, is shown here trying to save Bunting: 'Drown the others if you like, but save, o save this innocent one!' An associate murmurs to Tory leader W.R. Meredith, 'If the worst comes, I do hope none of 'em will squeal!'

CUTTING THE APRON STRING; OR, THE "TRUE POSITION" MADE PLAIN.

Grip, 7 May 1881. After George Brown's death, control of the *Globe* passed briefly to his brother Gordon, who was seen by some as an abler editor than George, though he clearly lacked his brother's force in commanding politicians and political events. *Grip* was relieved to see that the *Globe* was no longer intent on bullying the Reform Party. The sign on the wall in the centre of the cartoon, a take-off on the *Globe*'s motto, reads: 'The subject who is truly wise will not attempt to control any person bigger than himself. – Junius (Amended).'

SPECIMEN YOUNG LIBERALS.

(DELEGATED TO REPRESENT THE "GLOBE" WING OF THE
PARTY AT THE CONVENTION IN MONTREAL.)

Grip, 5 June 1886. This cartoon, typical of the small sketches spread throughout
Grip, kept alive the idea of a reactionary '*Globe* wing' in the Liberal Party, even
though no serious gap existed between the leaders and the *Globe* after Gordon
Brown was forced out in 1882.

ready to compromise. Brown, the magazine said, was prepared to split the party if necessary in support of his hatred for the protective National Policy: 'This is the sort of stuff great men are made of, and Canada has only a few of them.'[4]

Gordon Brown's successor, the colourless John Cameron from London, Ontario, was a confirmed Blake man and a poor target, though Bengough occasionally sent a shaft his way. A more promising victim was Timothy Warren Anglin, the former Commons Speaker and New Brunswick journalist, who in 1883 was brought to Toronto by the party to edit the *Catholic Tribune* and write editorials for the *Globe*. *Grip* correctly interpreted Anglin's role as a cynical bid for Irish Catholic votes: 'His principal chore will be the feeding of the political pig [Irish vote] with good Grit swill, with a view of having it fat and docile "agin the next election."'[5] At times, too, the magazine still attacked the *Globe* 'wing' of the party ('Specimen Young Liberals'), but without much conviction. By this point, there was far less distance between the newspaper and the party, so it was hard to attack one without attacking the other. *Grip* was increasingly seen as a member of the Liberal family, and at heart it probably was, despite a pretence of balance, as in this 1892 poem:

THE PARTY PRESS

> Here's Grit and Tory, – small the odds, –
> Swearing by their respective gods,
> Each their own organs patronize,
> Suppressing truth or telling lies.
> Of all reforms beneath the sun,
> 'Tis time reform was here begun,
> For what compares, in wild excess,
> With our Canadian party press? ...[6]

Material of this kind disguised *Grip*'s own party leanings – though the slant was perhaps most apparent not in what the magazine said but in what it left out.

An anecdote told by Thomas Bengough reveals *Grip*'s sensitivity to the Liberal leadership. When Thomas was working as Premier Mowat's private secretary, he sometimes took shorthand dictation from Mowat at his home. On arriving there one evening, he was met by the premier's wife, who 'gently remarked to me that while she admired *Grip* she thought it unfair that they should "put ladies in the paper."' She was referring to a comment by W.A. Foster that 'if it were not for his amiable spouse the Premier would not know when it rained.' While this remark seems relatively harmless, Thomas shared Mrs Mowat's reaction: 'This was an ungracious and uncalled for slam at my chief.'[7] Undoubtedly, his brother soon heard of his concern.

In his own memoirs Bengough said nothing of any closeness to the party apparatus and shed no light on a later allegation that at one point before the 1882 election he wrote a controversial Liberal campaign song, the famous and bigoted 'Ontario, Ontario.' The claim was made only after Bengough's death, and as it came from the witty but unreliable pen of Hector Charlesworth, it deserves to be viewed with a large measure of caution. Charlesworth's account was extremely circumstantial (and, incidentally, may provide a glimpse into government-media relations of the day). Charlesworth said that a committee meeting of Toronto Liberals was held on a rainy afternoon in the grocery store of one John Macmillan. It was attended by a baritone named E.W. Schuch, who had worked as a 'campaign singer' in an Ohio election and was offering the same service to the Grits, provided suitable lyrics could be created. At that point, said Charlesworth, Bengough 'went into retirement behind the counter and penned "Ontario, Ontario," in less than half an hour.'[8]

If the story is true, the jingle would later have been an embarrassment for Bengough. Its message, sung to the tune of 'Maryland! My Maryland!,' warned against the designs of French Canada and the Catholic Church: 'The traitor's hand is at thy throat, / Ontario, Ontario! / Then kill the tyrant with thy vote, / Ontario, Ontario!'[9] At the time, many Ontarians were convinced that Quebec was conspiring with Macdonald to give away large sections of northern Ontario to Manitoba, so the song struck a tender nerve. Before the campaign was over, it had given rise to a furious dispute; Blake, according to Charlesworth, called it 'damned rubbish' and said it had lost Quebec for the Grits.[10]

If Bengough did indeed write the jingle, he would have been slow to admit it later when he became enamoured of Laurier and national reconciliation. But authorship of the song is still in doubt, partly because of Bengough himself. At one point, Farrer of the *Mail* facetiously tried to pin the authorship on J.D. Edgar, a well-known poet as well as a politician, and Bengough drew a cartoon that seemed to place the responsibility on Farrer. He pictured a puzzled Farrer listening to Edgar's repudiation and commenting: 'Not his? Who the divil else's?'[11] The mystery thus remained unresolved. It is interesting to note, though, that in

Bengough's papers there is an oblique reference to at least one other campaign song he wrote for the Grits.[12]

In the middle of the 1870s, *Grip*'s desire for an independent image was given fresh impetus when the raucous Toronto *News*, under Sheppard and Thompson, made a surprising breakout towards radicalism, including support for Canadian independence and republican principles ('The Journalistic Cowboy,' p. 126). Sheppard had absorbed American ideas while roaming the United States, where he had worked at times as a cowboy and stagecoach driver, and some of his irreverence appealed to *Grip*, even though the *News* style reminded it of 'a Texas steer trying to cough up cactus.' Bengough's support was limited, however. As an early convert to Henry George's tax reform ideas, he would have been delighted by a *News* editorial (almost certainly Thompson's work) that condemned the land monopolist as 'a parasite, an incubus ... subsisting in luxury on the toil and sweat of others.' He would also have been sympathetic to the *News*'s constant attacks on the main party organs and its support for labour unions and a third party, but he would not have approved of its admiration for independence and American political institutions.[13]

The *News*, however, was only a minor and rather shrill nonconformist, scrapping with Maclean's *World* and Robertson's *Telegram* for a share of the downscale market. Bengough was more significantly affected when the elite *Mail* (with Griffin gone and Ned Farrer back in the editorship) made a carefully crafted departure from the Tory camp in 1885–87. At first, Bengough reacted to this development with cynicism, suspecting a Tory plot. He cartooned the editors of the Montreal *Gazette* and the *Mail*, the two main Tory organs, as quarrelling monkeys both controlled by the same organ-grinder as they gave contradictory messages to Ontario and Quebec ('The Discordant Organs,' p. 128). But over the next few months he began to believe in the *Mail*'s independence and to get caught up in its campaigns. When the Tories in 1887 set up the doctrinaire and tightly controlled *Empire* to replace the *Mail*, *Grip* happily pitched into it. Through the late eighties, *Grip* seemed to admire almost everything the *Mail* had to say on such subjects as race and creed, and commercial union – until 1889, when the paper mysteriously dropped its support for the latter policy.[14] Thereafter, Bengough grew increasingly suspicious as signs emerged that Farrer and his ally Goldwin Smith were heading towards a policy of outright political union in alliance with American business leaders, who were not at all interested in a merely commercial fusion.[15]

By this time, Phillips Thompson had rejoined *Grip*, and the magazine's

THE JOURNALISTIC COWBOY.

printed material had begun to reflect his radical agenda rather than the *Mail*'s. During this period, *Grip* must have experienced a good deal of internal tension of the kind Bengough loved to point out in other papers. Thompson had never been the kind of writer who quietly adjusted his views to his managers, as his constant moves showed. Also, he was one of the first Toronto writers to see the *Mail*'s race and creed campaign as a deliberate effort to break up the country and bring about political union with the United States.[16] He would certainly have discouraged Bengough's admiration for the *Mail*'s aims. But unfortunately Bengough, in his reminiscences, says nothing about difficulties with Thompson. He does not even mention Thompson among the contributors to the magazine or among those who 'briefly' edited it, although Thompson was formally listed as associate editor from 1890 to 1892 and took over as editor when Bengough was forced out in the middle of 1892. Thompson was still alive when Bengough published his reminiscences, and he still had a sharp bite, so Bengough may have preferred to stay silent rather than stir up old tensions. Similarly, Bengough made no mention of Peter McArthur, who was said by one writer to have been a major *Grip* contributor before he went on to greater fame in New York.[17]

In his later writings, Bengough did offer sketches of some of the magazine's less controversial people, and the quality of these pieces indicates that he might have told a fine story of the magazine and of Toronto journalism if he had been willing to be frank. He told, for instance, of R.W. Phipps, a man of scholarship and talent but also a 'phenomenon of egotism,' who thought he should have been named finance minister to implement the National Policy. 'In manner of dress and deportment, Phipps suggested the countryman come to town for the first time, and this no doubt gave his self-conceited speeches an extra power of shock, but they were spoken with a frankness and sincerity which made the shock only amusing.'

Bengough also described Tom Boylan, a totally different type, who would come down the stone steps to Bengough's little basement 'sanctum' with an embarrassed hangdog look and the comment, 'Here's a little thing for the next issue – can you give me something for it?' Boylan

---

Grip, 15 Dec. 1883 (*opposite*). E.E. Sheppard (backed by Phillips Thompson) surprised Toronto in 1883 with a radical pro-independence and 'democratic' rampage at the *Evening News*. The other journalists shown here include John Cameron of the *Globe*, John Ross Robertson of the *Telegram*, Goldwin Smith, and Martin Griffin of the *Mail*.

THE DISCORDANT ORGANS.

was not always quite sober and thus showed occasional flashes of cheerfulness, despite his usually gloomy frame of mind. He may well have been the model for one of Bengough's most effective cartoons, 'The Last of the Paragraphers' (see p. 223). In any event, the sketch says a good deal about the tenuous existence of the magazine's contributors.[18] Others in the magazine's stable included W.A. Foster (a barrister and promoter of the Canada First movement) and Edward Edwards, a gloomy critic on local issues (he was, Bengough recalled, apparently a clergyman who had 'thrown aside his clerical garb as a protest against incurably wrong conditions').[19]

Although Bengough described some of his writers, he said nothing of the infighting at the magazine, nothing of the tensions with backers and politicians, nothing of the doubts and recrimination provoked by his work. It is ironic that although *Grip* had a good deal to say about other press warriors, it has told us so little about its own. This lack of material makes it hard to trace the internal thinking at the magazine as it descended in the late eighties into the swamp of resentments that followed the Northwest Rebellion.

Grip, 11 Sept. 1886 (*opposite*). After the Northwest Rebellion, the Toronto *Mail* – under the resumed editorship of Edward Farrer and with the collaboration of Goldwin Smith – mounted a strong campaign against the political influence of French Canada and the Roman Catholic Church. Bengough was at first amused by the embarrassing gap between the two leading Tory organs, the *Mail* and the Montreal *Gazette*. But as the *Mail* broke with the Tories, he gradually became caught up in its campaigns. The monkey shown on the left is either Farrer or Christopher Bunting of the *Mail*, while the one on the right is presumably Thomas or Richard White of the *Gazette*.

6

Race and Creed

In Canada's great race and creed battle of the late 1880s, *Grip* generally bent with the prevailing Protestant winds. Its cartoons are valuable mainly in the way they reveal the wave of unreason that pervaded the country after Louis Riel's second rebellion in 1885. As well, they show something of the intricacy of party infighting that was generated by the troubles over race and religion.

Although *Grip* in its early years had reflected Toronto's well-known biases, it had done so in a notably mild way, considering its editor's conditioning. As a youth in the Ontario heartland, Bengough had been exposed to the usual Protestant influences. He had pored over Thomas Nast's powerful cartoons portraying the 'Romish' forces as wolves, snakes, and crocodiles. He had listened to Presbyterian clerics denouncing the Syllabus or the Doctrine of Infallibility as evidence that Rome was undermining the Enlightenment.[1] He had grown up at a time of regular street fights between fanatical Green and Orange youth gangs. In view of this background, it is interesting to see that the young Bengough at first reacted with restraint to Toronto bigotry. At a time when much of the Protestant anger still focused on the death of Thomas Scott, the Orangeman executed in Riel's Red River Rebellion of 1869–70, Bengough did not share it. As James Beaty's *Leader* writhed in fury over Riel's escape from punishment (and it did so with great regularity), a typical *Grip* commentary showed its editor's impatience: 'The *Leader* is nothing if not sanguinary. The old lady has blood in her eye, and shouts, "While the remains of Thomas Scott are decaying in the Red River those who dare to extend mercy to his brutal murder [*sic*] must be wiped out of existence." 'Sdeath, but she's a violent old hag, that would show no mercy to the merciful!'[2]

In the 1870s and early 1880s *Grip* showed occasional signs of being drawn (but only modestly) into the 'No Popery' campaign that reacted against the ultramontane claims of church supremacy in education and politics. In the tangled furore over the burial of freethinker Joseph Guibord, for instance, it took the Protestant line but preserved enough humour to show the wonderful convolutions of the affair. ('Civil Law Must Triumph!'). In this bizarre legal case, the courts ultimately forced the Catholic Church to allow Guibord's body to be buried in the plot he had bought in a Catholic cemetery; but after the body had been taken there under heavy guard and duly buried, Bishop Bourget deconsecrated that piece of ground. *Grip* saw the ironies of the situation as well as the politics:

IN RE GUIBORD

The Queen to Bishop Bourget
I decide you were wrong by church law, my Lord,
In refusing to bury poor Joseph Guibord;
I therefore command you to cease further fights –
You must give him his *dues*, tho' he can't have his *rites*.

Bishop Bourget to the Queen
Madame, just as you say, I will open the gate,
Waiving will of the Church before law of the State;
It's none of my funeral, so drive in your hearse,
But I tell you I'll stand on the gate-post and *curse*![3]

The comment accompanying Bengough's cartoon insisted that the church must bow to the will of the courts, even on a religious matter – an interesting inconsistency in view of *Grip*'s usual demand that the affairs of

---

Grip, 18 Sept. 1875 (Civil Law Must Triumph! p. 132). *Grip* was relatively tolerant in the 1870s, but it attacked Montreal's Bishop Ignace Bourget for refusing to allow the body of freethinker Joseph Guibord to be buried in holy ground. Here Bourget is shown obeying the Queen's order to open the gate while muttering, 'Certainly Madam. But I thought *I* was running this Province.'

Grip, 9 Oct. 1875 (Guibordism Reversed ..., p. 133). A few weeks after the Guibord cartoon, Bengough was equally hard on the Orange Young Britons who disrupted a Catholic procession in Toronto. The young hoodlum is saying, 'I can't bear to see the Sabbath Day desecrated. Let me at him!'

CIVIL LAW MUST TRIUMPH !

GUIBORDISM REVERSED--CIVIL LAW MUST TRIUMPH!

state and church be kept separate. A few weeks later, Bengough was equally critical of a mob of Protestant rowdies who threw stones at a Catholic procession in Toronto. But at the same time, he could not resist telling Catholics that they owed to British law and Protestant magnanimity the protection of their religious freedom ('Guibordism Reversed').[4] More extreme (but also unusual) was an 1876 poem, 'An Ultramontane Paean,' which had the Pope bragging about how he had managed to bring both Macdonald and Brown to their knees before him:

> All Quebec is Ours already – faithful province of Our own,
> Manitoba – fair Columbia – soon they shall be Ours alone.
> True believers – Irish – Frenchmen – shall their vacant spaces fill,
> Who shall hinder? Who shall stay it? Is it not Our sacred Will?[5]

This pandering to prejudice was balanced by an occasional plea for racial and religious tolerance, of a kind that would have put the magazine on the more moderate wing of Toronto opinion. But even these pleas had a distinctly Protestant spin. In 1878, for instance, a poem addressed to Catholics naively suggested that they should join Orangemen in celebrating the Battle of the Boyne on the 'Glorious Twelfth,' since they, too, had gained so much British liberty from the victory:

> Put Priestcraft all aside, and calm remember
>   Those common rights, important, broad and great,
> Which any day, bright May or dark December,
>   You with your rivals well might celebrate.[6]

The same ambivalence was evident in 1880 during one of the many controversies involving censorship by the Roman Catholic archbishop of Toronto, John Joseph Lynch. *Grip* showed the formidable prelate stabbing the snake of free thought with the dagger of faith,[7] but the comment beneath the cartoon was much less critical. It observed, seemingly without irony, that the archbishop was being strictly logical in barring his people from free-thought lectures and infidel books, even though this would be looked on as narrow and bigoted by some who considered themselves broad and cultured.

A few years later, in 1885, Bengough's first reaction to the Northwest Rebellion was similarly tolerant if narrow. Before the actual outbreak of the rebellion, he had shown more sympathy for the Métis than might be expected of a Protestant Torontonian, often warning the government to

MERELY A HUM-BUG-BEAR!

THE EDITOR OF THE *MAIL* NOT A BIT SCARED.

Grip, 24 Nov. 1883. Bengough predicted trouble on the prairies well before the Northwest Rebellion of 1885, and he ridiculed the efforts of *Mail* editor Martin Griffin to make light of the danger. Griffin's words here are 'Don't be alarmed, Madam, it's only a Grit Bear movement!'

"CRY HAVOC! AND LET SLIP THE DOGS OF WAR!"

Grip, 4 Apr. 1885 (*above*) and 23 May 1885 (*opposite*). At the outbreak of rebellion, *Grip* was thoroughly caught up in Toronto's burst of jingoism. The general shown being 'proud of his boys' is Sir Frederick Middleton, whose reputation would soon start to slide.

pay attention to the grievances of the region. For instance, 'Merely a Hum-Bug- Bear!' (24 Nov. 1883) ridiculed *Mail* editor Martin Griffin, who was shown assuring the prime minister that talk of disaffection was merely a Grit plot. Once the fighting started, however, the magazine was caught up in the glory of the moment. Its early support for the military appeared both in accounts of the campaign and in such cartoons as the maudlin 'Cry Havoc!' (4 Apr. 1885), which showed two soldiers striding off to war, their bayonets fixed and their eyes determined, while Macdonald clasped hands with Blake in unity, and an implacable figure of Canada pointed to the path of duty.

'The departure of the gallant volunteers for the scene of the rebellion in the Saskatchewan country was, perhaps, the most stirring event which Toronto has ever witnessed,' the magazine said, reflecting Ontario's surge of jingoism. 'The alacrity with which the noble young fellows sprang to the call of duty excited infinite pride, and the enthusiasm of

PROUD OF HIS BOYS, AND NO WONDER!

the enormous crowd assembled to see them off Monday was never surpassed.' With matching alacrity, *Grip* launched a separate *Canadian Pictorial and Illustrated War News,* which was filled over the next four months with sketches of soldiers pursuing the Métis or driving them from their entrenchments.

As the first word of victories came in, the prose and images of all Toronto journalists was more or less the same – modelled, perhaps on the American Civil War coverage they remembered from their youth or on the coverage in British papers of imperial ventures abroad. Later, both General Frederick Middleton and his troops were to come under a good deal of criticism, but in May *Grip* had no such reservations: 'The gallant fight at Fish Creek and the brilliant charge at Batoche proved that British blood will tell wherever you find it' ('Proud of His Boys ...').[8] At the same time, Bengough joined other Grit editors in placing the blame for the rebellion on the prime minister. He recalled that Chief Piapot had bestowed the title of Old Tomorrow on Macdonald and said it was well borne out by the way Macdonald had waited until the rebels took the war-path before setting up a commission to look into their grievances.[9]

With the rebellion quickly suppressed and Riel captured and sentenced, both Tories and Grits were deeply divided about his fate. Bengough, like most Grit-leaning editors, strained to keep his options open. Like the others, he could see that Macdonald was caught in a classic dilemma: if he (or his cabinet) commuted Riel's sentence, he would alienate Ontario; if he allowed the law to take its course, he would alienate Quebec. Either way, he would be well and truly impaled, and the Grits would be ready to pounce. To turn up the pressure, Grit editors recalled how Macdonald had hustled Riel out of the country after his first rebellion fifteen years earlier. They suggested that the prime minister would do something of that kind again in order to appease the *Bleu* Quebec wing of his party, and they made ready to stage a tantrum when he did.

During the spring and summer of 1885, *Grip* seemed to be following this pattern. In May it noted that with the arch-rebel 'safely caged,' the Tory *Mail* was promising that the law would be allowed to take its course. 'But it would be too much to suppose that no political effort will be put forth to thwart the aim of justice.' Later in the summer, Bengough seemed more neutral, portraying Macdonald as a magician who would manage somehow to satisfy both sides. But a small cartoon and an emotional poetic plea signed by Fidelis seemed to tilt the magazine towards reprieve. Entitled 'Quebec to Canada,' the poem included the lines:

> Pity the captive in your hand.
>   Pity the conquered race –
> *You* strong, victorious, in the land,
>   Grant us the victor's grace![10]

Despite the decision to print this poem, the magazine remained editorially neutral about Riel's execution. It seemed to be following the lead of the *Globe* which, in a classic bit of tightrope walking, was arguing that Riel deserved death – but that Macdonald as author of the rebellion would 'commit a hideous crime if he executed his victim.'[11] *Grip* was similarly elusive. Driving home the point that Macdonald could never satisfy both sides, Bengough showed the prime minister torn 'Between Justice and Mercy.' The commentary accompanying this cartoon stated: 'The life of Louis Riel now hangs upon the word of Sir John A. Macdonald ... The awful responsibility which is at this moment in his hands is but the natural result of the "tactics" which for a long time he has practiced under the name of statesmanship.' Like the other Grit editors, Bengough seemed poised to make the most of either execution or reprieve.

BETWEEN JUSTICE AND MERCY.

Grip, 31 Oct. 1885. After the rebellion, *Grip* made the most of the problem
Macdonald faced in choosing whether to commute Riel's death sentence (and
alienate Ontario) or refrain from doing so (and alienate Quebec).

JUSTICE STILL UNSATISFIED.

Sir John.—Well, madam, Riel is gone ; I hope you are quite satisfied.
Justice.—Not quite ; you have hanged the EFFECT of the Rebellion ; now I want to find and punish the CAUSE.

Grip, 21 Nov. 1885. When Riel was executed, *Grip* (unlike many Grit papers) defended the action, though its main emphasis was on Macdonald's role in provoking the rebellion.

But curiously, when the government ultimately decided not to intervene and when, in November, Riel went to the gallows in Regina, Bengough failed to exploit the decision. Most other Grit editors suddenly decided that they had all along favoured mercy. (The *Globe*, for instance, while not actually condemning the hanging, said it was understandable that French Canadians' resentment should focus on Riel's death and that they ought to unite with English Canadians to overwhelm the 'lords of misrule.')[12] But Bengough hung back. He took what he was convinced was the high road, defending the course of the law while condemning the government for letting the Métis discontent get out of hand.

In the tense days after the hanging, with French Canada in a fury, *Grip* rejected the 'horrible idea' (advanced by a number of Grit organs) that Riel had been sacrificed to regional prejudice: 'Let us believe that justice has been done, as we do most sincerely believe that the only aim and intention of the government was to do justice.' But justice would not be satisfied, the editorial continued, until the actual authors of the rebellion were exposed and punished, whether these turned out to be 'the plotting speculators at Prince Albert or drowsy Ministers at Ottawa.'[13] A very strong cartoon showed the female figure of Justice sternly turning her back on Macdonald, demanding that those who had caused the rebellion be punished ('Justice Still Unsatisfied'). The figure of Mercy had disappeared. One week later, with very little justice, Bengough portrayed Macdonald as a coward fleeing to England to escape the post-execution fuss (''Portant Engagement Elsewhere,' p. 142).

Given this hostility, Bengough's stand in supporting the execution is curious. It may partly have been a personal reaction against the blatant hypocrisy of the Grit editors and their political masters. But Bengough may also have been influenced by the *Mail*, which, in a series of forceful editorials by Edward Farrer and Goldwin Smith, had argued that French Canada was a drag on the rest of the nation and that it would be better to destroy Confederation than submit to Quebec's demands for 'special privileges.'[14] Bengough began to echo this argument, at first sporadically and later with more enthusiasm. In one cartoon, which is very revealing of the attitudes of the day, he argued that it would have been absurd to let Riel off just because he was a French Canadian – as absurd as repriving Wandering Spirit (Kapapamahchakwew) and the seven other Indians who had been hanged at Battleford for their part in the rising ('French Nonsense,' p. 143). The force of the cartoon lay partly in the fact that no one, or almost no one, saw any problem about hanging the Indians. The other underlying assumption reflected English Canada's conviction that

BACK LANE SHORT CUT TO BOAT LANDING

CHEAP TICKETS TO ENGLAND

GET GRIP'S COMIC ALMANAC FOR '86

QUEBEC

"'PORTANT ENGAGEMENT ELSEWHERE; JUST THOUGHT OF IT!"

Grip, 28 Nov. 1885. With little justice, *Grip* accused the prime minister of arranging a hasty trip to England to escape Quebec's fury over the hanging of Riel.

---

the Quebec protest was simply an attempt to extricate one of its own from the just application of the law.

Public opinion in English Canada was by no means uniform, however, especially on the execution itself, and the Grits were just as divided as the Tories. Many Ontario Grits were delighted to see Riel dead, and they were uneasy when some of their leaders argued that the rebels should have been treated as political dissidents, not as criminals. The party's leaders tried to pull their followers together by concentrating on the government's mistakes that had led to the rebellion and by glossing over the execution. But they were disconcerted by accusations that this put them on the side of the 'Rielites,' the nationalist protest party that emerged in Quebec behind Liberal Honoré Mercier. They felt vulnerable to the Tory cry that Blake was wooing French Canada by building a political platform out of the Regina scaffold.

In the Commons, this vulnerability led to a cunning turn by the Tory strategists, who forced a vote not on the question of the government's

FRENCH NONSENSE; OR, "REDUCTIO AD ABSURDUM."

Grip, 5 Dec. 1885. This cartoon was based on an interesting reading of public opinion, to the effect that no one could possibly object to the hanging of Wandering Spirit and seven other Indians in the wake of the Northwest Rebellion. The overt message was that Quebec's anger over Riel's hanging was simply a matter of racial resentment and that it would be as absurd to pardon him on these grounds as to have pardoned the eight Native people. It is notable that the artist's normal image of complaisant Quebec and Aboriginal maidens was replaced by more threatening figures.

errors (which would have unified the Liberal side) but on the narrow issue of condemning the government for hanging Riel. On that issue, of course, the Liberals could not unify. When the crunch came, Blake voted to condemn the hanging, while many of his Protestant followers bolted. *Grip* in this instance took the easy way out, avoiding the core of the argument and focusing on the government's ingenious ploy. It lectured Liberal journals that had been caught up in the argument and had criticized Blake, thereby giving the *Mail* the chance to quote them gleefully ('*Nolens Volens*' [Willing or Unwilling]).

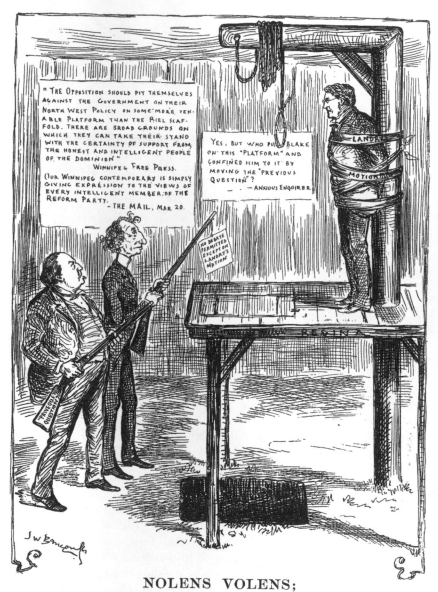

NOLENS VOLENS;

OR, WHY BLAKE MADE THE REGINA SCAFFOLD HIS PLATFORM, AFTER SAYING HE WOULDN'T.

Over time, both *Grip*'s sympathy for the Métis and its condemnation of Macdonald became sharper. It never recanted its support for the execution and continued to echo the *Mail*'s powerful arguments that justice demanded Riel's death even though the Métis had had cause to rebel. Even so, it appeared over time to move towards that sector of the party that deplored the hanging. In January 1886 it argued that the Métis were more sinned against than sinning, and it censured the authors of a music hall song which bragged that if the rebels ever rose again 'we will string them up.'[15] In May, just a year after the rebellion, it even ran a small cartoon – unsigned but very much in Bengough's style – that put the Métis fighters on a plane of moral equality with the government soldiers. Printed at a time when there was much discussion of medals for the Canadian soldiers, the cartoon showed a forgiving Canada bestowing on a Métis soldier a decoration marked 'Redress of Wrongs' (see p. 146). The caption, headed 'Another Decoration Now in Order,' said that the 'half-breeds' should now be granted the rights they had fought for.

In the context of post-revolt bitterness, this little cartoon was very much out of tune with the mood of Toronto, although it could be seen as part of a Liberal attempt to find a basis for party consensus. Macdonald's part in provoking revolt was still the common theme on which all Liberals could agree, and it emerged in *Grip* (following both the *Globe* and *Mail*) as a dominant refrain. An 1889 satire was especially savage in using to this end the unveiling of a Port Hope statue for Lieutenant-Colonel Arthur Williams, an officer who had died at Batoche. Billed as a draft of Macdonald's speech for the occasion, it included the lines:

This magnificent statue will worthily perpetuate [Williams's] fame as a soldier to distant generations, but as for me, his old friend and leader, I can only have the consolation of knowing that *I* supplied him the opportunity of dying in action. Had it not been for the imbecility, the stupidity, the wanton carelessness and the hard-hearted stubbornness of myself and colleagues, there would have been no rebellion, and consequently no battle of Batoche, and consequently no slaying of this hero, and consequently I would not have been here today unveiling this memorial.[16]

Grip, 27 Mar. 1886 (opposite). Bengough was furious when Macdonald and Sir Hector Langevin, in a brilliant bit of parliamentary footwork, managed to limit debate to Riel's execution rather than letting it include the government's role in provoking the rebellion. This cartoon was a complicated attempt to show that Blake had been forced against his will to split his party, attacking the execution while many of his followers supported it.

ANOTHER DECORATION NOW IN ORDER.

THE GALLANT VOLUNTEERS HAVING RECEIVED THEIR WELL-
EARNED MEDALS, MISS CANADA WILL PROCEED (IT IS
HOPED) TO RECOGNIZE THE EFFORTS OF THE
HALFBREEDS, BY GIVING THEM THE
RIGHTS THEY FOUGHT FOR.

Along with its growing sympathy for the Métis in the late 1880s, *Grip* was paradoxically developing a stronger antagonism to French Canada and the Roman Catholic Church. In so doing, it clearly took much of its line from the *Mail*, but it drew as well on the general mood of Toronto. It was thoroughly caught up, for instance, in the racial *cause célèbre* that arose after one of E.E. Sheppard's editors at the *News* wrote a story imputing cowardice to a French-Canadian unit in the rebellion. When Sheppard as editor was charged with criminal libel and taken for trial to Montreal, *Grip* joined in English Canada's wrath. It said that Sheppard's defence speech – in which he had declared, 'We can never be a great and united people until we have one language and one ambition' – was 'magnificent' and 'could not have been equalled by any other man in Canada.'[17] At the same time, *Grip* was drawn into the faddish 'equal rights' demand for a new constitutional deal that would eliminate the 'special privileges' of Catholicism and French Canada. The change at the magazine was gradual and may not have been noticed by readers deafened by the shrill comment of other Toronto media, but it is startling when *Grip*'s issues of the early and late eighties are compared.

The peak of irrationality, for both *Grip* and Toronto, came with the so-called Jesuits' Estates issue of 1888–9, a hysterical reaction to a complex piece of Quebec legislation that was aimed at settling claims of the Roman Catholic Church and the Jesuit Order for lands confiscated in a period when the order was banned by the Pope. Ontario saw special Catholic privilege in the act and called for the federal government to disallow it. Again, the *Mail* was in the lead (in the campaign that Thompson and others thought was aimed at breaking up the country to bring on annexation), but *Grip* was not far behind.

A few years earlier, *Grip* had urged the *Mail* not to exacerbate religious problems. 'We advocate,' it had said, 'the bringing up of Canadian youngsters in the way they should go, that is, in love and unity as Canadians, so that when they are old they will not go through the streets of Canada fighting the Battle of the Boyne annually, and making assess of themselves generally.' As recently as the beginning of 1888, it had made fun of the *Mail* as a recognized stamping ground for cranks. But now it outdid the *Mail*, portraying the *Grip* raven as a Martin Luther nailing on the church door his demands for abolition of separate schools and disal-

---

Grip, 22 May 1886 (*opposite*). In the months after the rebellion, *Grip* became even more hostile to Macdonald – and more sympathetic to the rebels. In a tiny cartoon that would have won little sympathy in Toronto, he even suggested that the nation should now redress the wrongs committed against the Métis.

lowance of the Jesuits' Estates Act. 'A cry has gone up for a leader to step forward to deliver the Canadian people from the dangers which beset them,' it said. 'He has come! ... Like Luther of old, the new Deliverer has nailed his thesis to the church door, but the controversy he has with Rome is not, like Luther's, concerning religious doctrine – it is purely a question of civil politics ... The pretensions of any Church or sect to control the political acts of citizens we repudiate and reject.'[18]

Grip even published a cartoon that depicted the once-despised Christopher Bunting as a crusader, magnanimously grasping the hand of Mother Church and declaring that the *Mail*'s quarrel was not with her but with the devious Jesuit 'son' skulking behind her. *Grip* said it wanted to stress this point because it fully agreed with the *Mail*: 'There is no attack being made on the Catholic Church or on any of her doctrines or practices as a religious institution ... The fight is against the *political* doctrines and ambitions of a single one of these Orders – the Society of Jesus.'[19]

Despite this claim, Bengough's cartoons of church leaders in this period mark a low point in his life. 'The Vatican Tandem' is just one of many that showed arrogant, bloated prelates bullying political leaders.[20] The depths of Bengough's fervour became all too clear as *Grip* lacerated the 'contemptible' waffling of the *Globe* on the Jesuits' Estates Act, proclaimed that the heart of the Canadian people was 'on the side of the *Mail* and British Liberty,' and sneered at the *Globe*'s opportunism:

RECIPE FOR A 'GLOBE' ARTICLE

Mix business and duty –
Lay on the flail,
One crack for the Jesuits
And ten for the *Mail*...[21]

When the Commons rejected disallowance of the Jesuits' Estates Act, *Grip* threw itself behind the equal rights movement, pressing for elimination of the 'monstrosity' of bilingualism and dual schools throughout the country. It was delighted when the dissident Tory MP Dalton McCarthy moved to abolish official bilingualism in the North-West Territories – a region that included today's Saskatchewan and Alberta – and it promoted him as a possible leader of an Anglo-Protestant party. A Bengough cartoon showed Commons leaders of both parties as a bunch of old ladies who had blundered into imposing bilingualism on the region ('The Women Folks Alarmed!' p. 150). The commentary said that the leaders

THE VATICAN TANDEM

(Suggestion for an effective and highly instructive turn-out in the Fancy Drive Procession at the Montreal Carnival.)

Grip, 9 Feb. 1889. This cartoon is one of many, at the height of the so-called race and creed troubles, in which Bengough portrayed the Roman Catholic Church as a bloated tyrant, interfering in Canada's legislatures, courts, and schools. The politicians pulling the sleigh are Macdonald, Cartwright, Mowat, and Meredith. The figure at the top of the tower is Honoré Mercier, the Quebec nationalist premier who had gained office on the wave of anger that followed Riel's death.

were too terrified of Quebec opinion to voice their real conviction – that 'Canada would be a great deal better off if its entire people spoke the English language and that alone.'[22]

In the following weeks, Bengough's cartoons were backed by editorials proclaiming bilingualism to be a plot by the Catholic hierarchy to take over the West. They insisted that 'any institution, however ridiculous or burdensome, which is calculated to serve the turn of the hierarchy,' was sure to get the support of French-Canadian MPs and that the dual language policy in the North-West Territories was one such institution. 'The futile hope that in some miraculous way the great lone land may be

THE WOMEN FOLKS ALARMED!

THAT DREADFUL BOY McCARTHY HAS BROUGHT A LIVE ISSUE INTO THE HOUSE!!

TWO OFFICIAL LANGUAGES.
"AS USELESS AS TWO TONGUES ON A NORTH-WEST CART."

Grip, 1 Feb. 1890 (*opposite*) and 15 Feb. 1890 (*above*). Some of Bengough's least
attractive cartoons were drawn in campaigns to end bilingualism and cut off support for separate schools. 'The Women Folks' has the leaders of both parties in a
panic over Dalton McCarthy's motion to eliminate bilingualism in the North-West
Territories. Cartwright and Laurier are on the left, Sir John Thompson is disap-
pearing out of the window, and Sir Hector Langevin is shown next to Macdonald,
while Blake is on the floor. Bengough sometimes portrayed men as women when
he wanted to show them as craven or unreliable.

transformed into a second Quebec, is also present in the minds of these
gentlemen' ('Two Official Languages').

When the parliamentary debate ended in a compromise that threw the
decision back to the people of the region, *Grip* saw this as a victory for
McCarthy over Macdonald, ensuring the right result by default.[23] For a
time, it seemed that *Grip* might be transferring its allegiance to a Protestant party headed by McCarthy. But at the end of the debate a hint came
that its allegiance remained with the Grits. In contrast to earlier com-

ments about the wisdom of unilingualism, it said that McCarthy's apparent desire to abolish French even in social and business life was an absurd idea, undesirable even if practicable.

As this comment indicates, Bengough was beginning to develop an admiration for Laurier. While he still refused to give Laurier full support in the race and creed battles, he had become impressed by the personal qualities of the New Liberal leader. The conversion seems to have taken place when Laurier courageously confronted a Toronto audience in the fall of 1889, at the height of the equal rights hysteria. Suddenly, Bengough found Laurier to be a model of wisdom, an apostle of concord who had shown eloquence and common sense even in arguing the virtues of compromise:

The Canadian nation – if we ever reach the dignity to which every Canadian patriot aspires – must be at least for a few centuries to come composed of two races, different in their characteristics and dissimilar in their genius, but not necessarily antagonistic. Unless history witnesses the miracle of Quebec voluntarily abandoning its French traditions and suddenly becoming Anglo-Saxon, time alone can bring about such a unity as some are talking of as possible. Mr. Laurier demonstrated in a most convincing manner that such a unity can never be brought about by force, whether that force be exercised in the shape of encroachments by the majority upon the cherished and heretofore guaranteed rights of the minority, or in the more violent form of armed assault.[24]

Clearly, Bengough was showing the loyalty that would make him a committed Laurier supporter for almost three decades. He was also, perhaps, serving again as a barometer of Canadian liberal, or 'progressive,' opinion. At the depths of the Jesuits' Estates furore, that sector had joined in the hysteria, convinced that Protestant Anglo-Saxons needed to fight the monster of clerical and racial privilege. Now it was returning to a saner view. While still flirting with the equal rights movement, Grip avoided the more extreme and less credible Protestant Protective Association that followed it. At the same time, Bengough began to agree with Thompson that the Mail's brave talk of breaking up the country to ensure equal rights might actually be an annexation ploy, and he began to distance himself from the paper. For both Bengough and his community, it seemed, the worst of the race and creed fever had passed.

7

Opening of the West

The peak period of John Bengough's career was also the time of the opening of the West. It was the time of the Canadian Pacific Railway, the Winnipeg boom, the settlers' disturbances, the establishment of Regina. It was the time of the North-West Mounted Police, the Northwest Rebellion, the tension between Ottawa and British Columbia, and the Manitoba schools crisis. Like most of his fellow easterners, Bengough was fascinated by the West, though not necessarily knowledgeable about it. He was impressed by its huge potential, its mystery and challenge, though he was dismayed at times by its cruelty. Among his thousands of sketches there were very few on the Maritimes, but there were hundreds on the West. There is a certain justice in the decision (apparently based on a surveyor's whim) to name a south Saskatchewan town for the cartoonist.[1]

'*Grip* has always felt and expressed a warm interest in the affairs of the North-West,' the magazine said late in 1883. 'His sympathies are always with our hardy countrymen who have gone into the great lone land to lay the foundation of future greatness, and wholly against any government policy that retards them in their endeavor.' Paradoxically, *Grip* portrayed the West as suffering under the National Policy, yet also spoke of easterners migrating to the West to escape the same policy. A typical 1881 poem, 'To the West,' went:

> To the west, to the west, to the land of the free,
> Our sons and our daughters are longing to be ...

> To the west, to the west, to the land of the free,
> From the baneful effects of the National P.

Where the blessings Sir John promised under his sway
Are reserved for his friends – and for which we must pay ...[2]

Bengough's interest in the West and his simplistic view of it show up in his later correspondence as well as in *Grip*. In 1906 he wrote to Prime Minister Laurier furiously condemning the speculative profits which the Saskatchewan Land Company was making by selling land to settlers – land which he thought should have come directly from the state. Bengough said that for years he had been full of hope and enthusiasm for the West, and he earnestly hoped and prayed it might 'develop as a noble Christian community.' But its foundations would have to be laid in justice, he said: 'I denounce in the name of God and Humanity this legalized system of heartless robbery.' Laurier's reply, while friendly in tone, took apart Bengough's argument and virtually supported the Tory policy of land payments for railway building. Laurier told Bengough that he too deplored the speculation, but the land in question had been given as grants to finance the railways, and the process was necessary: 'Unless early railway construction had been effectively helped out of the public treasury, the settlement of the Prairies might have been retarded ... Unless we had taken means of promptly developing our country, we stood to lose our own population.' Reading between the lines, one can find a note of impatience with Bengough's naiveté. The same tone comes through in another letter, in which Laurier told Bengough in passing, 'I know how earnest you are in your convictions.'[3]

The same passionate beliefs inform Bengough's cartoons on the West, which leave a picture that is both distorted and incomplete. Although Bengough made at least two western trips in the 1880s and was familiar with some leading characters and problems in western politics, his source material was thin. He later toured and entertained in most of the western towns, but in these early days his view was more than usually limited by political biases, including a conviction that all Tory policies, especially railway policies, were designed to hurt the region.

A typical cartoon, in November 1882, portrayed Manitoba as an Indian maiden about to attack Macdonald. It was accompanied by a warning that the prime minister could never 'make a passive squaw out of a young woman who has white blood in her veins and a love of freedom in her heart' ('Let the Big Chief Beware!'). Another, the following year, had Macdonald and a couple of his ministers scratching their heads to think up ways to hurt the West, adding to a list that already included such things as reservation of the best land for speculation, disallowance of

LET THE BIG CHIEF BEWARE!

Grip, 18 Nov. 1882. This vivid cartoon helped persuade Manitobans that Ottawa's deal with the Canadian Pacific Railway syndicate had imposed an unbearable burden on their new province.

local railway charters, and high taxes on implements: 'We say deliberately
... that it would tax the ingenuity of any Cabinet to devise more cunning
means of retarding the settlement of the North-West.'[4] On another occasion, *Grip* suggested that the grievous wrongs against the West could easily
be set right: 'These troubles arise almost exclusively from evil legislation,
and can be cured effectively by the simple method of abolishing the
enactments complained of.'[5]

Long before the Northwest Rebellion, Bengough gave serious attention to western alienation. When a series of meetings in the Prince Albert
region in 1883 aired complaints about, among other things, the North-
West Territories' long fight for representation in Ottawa, Bengough
pictured the region being ignored. A year before the rebellion, Interior
Minister Sir David Macpherson was shown as a country bumpkin oblivious to pressing dangers. The same year another senior minister, Sir
Hector Langevin, was shown as perversely refusing to find any grievances
among westerners.[6]

Despite his concern for western Canada, Bengough lacked any clear
appreciation of the potential of the region, especially of British Columbia
and the North. From the beginning, he echoed Edward Blake's doubts
about the basic worth of the transcontinental railway tying British Columbia to the rest of Canada. In 1876 – a time when Alexander Mackenzie, as
prime minister, was quarrelling with British Columbia over terms for
completion of the line – *Grip* spoke patronizingly of how few residents
there were in the province and suggested that when they finally got their
expensive railway, they might well take their end of it into the United
States. Three years later – with Macdonald back in office, vigorously pro-
moting the railway – the magazine called the project a gigantic piece of
nonsense undertaken only to 'stop the howlings of a handful of people'
on the coast and to sustain the fiction of union.[7] In 1881 it was still convinced that Macdonald was paying far too high a price to 'keep British
Columbia British' ('The Pacific Youngster Pacified'). It would be years
before Bengough included British Columbians among the westerners
who deserved sympathy because they were bound to the Canadian Pacific
Railway by 'chains of slavery.'[8]

While he was vague about British Columbia and the Far North,
Bengough was consistently more sympathetic to Manitoba and the North-
West Territories – the latter including today's provinces of Saskatchewan
and Alberta. This applied especially to railway policy. Bengough slavishly
followed the Grit line, condemning the price the government had paid
the Canadian Pacific Railway Company (in loans, land, and monopoly

THE PACIFIC YOUNGSTER PACIFIED.

SIR CHARLES.—"WELL, THEN, AND DID HIS BAD, BAD MACKENZIE MAKE A FOOLEY TOOLEY OF HIM, SO HE
DID; BUT HE SHALL HAVE HIS ISLAND RAILWAY, SO HE SHALL; AND HE'LL ALWAYS VOTE FOR HIS
SIR CHARLEY, SO HE SHALL!"

Grip, 17 Sept. 1881. While Bengough often promoted Manitoba's interests, for
many years he considered British Columbia a spoiled, insignificant territory, not
worth the effort Canada was making to keep it in Confederation. The BC politicians watching Sir Charles Tupper are Amor De Cosmos, the eccentric Nova
Scotia–born editor who became premier of British Columbia and a federal MP,
and (in the dress) MP Arthur Bunster.

THAT TROUBLESOME YOUNGSTER.

INDULGENT MAMMA MACDONALD.—"IT MUST BE A GOOD LITTLE MONOPOLY, AND IT MUSN'T CRY FOR OLIVER'S
    THINGS, OR MAMMA 'LL HAVE TO——"
SPINSTER BLAKE (SOTTO VOCE).—"OH, IF *I* ONLY HAD THE MANAGEMENT OF THAT CHE-ILD!"

Grip, 5 Nov. 1881. Timber lands in the northwest disputed by Ontario and
Manitoba were also coveted by the CPR syndicate and other friends of the federal
government. In this cartoon Premier Mowat is holding onto the 'timber limits'
coveted by the railway.

guarantees) while suggesting no serious alternatives. He failed to see the importance of the line to Canada – or even to Ontario. On one occasion, with astonishing short-sightedness, he observed that the CPR would 'certainly not do *us* [Ontario] any good, however much it may benefit Quebec or any other province.'[9]

On his kindest days, Bengough saw the railway as a soulless corporation that cursed the West (especially Manitoba) with its hoggish behaviour – with a combination of gall, impudence, and greed that had goaded westerners to the verge of rebellion. His view on this issue admitted of no alternative explanation ('That Troublesome Youngster'). He was totally blind to the balancing view presented by a later generation of pro-Macdonald historians such as Donald Creighton: 'The whole difficult and ungrateful effort to preserve the east-west transport system from the damage which Manitoba seemed determined to inflict upon it was breaking against Manitoba's unreasoning, almost maniacal, resistance.'[10] Along with his fellow Grits, Bengough was especially hard on the CPR's twenty-year monopoly, which forbade the building of competing lines down to the U.S. rail system ('Macbeth Hath Murdered the Manitoba Charters'; '"Ministerial" Consolation': pp. 160–1). Just as constantly, he opposed government loans and guarantees for the CPR itself.[11]

Some of Bengough's blind spots about the railway and the West Coast eventually disappeared, but not until he toured British Columbia in 1889. Until then, although he would certainly have insisted that he was sympathetic to the West, he had not gone physically or psychologically beyond Manitoba. He visited that province first in the spring of 1882 at the height of the boom and acquired prejudices about western speculators and western weather that stayed with him for years. (A train taking him to Portage la Prairie was blocked by an April blizzard.) Nevertheless, some of his quick sketches of Winnipeg have a simple and effective quality, catching the frontier verve. Like other eastern journalists, he was both fascinated and appalled by the hysteria of the boom in the early 1880s ('Bird's-Eye View of Manitoba,' p. 162). He enjoyed the excitement but found the frenzy of speculation decidedly sordid and responded not only with cartoons but with a number of satires and poems like this 'Song of Manitoba':

> Sing a song of millions,
>   Spent like random shots
> Up in Manitoba,
>   Buying corner lots.

MACBETH HATH MURDERED THE MANITOBA CHARTERS.

MACBETH.—"I HAVE DONE THE DEED."—ACT II., SCENE 2.

Grip, 21 Jan. 1882 (*above*) and 9 Dec. 1882 (*opposite*). Like its Grit allies, *Grip* underplayed the importance of the Canadian Pacific Railway and the government's difficulty in building it. These cartoons are from a strong and effective series attacking the CPR's monopoly and Ottawa's disallowance of subsidiary lines authorized by Manitoba. In 'Ministerial Consolation,' Premier Norquay tells

"MINISTERIAL" CONSOLATION.

(*continued*) Manitoba, 'Courage, my dear, you'll not mind it when you get used to it,' and Macdonald intones, 'I'm sorry, but the "Bargain" demands it.' The death warrant pinned on the scaffold is from the Winnipeg *Times*, the government organ, and says, 'Where is the Reason in the cry against Disallowance since it is understood to be the settled Policy of the Dominion Government?'

BIRD'S-EYE VIEW OF MANITOBA.

Grip, 4 Mar. 1882. On his first trip west, Bengough captured in sketches and poems the soon-to-collapse Manitoba boom.

> Fancy paper city –
>   Pretty Indian name –
> Is it very naughty,
>   Playing such a game? ...[12]

When Lieutenant-Governor Edgar Dewdney chose Regina as the capital of the North-West Territories, apparently to forward his own interests, *Grip* joined the Liberal newspapers (and at least one Tory paper, the Winnipeg *Times*) in a storm of criticism that covered everything from Dewdney's land jobbery to his exploitation of the Native people. And when the prime minister brought Dewdney into the cabinet in 1888 and named him minister of the interior, *Grip* called it little short of a public outrage: 'Dewdney's name is execrated throughout the North-West Territories as that of a sordid, self-seeking adventurer, and it is humiliating to think of his being elevated to a position of honor and influence over the heads of men who possess both character and ability.'[13]

Towards John Norquay, the erratically Conservative premier of Manitoba, Grip's stance was consistent. It praised him when he fought Ottawa for provincial rights and condemned him when he compromised.[14] At times its exasperation with Norquay extended to the whole province. In 1887 (after yet another discouraging Liberal loss in the federal election), Grip addressed Manitobans directly, telling them that their problems were of their own making. First, they had voted solidly for Sir John A.'s party and in favour of the bargain with the railway syndicate. Then, when the monopoly clause had been enforced, they had yelled with rage – but they had then gone to the polls to vote for Sir John again: 'Now, how does the average politician deal with people of your kind – partisans, whose blind slavery to party overrides even their own personal interests? Why, just as the shrewd Old Man has been dealing with you – smooths them down with a few soft words and sending them home happy, and then goes right on disallowing their [rail] charters as before. And serves them jolly well right if they haven't any more spunk than to lick the hand that smites them.'[15]

Grip's rejection of every federal position was by now predictable, especially on railways and trade. Typical was an awkward 1890 poem signed by Wallack Sacul and entitled 'The Manitoba Farmer':

> Oppressed by laws iniquitous
>   By blindfold rulers made,
> Not strange so many loyal hearts
>   And eyes have southward strayed.
>
> And some have thought to give the head –
>   Where heart might never be –
> If Annexation with the States
>   Would bring true liberty.
>
> They tax the farmer's food, his clothes
>   His instruments of trade;
> Whilst manufacturers bonused are,
>   And Party friends are paid ...[16]

In the late 1880s, when the Manitoba government decided to cut off public funding for its Catholic schools, *Grip*'s Ontario Protestant outlook (as well as its anti-Macdonald stance) inevitably led it to support the provincial action. Like most Ontarians, Bengough chose to see the issue as one of provincial, not minority, rights. In a tone of exasperation, he implied that no right-thinking person could see it otherwise. No one was stopping Manitoba Catholics from building their own schools – the government was simply insisting that they not be paid for by taxpayers. 'If such schools are so absolutely necessary, so essential to the moral and spiritual well-being of the children, surely they are worth paying for.'[17]

This assessment was to be a constant theme of Bengough's cartoons for many years, both in *Grip* and in his later Liberal propaganda cartoons in the *Globe*. At the same time, he hammered away at the harm done the West by high freight rates and by the National Policy of high tariffs, which forced westerners to buy high-priced implements in eastern Canada.[18] As well, he endorsed western efforts to end official bilingualism – again, an imposition of Ottawa. In all these instances, *Grip*'s attitude was dictated not so much by an understanding of western conditions as by Bengough's own prejudices – on opposition to the Tories, on free trade, on capitalist exploitation, on prohibition, and on race and religion. While he was quick to condemn the policies for the West that were made in Ottawa, he seems not to have seen that his own solutions were just as surely made in Toronto.

8

The Radical Times

At the end of the 1880s and the start of the 1890s, *Grip* increasingly showed the influence of T. Phillips Thompson, who was now a veteran and embittered radical far removed from his beginnings as a homely humorist. His work made a profound difference to the magazine, probably helping to give it its finest years – but also contributing to its collapse. Thompson had not only worked with *Grip* on and off from its birth but had sent in material even when he was away in the United States or Britain soaking up radical ideas. The beginning of his period of major influence at *Grip* seems to have been signalled in 1889 by a note reporting his return from England and hinting at his habitual discontent. It said that Thompson had returned after a year-long attempt to live in the 'distressful climate and constrained social relations' of the Old Country and added, 'The fact is, that to a man in sympathy with the life of this continent and imbued with its spirit of freedom, the air of Europe is stifling ... In this instance, what is *Punch's* loss is *Grip's* gain and we welcome 'Jimuel' back.'[1]

Thompson was formally listed as *Grip's* associate editor from 1890 to 1892, at the same time as he was failing to keep alive the *Labor Advocate*, also printed by the Grip company. When the company's new managers forced Bengough out in mid-1892, Thompson took over as the editor of *Grip*. His name did not appear on the masthead – no editor was listed in this period – but when Bengough revived *Grip* at the beginning of 1894, he reported that Thompson had indeed succeeded him as editor. It is not certain, though, that Thompson was fully in charge or remained so throughout the year of Bengough's absence. The editorial comments for a time echoed Thompson's ideas, but later this rhetoric faded and many of the items – not very good ones – were signed with the initials G.C.[2] Thomas Bengough later blamed *Grip's* decline on manager T.G. Wilson, saying that under his leadership the magazine 'lived at a poor dying rate, absolutely devoid of humor, sarcasm, criticism worth anything, with cartoons lacking point and reading matter having no interest or punch or snap.' This assessment was clearly jaundiced, but it was not without merit. The magazine by this time was obviously skidding, apparently out of touch with its audience.

Thompson's views, most of them offered anonymously or under such well-known pen-names as Jimuel Briggs and Enjolras, were well known to the Toronto readers of his day, but later analyses may have attributed some of his sharper lines to others. While he was writing editorials for the *News*, for instance, the proprietor E.E. Sheppard acquired a reputation as a tough and radical 'democratic' editor, boosting labour unions and favouring republican independence for Canada. Just a few years later, Sheppard was running for the Conservatives and showing his true Tory colours in *Saturday Night* columns, so it seems likely that Thompson was responsible for some of the more extreme views attributed to his chief.[3] Similarly, Bengough was undoubtedly credited with (or blamed for) some of Thompson's sharper lines. Thompson probably wrote the cutting attack on the Massey family that has been attributed to Bengough. It commented sarcastically on the joy in Methodist ranks over a Massey family donation of $40,000 to endow a chair at Victoria College and said it was a fine thing for capitalists to keep prices high with their combines while manfully cutting wages so as to 'acquire the means of being charitable and munificent on a great scale.'[4]

While the professional relationship between Bengough and Thompson is veiled, it would appear that Thompson was the dominant personality as well as being the more experienced and more radical of the two. When Bengough revived the magazine in 1894, he tacitly admitted that he had erred in letting others (presumably Thompson) impose radical ideas on his publication. Bengough had always had a keen sense of his public's sensibilities – formed, perhaps, by his regular public appearances throughout the country. He also showed a greater inclination to be agreeable. Thompson, by contrast, loved a fight and cared not at all for public opinion. He sneered even at his prime readers in the labour movement, telling them they were not bright enough or courageous enough to appreciate what he was trying to do for them. It seems clear that Thompson's intransigence did indeed set *Grip* on the slope to oblivion, although hard economic times greased the path.

Bengough's recognition of his fatal error was set out in the first issue after he revived *Grip* in 1894, in a note promising that 'the old bird

[*Grip*] ... would not allow himself to be made a vehicle for "fads" and "hobbies" even so much as in earlier days.' This touched off a revealing exchange with a leading *Saturday Night* writer, Joseph T. Clark (Mack), who was not satisfied with the assurance and warned *Grip* (in a comment that probably reflected a widespread Toronto opinion) to repent of its radicalism. Bengough, he said, was rated as the country's best cartoonist, but his mistake had been to abandon the vantage ground of critic and caricaturist to take the most violent side in every public question:

Those who were not enthusiasts on temperance, single tax, Henry Georgism-in-general, free trade and annexation, all at once, took their doses of old *Grip* during Mr. Bengough's last year of management with feelings almost of nausea. If Mr. Bengough can shake himself loose from his trammels and ply a free crayon, he has the skill to win for the new *Grip* a place never occupied by the old *Grip* even in its palmiest days. The success of the paper should be a matter of national pride, but if it is run in the interests of a wild-eyed *coterie* it will share all the vicissitudes encountered by those faddists and their fads. Here's hoping that *Grip*, purified in the grave, will now shake away from its ragged foundlings and become respectable and great.[5]

Bengough accepted the general rebuke but sharply denied any annexationist leanings. 'It is true,' he said, 'that (through an enthusiasm for humanity which we hope was pardonable) *Grip* used to be perhaps too much in earnest for a mere jester on the questions of Prohibition, Just Taxation, Free Trade and other great questions, but not a line was ever written or drawn in support of Annexation.'[6]

This reply seems to show that Bengough regretted giving so much latitude to Thompson, though his later silence about Thompson makes it difficult to be certain. In his memoirs, Bengough wrote that he himself had edited the magazine almost exclusively until his retirement, with the exception of two short periods in which it was edited by *Globe* editors R.H. Larminie and E.W. Thomson. He made no mention of the periods in which Thompson was listed as editor (in the early days, under the Jimuel Briggs pen-name) or associate editor, or of his succession to the editorship in 1892. This omission is especially ironic since Bengough's formal collaboration with Thompson, from 1889 to 1892, gave *Grip* some of its best days, at least from the point of view of later readers. In those eventful years (which covered the Jesuits' Estates aftermath, the 1891 election, Macdonald's death, the McGreevy scandal, and the beginning of the

"THOU SHALT NOT KILL!"

Grip, 3 Nov. 1883. Cartoons like this one reflected Bengough's new-found enthusiasm for the anti-capitalist populism that was gaining power in the United States during the 1880s. Late in the decade, his collaboration with T. Phillips Thompson strengthened this tendency.

Manitoba schools crisis) *Grip* was tough, biting, socially aware, independent – certainly a force in Canadian politics. Bengough's cartoon work was at its best, with a sharp albeit bigoted edge to it; and the best of Thompson's social conscience was on display, while the worst of his dogmatism seemed to be checked.

While Thompson's influence in this period is apparent, it is not clear how much of a role he played at other times. An 1883 comment favouring public telegraph lines and railways while opposing monopolies, 'especially such heartless money-bloated grabbers as Jay Gould,'[7] sounds like his work. But it could conceivably have been Bengough's; like Thompson at the time, he was under the influence of Henry George and was developing stronger views on industrial justice. These views appeared in such cartoons as 'Thou Shalt Not Kill!', which showed a manufacturer cutting wages and sentencing families to death, and ran with the comment: 'The explicit curse of Heaven has been declared against those who grind the faces of the poor, and no invective of ours can add to the weight of that denunciation.' Either Thompson or Bengough could have written that line, as well as many others of the same kind that reflected the surge of American populism in the eighties. The same tone was shown in 1887 when Thompson brought out his major work, *The Politics of Labor. Grip* gave it generous attention, including a poem that began:

> Would you lend your ear and heedfully hear a terrible tale of woe,
> How the millionaire with the iron glare grinds down the workmen low,
> And capitalists on heights of mist reside in hills of gold
> And with angry frown keep poor men down in hovels damp and cold ...[8]

Thompson's more extreme rhetoric becomes increasingly evident in some of the anti-capitalist material towards the end of the decade. It seems to show, for instance, in a commentary early in 1888 to the effect that the country's coal monopoly existed because the mines were owned by people who assumed that God had created coal for their particular benefit. It also shows in a column which appeared that summer complaining that the British navy was spending millions on naval exercises while 'thousands' in England starved each year; and which went on to say that the country's problem was 'the unfortunate fact that the tight little island is owned by a handful of peers, who charge the people very high prices for living on it.' It is apparent again in a column in the fall of that year, which complained that 'even the most stupid workingman' should be able to see that protection could not help labour, and which then launched into a dogmatic socialist screed declaring that labor was 'the source of all wealth, and not, as the Protectionists teach, the puny child of Capital, needing to be coddled by monopoly.'[9]

After Thompson was listed as associate editor, his style showed in a comment on a mine disaster at Springhill, Nova Scotia, urging the government to provide for families of workers killed or disabled during perilous duties: 'It is a monstrous thing that men should be engaged in occupations such as sailing, railroading, mining, etc., absolutely necessary to our civilization, for a mere subsistence out of which nothing can be saved, and that when they are killed or maimed society takes no care for their families beyond extending a little temporary "charity."' The Thompson touch showed as well in an 1890 note that attacked the 'specious humbug' of a Manufacturers' Association claim that it was working for the benefit of labour, and in an 1891 description of an American incident in which 'nine working men, rendered desperate by heartless and systematic oppression, were shot down like dogs by the tools of the protection-created monopolies.'[10]

More broadly, Thompson probably had a hand in changing *Grip*'s orientation after the election of 1891. During the campaign itself the magazine kept to the Liberal line, attacking Macdonald, supporting reciprocity, and downplaying Macdonald's charges that reciprocity would lead to annexation. But after the Liberal Party's defeat (its fourth in a row), *Grip* took a radical turn and came out with its own political platform, which included control of monopolies, along with such planks as direct taxation, national independence, women's suffrage, equal rights, free trade, and prohibition.[11] At the same time, it became more hostile to the Liberals in both Ottawa and Toronto, and more outspoken in attacking political corruptionists of both parties ('To the Rescue!'). It became more dogmatic, too, in its anti-business tone, in a way that must have annoyed the party chiefs. On public ownership it said that 'the mines of Ontario were not intended by the Creator for a few favored monopolists, but for the benefit of the people as a whole.' On international capitalist exploitation it said (concerning a South African crisis), 'Imperial troops should not be asked to fight for the interests of private business speculators.'[12] These anti-capitalist views seem notably stronger than those of Bengough, who always insisted that he had no objection to private ownership, only (after Henry George) to ownership of *land value* that had increased because of general progress.

On Bengough's departure in July 1892, the most noticeable change in *Grip* was the quick decline in cartoon quality, as a handful of substitutes (Sam Jones, S.J. West., A.G. Racey, Sam Hunter, Buckton Nendick, and 'Napoleon') tried to take Bengough's place. But changes in the serious commentary were also noticeable. The magazine lost its whimsical quality and took on an air of unrelieved didacticism, replete with references to capitalist exploiters, arrogant militarists, and the like. Meanwhile, the rest of the sheet seemed increasingly to be filled with borrowed material – shoddy humour, frothy drawing-room cartoons, cheap and often racist American boilerplate, and Canadian cartoons that were often amateurish and unconnected to the text. While some of its views echoed its earlier ones, the magazine's unique quality was gone. What replaced it was an outlook of unrelieved biliousness.

A typical tirade was directed at the 'privileged class' that had condoned

TO THE RESCUE!
Or, Miss Canada in the Clutches of the Foul Fiend of Corruption.

Grip, 29 Aug. 1891. Public horror over 'boodling' in the early 1890s focused mainly on contract kickbacks to the Quebec Tory, Thomas McGreevy, the brother-in-law and nemesis of Sir Hector Langevin. By this point, *Grip* was becoming exasperated with both parties, and it may be significant that the little figures attacking the monster include not only Laurier and Cartwright but also Sir John Abbott and Sir John Thompson, the current and future Tory prime ministers.

the punishment of an Ohio militiaman for the offence of cheering an anarchist. The militiaman, according to the commentary, had been suspended by the thumbs for thirty minutes, until his life was endangered: 'Taken in connection with the wholesale arrests of citizens on the most frivolous pretexts on mere suspicion of anarchism, and the repeated suppressing of free speech, it shows that the bloated institutions of the United States in their practical working are little if any in advance of the methods of Russian despotism, and that the people who thus tamely permit their liberties to be sacrificed are a race of trucklers and cowards.'[13] The editorial added that the incident might have some benefit if it showed young men the folly of volunteering for military service in which they could be forced to 'do the dirty work of whatever gang of selfish and corrupt politicians may happen to be uppermost.'

A few weeks later the magazine linked the same themes to a switchers' strike in Buffalo and the Homestead strike at Andrew Carnegie's Pennsylvania steel mill. In both cases the workers had been more than a match for their adversaries until the forces of the state had come in on the side of capitalism, it said. This proved that the workers should not waste their time on strikes but should 'overwhelm capitalism with their votes.' It also showed the working class the folly of supporting the military system: 'Practically, on this western continent there is only one use for soldiers, and that is to defend the interests of the wealthy and privileged classes against the workers. Yet ... the poor idiot of a laborer does not see it, and carried away by his fool notions of "glory" and a good time, dons the blue or red uniform, and undertakes to slaughter his comrades at a word of command.'[14] This contempt for the 'poor idiot of a laborer' constantly showed up in Grip's commentary during this era, and it is not clear whether it was genuine or was an attempt to shock workers into action. At times, the magazine spoke of the workers as 'the willing slaves of party and sectarianism,'[15] and as 'besotted idiots who tamely allow themselves to be fleeced by laws of their own creation.'[16]

Repeatedly, Thompson displayed anger at labour's failure to support its leaders, and it is clear that he himself was bitter over the failure of his attempts to create a labour press. On one occasion, he grumbled about the costly folly of a planned parade to celebrate labour's accomplishments: 'What in the name of common sense has organized labor in this city done to demonstrate over? The supporters of a movement that has been repeatedly defeated at the polls – that cannot elect so much as an alderman or a school trustee, let alone an M.P. – that cannot win a strike on a large scale, or even support a newspaper, only expose themselves to ridicule by wasting means and energy on triumphal parades.'[17] All this reads like a strong echo of the material Thompson had written at the *Labor Advocate* until its death late in 1891. There, too, he had denounced workers for failing to support labor papers: 'It is much to be regretted that the wage-earners are so stupidly blind to their own interests that they cannot see the advantage of having a live outspoken journal to plead their cause.'[18] In his politicking, too, Thompson showed a supercilious-ness that probably defeated his best aims. When he was running indepen-dently in an 1893 provincial election, *Grip* carried this short summary of his candidacy (with, incidentally, no indication that Thompson was then also editing the magazine):

Phillips Thompson. – Journalist. Nominee of the People Who Think. Represents living issues and believes in something definite. The only candidate of the four who stands for anything worth talking about. General platform – Extinction of the drones, and securing to those who work the full results of their labor.[19]

On other national issues, Thompson was a gloomy Cassandra, despair-ing of the depression-wracked country and disgusted by all parties. The rottenness of Ottawa's 'boodling,' combined with its economic favourit-ism, had put the country unquestionably on the way to disaster, he wrote. If the Americans wanted to annex Canada, they would find it an easy enough task: 'They were willing to pay seven million dollars for Alaska – half that amount judiciously expended in buying up leading Canadian politicians and newspapers would secure ... annexation.' When members of Toronto's St George's Society moved to expel Goldwin Smith for his annexation plotting, *Grip* expressed its view in Thompsonesque language of a kind that Bengough would never have used: 'If that shallow pated supercilious imbecile Castell Hopkins is a fair representative of the St. George's Society, Prof. Goldwin Smith could have no stronger testimonial to his moral and intellectual worth than expulsion from such a body.' In general, though, the magazine continued to argue that Canada would never submit to annexation and that trade reciprocity would be enough to satisfy the complaints of those flirting with political union. Bengough was on sound ground in his later insistence that the magazine had never backed annexation.[20]

On the federal scene the magazine cursed both parties. While con-tinuing to show respect for Laurier, it brushed aside the Liberals as a bunch of cowards and trimmers who had learned nothing in opposition: 'They are hungry for the fleshpots of office, but they are too much afraid of the forces of the corruption [*sic*] and vested interests, now ranged in solid support of Toryism, to risk offending them in a bold, straight-forward appeal to the masses of the people.' On another occasion, the magazine made a more careful distinction between Laurier and his fol-lowers. In Laurier, it said, the Grits had a leader of growing prestige with an 'unsullied record and high standard of political morality,' but it was doubtful if he could check the rapacity of the predatory horde at his back. Nor did the magazine have much time for two emerging protest parties, the Tory splinter headed by Dalton McCarthy and the agrarian Patrons of Industry. It pronounced McCarthy a 'considerably over-rated man' and said the Patrons 'doubtless mean well, but they don't know very much.'[21]

Undoubtedly, Thompson by this time was thinking of very radical solu-tions to the country's woes, even toying with anarchist possibilities of a kind that would have been horrifying to Toronto's middle class:

No intelligent person these days – unless hired to think otherwise – regards gov-ernment as a sacred, inviolable institution. Divine right is an exploded notion. Government exists merely as a public convenience, by the consent of the gov-erned. There is no more sacredness attaching to it than to a bank ... Any citizen of any country has a perfect right to urge upon his fellow citizens changes in the form or scope of the government, a transference of the sovereignty from one gov-ernment to another, or the abolition of all government whatever. And anyone who denies him that right, or seeks to interfere with him in its exercise does not know the meaning of the word 'liberty.'[22]

In the United States, *Grip* stated on another occasion, both parties were controlled by the plutocrats, and the struggle between them was merely a sham battle to distract the masses from the real issues. The same was true of Canada. The progressive men of either party were powerless against the machine: 'The masses could easily, had they the sense and the cour-age, effect a peaceful reform by the ballot – but unfortunately most of them are fools and cowards. It is altogether likely that the class war will increase in intensity till it culminates in the bloodiest revolution of modern times.'[23]

A similar anarchist streak marked the magazine's view of the justice sys-tem. Governments, it said, had shown ingenuity in inventing new crimes and driving people by taxation and injustice to lawbreaking, while the presence of detectives tended to multiply crimes and endanger the inno-cent: 'They [the detectives] are, as a rule, utterly conscienceless and mercenary, and ready to resort to any methods to secure convictions and win blood-money. It is far better that a few criminals should escape.'[24]

This sympathy for anarchism stands in interesting contrast to *Grip*'s tough attacks on the movement a few years earlier, before Thompson's name appeared on the masthead. Late in 1887, for instance, after the execution of four anarchists accused in Chicago's Haymarket riot, Bengough had depicted Uncle Sam driving a pitchfork through the head of a snake representing anarchism and had commented, 'There is no excuse for Anarchy in a free country ... Uncle Sam has the endorsement of all the friends of civilization in the summary extinction of the poisonous snake.'[25]

While the extent of Thompson's authority at *Grip* in the post-Bengough period is unclear, it may be significant that the magazine was noticeably more anti-Catholic at this time, especially in its treatment of the new Catholic prime minister, Sir John Thompson. It stopped short of supporting the brutish Protestant Protective Association but went a considerable distance towards excusing it. The spread of the movement in Canada, the magazine said, was due as much to the revulsion inspired by the Catholic premier as to the efforts of anti-Romanist propagandists: 'There is a good deal that looks like intolerance in its principle of remorselessly knifing at the polls every Roman Catholic or politician supported by the Catholic vote – but if this feeling gains ground the Roman Catholics are themselves to blame for permitting themselves to be herded together like cattle and traded off to the politicians for special favors to their Church.'[26]

The post-Bengough *Grip* also said that Dalton McCarthy – who was widely regarded as one of the strongest Protestant politicians – was lacking backbone in advancing the Orange interests. Even the Orange Order itself was not strong enough in its Protestantism. When Sam Hughes, the 'fire-eating Orangeman,' agreed to support the Catholic prime minister, *Grip* said the switch showed how little reliance could be placed on the Orange Order as a defence against encroachments of the Romish hierarchy and its tools.[27] This tone was not unusual. Repeatedly, *Grip* condemned the 'shifty, weak-kneed and truckling' Ontario politicians of both parties who professed a belief in equal rights but were ready to sell out their principles for political gain.[28] A.G. Racey's cartoon 'Miss Canada Dreams' reached a new low in paranoia by depicting the Catholic hierarchy as a rapist invading Miss Canada's bedroom behind the mask of Sir John Thompson. A typical 'satire' of the day purported to be a revised catechism:

MISS CANADA DREAMS.

Grip, 10 Dec. 1892. After Bengough was forced out of *Grip*, the magazine vigorously pressed issues of social justice and gender equality but became more intolerant in racial and religious matters. A low point was marked by this A.G. Racey cartoon, which implied that the Roman Catholic hierarchy had used the new Catholic prime minister, Sir John Thompson, as a mask while carrying out its rape of the country.

YE VALIANT KNIGHT, SIR OLIVER, FARES FORTH TO VANQUISH YE
FEARSOME DRAGON!

Grip, no. 1067, 12 May 1894. When Bengough revived *Grip*, the magazine became
more tolerant in matters of race and religion. In this instance, it portrayed Premier Mowat attacking the Protestant Protective Association – the dragon disguise
of Ontario's Conservative leader, W.R. Meredith.

Teacher – 'What is the whole duty of man?'
Pupil – 'To live and die for the Church.'
Teacher – 'For whose special benefit was the constitution of this country framed?'
Pupil – 'For the benefit of the Church first, and the French afterwards.'[29]

In this period the magazine also carried a heavy sprinkling of anti-Jewish,
anti-black, and anti-Asian cartoons, many of which seem to have been
reprints from American magazines.[30]

In various areas, then, *Grip*'s views had become so extreme that it quickly lost support. Even some of the sentiments that seem more progressive were written in a way that managed to alienate the magazine's natural backers. As Thomas Bengough recalled it, subscribers fell away in their hundreds, and within a year the magazine was forced to announce its suspension.[31] Whether all these trends can be attributed to Thompson is debatable. The editorial comments in the last half of 1892 are certainly in his style, but he may not have controlled the content of the rest of the magazine. In the first half of 1893, before suspension of publication, his touch seems to be missing. It is fairly clear, though, that Thompson was a major force in alienating Grip's support as he steered the magazine in the direction of radical socialism, both before and after Bengough' departure.

The sharp change in Grip's tone when Bengough revived it at the beginning of 1894 also says much about the differences between the two men. In that period, the last year of Grip's life, the anti-Catholic tone virtually disappeared, and cartoons sought religious reconciliation while attacking the Protestant Protective Association ('Ye Valiant Knight,' p. 177).[32] On Sir John Thompson's death, Bengough wrote one of his famous poetic elegies.[33] The emphasis on prohibition and women's suffrage was continued, and the strong support for Laurier re-emerged (combined with regret at Laurier's retreat from a free trade platform). The emphasis on labour rights was much reduced. The anti-imperial tone and the sympathetic comments on anarchism disappeared.[34] These changes indicate the areas that Bengough considered 'faddish.' Overall, though, the magazine in its final chapter never regained its old vitality. Bengough's cartoons seem hurried and sketchy, as though he had to spend too much time on other elements of the editorship or on other jobs. The text was weak and discordant. When the end came, in the final days of 1894, it seemed more or less inevitable.

9

Imperialism and Independence

Few trends in *Grip* can be traced as clearly as the anti-imperial tone, which shows up early in the magazine's career, fades out of sight, and then re-emerges strongly in its late years, presumably under Phillips Thompson's influence. Its most extreme examples occur after Thompson returned as associate editor in 1890 and especially after he succeeded Bengough as editor in mid-1892. While the extremes are aberrational, they are interesting as a minority view that would probably not have been tolerated only a few years later. There is, for instance, a decidedly spiteful touch in an 1893 parody of the poem entitled 'Canada to England' written by James L. Hughes, the Tory Orangeman and school inspector who had joined with Colonel George Taylor Denison in a campaign to indoctrinate Canadian schoolchildren on imperial glories. Hughes's original started thus:

> Oh! Mistress of the mighty sea!
> Oh! Motherland so great and free!
> Canadian hearts shall ever be,
> United in their love for thee.

This paean of loyalty was apparently too much for Thompson, or one of the other *Grip* writers, so an amended version was devised; beginning:

> Oh! Mistress of the mighty sea!
>   (We owe her more than we can pay.)
> Oh! Motherland so great and free!
>   (Step-motherland, some people say)
> Canadian hearts shall ever be,
>   (On boodle set, in virtue lax;)

United in their love for thee,
  (And British goods we'll roundly tax.)

Chorus
Yes, Motherland! Dear Motherland!
  (Of English blood you have no trace;)
Beneath the Union Jack we'll stand,
  (Which still enslaves your father's race.) [1]

Since attacks of this kind showed up well before Bengough's departure, they raise questions both about his core views on imperialism and about the extent of his control over the magazine's editorial line. Bengough was to become a strong imperialist during the Boer War and the First World War, but Thompson continued to rail against the empire, even maintaining an extremely unpopular pacifist and isolationist stance in the First World War. [2] It seems likely that Bengough was influenced by Thompson to lean towards an anti-imperial stance, one that made him uneasy. Few of Bengough's cartoons implied criticism of Britain, and those that did were related to some of his pet causes, for instance, an 1887 cartoon that showed John Bull converting Africa with a Bible in one hand and a rum bottle in the other. [3]

Nothing in Bengough's cartoons matched the sarcasm that appeared in *Grip*'s text even before the change in editorship. In May 1892, for instance, the magazine had a brilliant satire on a jingoistic poem by Paul Cushing that called for a righteous war to restore England's manliness. The original poem and the satire, run side by side, started out thus:

FOR ENGLAND'S SAKE	FOR BUSINESS' SAKE!

Give us war, O Lord,
  For England's sake.
War righteous and true,
  Our hearts to shake.
We are drinking to the brim
What will poison heart and limb,
And our eyes are growing dim,
  For England's sake!
	Give us war, he prays,
	  For England's sake.
	'War righteous and true,
	  Our hearts to shake.'
	Things are getting sort of slow,
	War would make a boom, you know,
	Market prices up would go –
	  For business' sake!

Give us war, O Lord,
  For England's sake.
	Give us war, he prays,
	  For England's sake.

War righteous and true,	Let us wade in blood,
Such as our fathers knew,	'Twould really do us good
Our hearts to shake.	Some hearts to break.
Ere the tricks and arts of peace	Let us butcher fellow men
Make our manliness to cease,	Like porkers in a pen,
While our world-wide foes increase,	'Twould make things boom again,
For England's sake!	For business sake![4]

If Bengough actually approved this parody, it could mean he was briefly caught up in the flurry of anti-imperial sentiment that was promoted in Toronto during the late eighties by, among others, Thompson and Edward Farrer. When this agitation stirred an imperialist reaction by Colonel Denison and his coterie, *Grip* leaned towards the anti-imperial side and contributed to an interesting debate. The magazine's material is very much out of keeping with the common image of Victorian Toronto as a bastion of imperialism in a province whose school readers displayed the Union Jack and the ubiquitous motto 'One flag, one fleet, one throne.' A decade later, this tone did indeed predominate and the anti-imperial satires disappeared. *Grip*'s material provides evidence of a very different earlier tone.

Some of the anti-imperialists flirted with annexation. More commonly, at least at *Grip*, they explored the tension between democracy and authority, between a democratic New World vision and the elitism, militarism, imperialism, and clericalism of Europe. Bengough was drawn to at least some of this New World credo, but he also had a strong emotional feeling for the glories of empire (as shown in the Northwest Rebellion) and more broadly for British enlightenment, British honour, and British fair play. Over its lifetime, his magazine wavered between the two conflicting intellectual forces and occasionally blended both in a peculiarly Canadian synthesis. In the magazine's early stages, these mixed feelings emerged in passages like this one (by Demos Mudge):

England is the Uriah Heep of nations.

   Humility is her noblest attribute.

   How 'umble, umble' she was when the Yankees cheated her of Maine; how 'umble' she bore their San Juan encroachments; ... how generous with the property of the colonists, her fond children ... So we must be proud of our British connection, though the true, old, uncorrupted British blood in our veins boils with indignation at the cautious, cowardly bullying of our mother.[5]

Demos Mudge was in these early stages distinctly more sympathetic to

Canadian independence than Bengough, and the column was probably written by Thompson. In the same year a satire with the stamp of the same writer hit on the arrogance of British immigrants. It advised them not to think of immigrating to Canada until they had imbued themselves with a wholesome contempt for everything Canadian, and then, while crossing the Atlantic, to 'reconcile your conscience by the belief that your voluntary expatriation is pure philanthropy in the interests of a lot of poor devils who cannot possibly exist without you, and amuse yourself by picturing the grand civilizing effects to be produced by your advent.'[6]

This resentment over British airs of superiority and British betrayal was accompanied by antagonism to imperial expansion:

> ... Grab Britannia!
> Whenever you're inclined to –
> 'Necessity' your plea
> For all you have a mind to!
>
> Grab India, Ireland, Egypt – what
> You will. For you the lands subsist,
> They're meant as fuel for your pot,
> So chew them up just as you list ...[7]

Comment of this kind disappeared after *Grip*'s early years, but it re-emerged strongly in the late 1880s. While Thompson's influence is the most likely explanation, it is not easy to assign responsibility for the trend, given the anonymity of most *Grip* writing. Thompson's material, especially in the seventies, occasionally appeared under the Jimuel Briggs pen-name, and in later years it sometimes appeared under his own name. Similarly, Bengough's poems and satires were sometimes signed in full or with the initials J.W.B. The name William McGill appeared on some anti-imperial writing in the late 1880s and early 1890s. But the authors of many of the magazine's toughest and funniest comments were anonymous.

It is not known, for instance, whether Edward Farrer, the country's most brilliant and subtle anti-imperial writer at that time, ever contributed to the magazine. Bengough was a great admirer of the Irish editor, cartooning him scores of times and speaking admiringly of his wit and his trenchant analyses. It is known that Farrer, who undermined imperial loyalty at a series of newspapers, was as prolific as he was devious, writing anonymously for various publications. He worked actively in Toronto's close-knit journalistic community for seventeen of *Grip*'s twenty-one years and had a considerable reputation for satire, yet he never appeared openly in the magazine. He may, however, have been the author of some of its 'hits.' For example, an 1891 *Grip* comment on imperial honours may well have been by Farrer. It gravely thanked the imperial government for the honour it had done Canada in remaking Sir George Stephen into Lord Mount Stephen and then said:

We feel that what is most needed to transform this raw, rough and democratic community into a land of true culture and standing is the establishment in our midst of an Upper Class, enjoying privileges and immunities beyond the reach of the people at large. In the absence of live lords to whom on all occasions the common people may take off their hats and before whom our middle classes may cringe and grovel, the community is liable to be permeated with a most unhealthy independence of spirit.

This passage has a similar ring to one that appeared under Farrer's byline more than a decade later:

[The New Imperialists] have an idea, too, that by distributing titles ... they can plant an aristocracy here that will overawe the rough, raw and democratic Canadian farmer and lead him, like a little child, to the altar of Jingo.[8]

It also resembles material from the editorial pages of the Winnipeg *Times* and *Sun* when Farrer was editor there – for example, this 1883 passage from the *Times*:

Knights being essential to the growth of Canada, is it fair that the Northwest should have none? The Eastern Provinces are abundantly blessed in this respect ... But in this region of almost illimitless area and wholly illimitable prospects there is not a solitary Sir. The Northwest will not long tolerate this insufferable neglect of her interests.[9]

A similar touch is evident in an 1888 *Grip* satire on the Canadian practice of depending on British commanders for the militia:

We breathe more freely now that consent of the Imperial authorities has been obtained, at the earnest prayers of the Government, to extend the term of Gen. Sir Fred. Middleton as Commander of the Canadian forces for four years more. In the event of an invasion of our coasts by the natives of San Salvador, or the revolt of the Nova Scotia fishermen, it is of utmost importance that we should have a first-class military man to protect us.[10]

Nevertheless, even though some of *Grip*'s anti-imperial writing has Farrer's style, there is no firm evidence of a connection. Bengough's memoirs contain no mention of him, though this may be because Farrer's scandalous annexationist plotting in the nineties made Bengough reluctant to admit a link – just as he was clearly reluctant to speak of his collaboration with Thompson. There is thus no clear evidence on the authorship of some of *Grip*'s best anti-imperial material, such as this prescient piece, published in 1876, which foresaw (with no sympathy towards Britain) the very morass Europe would sink into four decades later:

It appears to *Grip* that the devil is in the air ... Here, according to [Disraeli], all the secret societies of Europe have suddenly flown at the throats of the Turks. Servia has pitched in; bloody noses and cracked crowns are to be had without charge anywhere along the frontier; Russia is coming along with her millions of fellows carrying guns, choppers and other life-preservers; Turkey is busy using on the Bulgarians and the Montenegrins all the latest inventions of a humanitarian age; all the myriads of Austrian camps of instruction are sharpening edge tools and cutlery, and swearing in Slav and High Dutch; Bismarck keeps his finger on the telegraph knob which will let fly his little contingent of a million and a half grim scarred veterans against any population which the interests of peace and goodwill require to be shot, hacked, blown up, spiked or drowned; France has grown bran-new talons and incisors since her last were pulled out, and is looking for a nation requiring scratching ... Britain is preparing all the agencies of iron, coal, gunpowder, nitro-glycerine, dynamite and asphyxiating preparation, for the purpose of committing instantaneously as many house burnings and homicides as ever were perpetrated in ten centuries before.[11]

The anti-imperial writing of William McGill was also of high quality and resembled some of the other material carried without a byline. Typical is a McGill satire in 1891 which savaged the imperial connection, saying that Canada had chosen imperial 'scullionship' and suggesting that colonials should be accorded special rights to kiss Victoria's big toe. It concluded: 'Canada as a republic would have no future before her which would not be overshadowed and belittled by her southern neighbor. But as a transatlantic repository of old world ideas, kingship, lordship, class distinction of every sort, as a kind of political junkshop ... her career might be pre-eminently unique.'[12]

In the running debates in the late eighties over whether Canada should opt for independence, annexation, or imperial union, *Grip* was especially hard on Colonel Denison, the city magistrate who was the zealous leader of the imperialist group and always ready to call out his cavalry to deal with annexationist scum.[13] A signed 1888 poem by Thompson (not one of his best efforts) described how the 'swaggering, blustering carpet-knight' had 'curled his moustache and pawed the air' while boasting that his fighting men would shed seas of gore before Canada would trade with the Yankees:

> Swashbuckler Denison – soak your head!
> Though ancient Pistol is long since dead,
> In your braggart speeches we seem to hear
> The voice of that revenue-patriot near.
> 'Fighting-men' – Bah! Put your brains to soak
> Such rant's too stale for even a joke.[14]

On another occasion the magazine noted a German news item predicting the end of open cavalry charges, and it produced a poem saying how devastated Denison would be to face the end of his glory:

> ... No more the trumpet call he hears
>   Or drinks the stern delight of slaughter.
> His name no more the foeman fears,
>   Who erst shed Yankee blood like water.
>
> The only charges he can make
>   Are from the bench's elevation,
> On hapless drunks his ire he'll slake
>   His sole and only consolation.[15]

An elaborate satire in the same issue suggested how Denison and his cohorts might pursue their plan to instil loyal thinking among children:

LOYALIST ARITHMETIC

Now that it has been determined to teach the principles of true loyalty in the schools, in order that Canadians may be imbued from their infancy with proper feelings of hatred and contempt for Yankees, Commercial Unionists, traitors, etc., it is felt that some changes in the school books in use are desirable ... Something like the following would probably be found appropriate:

1. A Canadian army, commanded by Col. Denison, comprising 2,000 men encountered a force of 10,000 cowardly Yankees – of whom they killed 1,025 1/2, wounded 2,665 and captured 4,087. How many Yankees ran away?[16]

In the same period, *Grip* ran a satire on putting colonies to their legitimate use – 'as cess-pools for the ne'er-do-wells of the English aristocracy.' Another satire had Lord Lawdedaw proposing that the proper role for Canada was to 'bweed and waise men for wah puhposes'; it went on, in the same kind of language, to point out that if Canadians were thoroughly imbued with their new role, this would stop their absurd craze for higher education. The tone was similar to an 1884 letter from Augustus Fitz-Snobbington, who argued that Englishmen should be appointed to all important Canadian posts, since 'it is absurd to suppose that a raw Canadian, but yesterday evolved from a painted Indian or a bear, is capable of fulfilling a position like this to which I have been appointed.'[17]

In another long-running issue – Britain's alleged sellout to the United States of Canadian fisheries – *Grip* at one point seemed to hint that Canada might as well give in and accept union with the United States ('How It May End,' see chap. 1).[18] This presumably was meant not as a serious recommendation but simply as another warning to the motherland about the hazards of neglect. A more typical sketch rejected American claims that Canada was eager for union ('The True State of Her Feelings'). On most days, *Grip* was impatient with both the British and the Americans, as shown in an 1888 satire that ridiculed a poem from the always respectful Toronto *Empire* which began:

> Britain bore us in her flank;
>   Britain nursed us at our birth;
> Britain raised us to our rank
>   'Mid the nations of the earth.

Grip's writer thought this might be updated to:

> Britain sold us to the Yank,
>   Britain gave our fish away,
> Britain to the level sank
>   Of those who are their neighbors' prey.

The same issue of *Grip* included cartoons, not signed by Bengough, on

THE TRUE STATE OF HER FEELINGS.

BROTHER JONATHAN (*soliloquizing*)—"Ah, she loves me ; I know it ; I feel it in my very bones. She wants to jine me in the holy bands of political union."

MISS CANADA (*overhearing the whisper*)—"Mr. Jonathan, pray don't deceive yourself on that point. My heart is perfectly whole I assure you. I simply want to trade freely with you, that's all."

Grip, 19 Jan. 1889. When an annexation movement emerged in Toronto in the late 1880s, *Grip* consistently opposed it, as in this cartoon – one of the few drawn for the magazine by Bengough's brother William.

the Imperial Federation Boom (a frog blown up near the point of explosion) and on the Imperial Bootlickers' League (showing 'the kind of Canadian John Bull despises' – a grovelling colonial licking Britain's oversized boots).[19]

On the Irish problem, too, *Grip* was unsympathetic to Britain in this period, comparing her policy to Russian tyranny:

> For Ireland I prescribe a course
>   Of strong, heroic treatment,
> Proceeding still from bad to worse,
>   With strictly no abatement.
>
> Apply the gag, lay on the lash,
>   Bind hand and foot in fetters;
> Bring down the baton with a crash,
>   And make 'em mind their betters.[20]

A William McGill poem in 1889 took a broader swipe at the imperial federation, a common subject for after-dinner speakers (especially, perhaps, the voluble Colonel Denison):

THE FEDERATION ORATOR

> He talks of Britain's glory as revealed in song and story
> And allowed by Whig and Tory to exist without a doubt;
> Of her present, past and future, how like a great free-booter,
> She has carved the world to suit her, and cut other nations out.
>
> How, the lion's share retaining, she is gaining the remaining
> Choice portions of earth's surface, claiming every corner lot,
> Till the Union Jack is floating, and a British eye is gloating,
> And a British heart is doting on it in each sunny spot ...[21]

In the same spirit, a sarcastic comment in 1890 rejected as 'gratuitous grovel' the motion of loyalty to the Queen moved in the Commons by William Mulock.[22] A few months later (on Victoria's birthday, to add to the insult), the magazine sneered at Britain's imperial exploits in Africa: 'It is very evident ... that the whole of the Dark Continent will very shortly be parcelled out between England, Germany, France, Portugal, etc., England, as usual, taking the lion's share while keeping up the greatest outcry about the aggressiveness and rapacity of others.'[23] Later the same year there was this unsigned poem, possibly by Thompson since it combined anti-imperial and anti-capitalist fervour:

THE STATELY HAULS OF ENGLAND

> The Stately Hauls of England!
> How powerful! How grand!

> With mortgages and syndicates
> They've covered all our land,
> Our dear step-mother country,
> (Long may Victoria reign!)
> Our substance in a thousand ways
> To fat herself does drain ...[24]

A few months later, a satire by William McGill imagined a future Canada with its very own monarch, who would be protected by an honour guard headed by Denison and financed by a special deal in which P.T. Barnum would be 'permitted to exhibit H.M. throughout the continent as the only king of the New World.' A more serious slap at the Royal Family came in a parody of Gilbert and Sullivan that attacked the Prince of Wales, the future Edward VII, who had been caught in a gambling scandal:

> When he isn't hiding aces in his boot ...
> Or of buxom Yankee females in pursuit ...
> It's just awful to observe his goings-on.[25]

Compared with these attacks on the imperialists, the annexationists got off lightly. When Premier Mowat dismissed Crown Attorney Elgin Myers of Dufferin County for his annexationist campaigning, Bengough (just before he left the magazine) cartooned the newly knighted premier as a medieval anachronism ('Be-Knighted "Liberalism!"'). An unsigned poem warned the premier that many of the wicked annexationists were Grits, who might well be alienated by his loyalist screed.[26]

The attacks on imperialism were sporadic and appeared among a mass of commentary and humour, but they are still surprising when set against the passionate imperialism Bengough displayed after Victoria's 1897 Diamond Jubilee and during the soon-to-follow Boer War. His poetry from that period is worse than maudlin. One example, entitled 'Heroic Britain,' ends with the verse:

> Noble old Isle, though foes of late
>   Have called thee many an ugly name;
> Though in their blind and frenzied hate
>   They've sought to dim thy ancient fame,
> In greatness that is truly great
>   Thou'rt still the one Imperial State![27]

BE-KNIGHTED "LIBERALISM!"

WHAT WE EXPECT THAT MEDIEVAL WORTHY, SIR OLIVER MOWAT, TO DO NEXT.

A poem on the return of Canadian troops from the Boer War reached the same level of bathos:

> Take them back, Canada;
> Proudly receive them!
> Each gallant son of thine,
> Bearing on head of him,
> Wearing in heart of him
> Britain's deep gratitude,
> Heart's benediction
> Of people and Queen ...

Even as early as 1895, a year after *Grip*'s death, a collection of poems put out by Bengough included one entitled 'The Charge at Batoche,' which began:

> Who says that British blood grows tame,
>   And that the olden fire is gone
> That swept the fields of deathless fame
>   When heroes led our soldiers on?[28]

The turnaround is difficult to understand. Presumably it arose from a combination of factors, especially the change of mood in the country and the disappearance of colleagues who had influenced the magazine. As well, Bengough's personal circumstances had changed: After *Grip*'s death, he was writing and cartooning freelance for a variety of publications and was eyeing a political career. So while holding fast to some of his favourite causes, especially the single tax and prohibition, he may have become more conservative on other issues. On the Boer War, his support for Canadian participation was in conflict with the stance of his former radical allies such as Farrer and Thompson. Now he was aligned with George Taylor Denison, Sam Hughes, Castell Hopkins, and others whom *Grip* had so often ridiculed.

Grip, 2 July, 1892 (*opposite*). While criticizing annexationists, *Grip* was even harder on the more fervent imperialists, especially in its text. 'Be-Knighted "Liberalism!"' accused the recently knighted Sir Oliver Mowat of reverting to medieval standards in his decision to fire an annexationist-leaning official, Elgin Myers. The man applauding is Colonel George Taylor Denison, leader of the imperialist group.

While the turnaround is striking, it may say more about a change in the times than a change in Bengough. In the eighties and early nineties there had been a sympathetic audience for anti-imperial satire; later, that audience disappeared. In historical terms, this is more significant than any consideration of who wrote what. By the time the First World War arrived, Bengough (like most Anglo-Canadians) had lost any sense that Britain might share the responsibility for imperial tensions, and he went all out in condemning the Kaiser:

> ... The world's at war,
> What for?
> Why turn all Europe to an abattoir?
> Why with dead Germans clog
> The trenches? – pen the dog –
> The foaming, frothing mad dog Emperor.[29]

The mood of the times had effectively silenced dissident views. Reverence for empire was the norm.

10

Grip's Social Conscience

When seen through the values of another age, *Grip*'s cartoons and verses on social issues are arguably more flawed than the general body of its political material. In Bengough's cartoons, women are artificial – often abstract representations of ideals, rather than portraits or caricatures. His farmers are stereotypical hayseeds. His workers are honest toilers or drunks. His capitalists are bloated cigar-smoking tyrants. His Aboriginal people are 'noble redmen' or victims.

However, these patterns must be seen in context. In part they arise from the satirist's need to simplify, to make an instant point, to choose well-known concepts. In part they are simply an expression of the era. Over time, of course, both the words and the visual symbols change, losing or gaining connotations. Words such as 'squaw,' 'darkey,' and 'celestial' – even 'capitalist' and 'redmen' – had a different value in Bengough's day. Pictorial symbols change as well. Whips and cudgels, which were commonplace in Bengough's time, seem offensive now, just as many of the commonplace symbols of our time would offend people of the 1890s. Even the hats worn by Bengough's subjects (the top hat of the plutocrats, the square cap of the mechanics) are significant. From our vantage point it is hard to 'read' these symbols, to be certain of either the creator's intention or the audience's reaction.

For all the limitations, though, Bengough deserves credit for breaking new ground in focusing on social, not just political, issues. Occasionally, too, he offers true insight on Canada's social conditions: the tragedy of starvation in Native communities, the loneliness and poverty of settlers, the despair of the slum. While Bengough's attitude towards women, Native people, Jews, Asians, and French Canadians can easily be classed as patronizing, it was for the most part progressive for its day. Even the images that stir anger can be of use to modern students. If 'history is a foreign territory,' the cartoonist's repertoire of symbols provides clues to the patterns of change.[1]

In *Grip*'s mature years its attitude on women's advancement was notably supportive, especially with regard to suffrage and education. In 1883 it described a government bill to extend suffrage to women as a reform that could be the crowning achievement of John A. Macdonald's career.[2] But Bengough's cartoons carry interesting subtexts, which are revealing of the times as well as of his own attitude. While he followed the tradition of portraying abstract ideals such as justice and liberty as strong female figures, he also portrayed men as women, especially when the cartoon metaphor demanded it. Usually, this was when he wanted to show the men as flighty or irresponsible.

Even in cases where female figures actually represented females, the message could be ambiguous. The cartoon 'Woman's Sphere' (p. 197) is a case in point. It shows two suffragists as the essence of respectability, making their requests to the premier as one bourgeois to another, and the younger woman clearly defers to her bossy elder. There is no hint in Bengough's world view that young working-class women or intellectuals might actually force the voting issue; rather, it was a matter to be worked out in a respectable fashion by respectable people. Further, votes for women seem to have been linked in Bengough's mind with particular campaigns – usually temperance or prohibition. There is no vision of women actually taking part in the raw life of politics. The idea seems to have been that women would vote for righteous causes and then withdraw into their homes.

Grip's support for women's education and women's votes thus seems hesitant – but even that was an improvement on its earlier attitude. Back in 1877, a typical poem had derided women who went to school and came away unable to cook or sew ('Husband who married her quickly found out / All she had learned she'd be better without').[3] The material on women's suffrage had been just as hostile:

THE FEMALE RIGHTER

I am a Female Righter, and
If you will list to me,
I soon shall make you understand,
What sort of rights they be.

I want upon the lounge to sleep,
Or read, or take my ease
And want the right my house to keep
As dirty as I please ...

I want the franchise of the land
Which now the men have got,
To vote on all I understand
And all that I do not.

These are the rights of women, and
You'd best oppose them not,
Or when we get the upper hand,
We'll teach you what is what.[4]

During this period Bengough showed some signs of following the lead of Goldwin Smith, who, despite his liberal reputation, was writing some notably conservative material in the *Nation*, material that supported capital punishment while deploring a broadening of the franchise and opposing the admission of women to medical education.[5]

Grip's patronizing tone was still very much in evidence in 1883, when a group of women presented a suffrage petition to Premier Mowat – a politician whose reputation for canny procrastination matched Macdonald's. The magazine reported that the women left in a happy and hopeful frame of mind, then added, 'The innocent little things! Grip, who is the true friend of the down-trodden of all sexes, takes the opportunity of explaining in a picture just what Mr. Mowat meant' ('Grand Triumph').

When women were admitted to the University of Toronto a year later, the magazine's comment and cartoon were just as condescending: 'In due time we shall have the "sweet girl graduates" after all. The doors of the university have been opened to the fair ones, and it is simply a question of four years' trial – if the girls sustain their reputation as students – when a batch of them will come forth with B.A.'s on their little satchels.' An 1890 satire on a fictional female reporter, Anna Nyas, arriving in Ottawa brought out the same language: 'My hand-satchel lost aboard that horrid train, with my dear little gold-lead pencil, my tatting, my blank note-books, my circular comb, my return ticket, my letter of introduction to Sir John, my smelling salts.'[6]

Throughout *Grip*'s history there were jokes and cartoons presenting the same stereotypic view of women:

GRAND TRIUMPH FOR THE WOMAN SUFFRAGISTS.
MR. MOWAT TAKES THEIR PETITION INTO HIS CONSIDERATION !!

Grip, 24 Nov. 1883. While *Grip* was notably progressive in its advocacy of women's rights, its images were often patronizing. The suffragists of 1883 were a flighty-looking group.

Here's to the ladies, God bless 'em,
What a pity it costs so to dress 'em.
But blow the expense,
Our feelings intense
Seek expression, and so we express em.[7]

In some more serious debates, too, the magazine followed the conventional line – as in its position on divorce. In one of its few areas of agreement with Macdonald, it praised him for resisting a divorce liberalization bill and endorsed his view that it would be 'a great misfortune to this country and promote demoralization if Parliament did not adhere to the

WOMAN'S SPHERE.

THE ATTORNEY-GENERAL, ONTARIO.—" Er—personally, I may say, I regret it, but you see the Legislature is still of opinion that woman's proper sphere is to look after the babies, and not to vote."

SUFFRAGIST.—" So it is; and yonder are a couple of political babies that require looking after in the worst way, but we must be enfranchised before we can take charge of them ! "

Grip, 16 Mar. 1889. By 1889 the image had improved, but Bengough seemed to imagine a political role for women that was restricted to bourgeois ladies campaigning on a narrow range of social issues.

principle of the law of the land and law of God that divorce could only be granted for adultery.'[8]

At other times the magazine was capable of a more progressive stance, especially towards those caught in abusive relationships. In the seventies, for instance, it combined law-and-order passion with a furious attack on brutal husbands in a humourless satire that advised men how to get away with murder:

Select as your object of attack your wife: if she be young, attractive, and affection-ate, all the better. Treat her for a length of time with the most disgusting brutality, beat her, insult her, torture her mentally and bodily by every available means. Finally, when you are tired of the amusement, cut her throat scientifically with a butcher knife. They will have all these circumstances in evidence, and in consider-ation of them, they will commute your sentence. They will not hang you. It would not do to put down this sort of thing too sharply; wives must learn their places; inferior creatures and all that, you know.[9]

This tone recurred often during *Grip*'s lifetime. In the early eighties the magazine satirized a husband who had assaulted his wife and then looked to her to pay his fine.[10] A few years later it protested a legal quirk that for-bade women to testify against husbands who had cut off support: 'As the law now stands, a woman who prosecutes her husband for non-support – or rather sues him for support – is not a competent witness. If the poor neglected wife ... is not the proper person to testify to the neglect of which she complains, it would be a more than interesting question to know just who is.'[11] However, *Grip* was never as fierce as the popular *News* in campaigning for battered wives or for the women who went on strike to protest $3.50-a-week earnings at shoe factories.[12]

In *Grip*'s later years, Phillips Thompson may have been the force behind its strong reformist stance. Certainly, the pressure continued or increased in the period when Thompson was in charge. On one occasion during his editorship, *Grip* reacted with fury against its former friend, Sir Oliver Mowat, when his government offered an array of excuses for rejecting a female suffrage bill: 'The friends of women's enfranchisement can now estimate at their true value Oliver Mowat's empty compliments and hypocritical expressions of sympathy ... [Mowat] shows himself in his true colours as a humbug and a trickster. He doesn't even rise to the dig-nity of a plausible hypocrite.' When a woman charged with theft was locked up along with her twelve-year-old daughter, *Grip* again brought out its harshest language, condemning the 'villainous' legal system run by callous martinets like Magistrate Denison and enforced by detectives who at best could only be called thugs and vampires.[13]

In the same period, the magazine gave the Ontario Bar rough treatment for its attempt to exclude from the profession Clara Brett Martin, who later became the first woman lawyer in Canada.[14] It said the action by the lawyers' 'trade union' was no surprise since the law was the most conservative and hidebound of professions. More surprising, is said, was the cowardly way in which the benchers had tried to shirk responsibility for their action. They had stated a year earlier that they could not legally admit women, and even when Martin had obtained a provincial act authorizing them to do so, they had still flatly refused. 'No doubt individually, and in their private capacities, the benchers are very estimable gentlemen, but professionally and collectively they are an unmanly, contemptible lot.'[15] In the same issue, *Grip* published a satirical poem by 'Ananias Limberjaw, Q.C.,' entitled 'The Law and the Lady':

> I think all lawyers must agree
> On keeping our profession free
> From females whose admission would
> Result in anything but good.
>
> Because it yet has to be shown
> That men are fit to hold their own.
> In such a contest, I've no doubt,
> We'd some of us be crowded out ...
>
> Praise to the benchers who have stood
> Against the innovating flood,
> To save us and our ample fees
> From tribulations such as these.[16]

The following week a rather elusive Sam Jones cartoon showed Martin as a peri – a fairylike creature of Persian mythology – barred from paradise by an angel in a legal gown ('The Legal Paradise and the Rejected Peri'). The Martin affair showed *Grip* at its reforming best. But again, it suggests that some of Bengough's later reputation as a fervent reformer may have been due to his radical colleague.

John Bengough's attitude towards the Native people was almost always

THE LEGAL PARADISE AND THE REJECTED PERI.

Grip, 1 Oct. 1892. After Bengough's departure, *Grip* reflected Phillips Thompson's more radical views on women's rights. In this cartoon by Sam Jones, it attacked the Ontario legal profession for trying to exclude Clara Brett Martin, its first female member.

sympathetic, both in cartoons and commentary, but it too was usually remote and somewhat idealized. His concern for the Natives appears more in the eighties than the seventies, though on occasion in the seventies the magazine protested killings on the American frontier, as in a poem entitled 'American vs. Indian' which included the lines:

> Shoot your Injun down at sight,
> When you chance to meet him,
> Let him know that might is right,
> From his country beat him.[17]

In the eighties, the Native people Bengough portrayed seem almost invariably to have been drawn from the prairies, as though no tribes existed in eastern Canada or British Columbia. (An exception was an 1890 cartoon on an early stage of the long-lasting Oka problem, depicting the church using Interior Minister Dewdney to eject Mohawks from the Oka area.)[18] The focus on the western tribes was a natural result of the concerns of the time. In the 1880s the plains tribes were in constant crisis as a result of the arrival of the railways, the encroachment of ranches, and the sudden disappearance of the buffalo. Thus, the plains tribes became for easterners a somewhat exotic group, much mythologized and analysed by teams of social critics and reformers who had passed through on the new railway. Meanwhile, the eastern tribes were more or less ignored both by the media and by social activists.

To modern eyes, it is striking that even the most well-meaning reformers seem to have accepted the necessity of a civilizing period of 'wardship,' leading to either assimilation or disappearance. Bengough shared this liberal view, believing that Native people (especially the young) must be helped to break with a barbaric past and adopt 'white' ways. But he was not unsympathetic, and to his readers he would have seemed decidedly progressive.

It is interesting that one of Bengough's earlier portrayals of Indians ('Startling Affair in London'; see chap. 1) uses two racial stereotypes to represent something other than their race. The Jewish stereotype is supposed to represent land companies, while the Indian maiden represents the Canadian West. It does not take a semiotics scholar to find in the portrayal a sense of sympathy to Natives, combined with hostility to Jews, capitalists, imperialists – and Tories.[19]

Something of this idealistic image of Native people recurred frequently in Bengough's work, at least until he first travelled through the prairies in

1889. Thereafter, the idealized Indian tends to disappear, indicating that Bengough may have found it hard to reconcile what he actually saw with the image acquired from magazines and classic paintings. During the 1889 trip, Bengough sketched hundreds of westerners and published the pictures along with diary-style observations. But none of those sketched were Natives, and his only comment on them is a derogatory throwaway anecdote concerning a fellow traveller, a painter named Woodcock: '"What a magnificent head for a model!" cries W. as some Indians in wild costumes come in at a way station to ask an alms. "Ah! how I wish I had it!" But Indian won't part with it: Wants it for his own use.'[20]

In championing the Native cause, Bengough normally followed rather than led. In the winter of 1886 he gave a good deal of attention to Native problems in the West, but he did so conspicuously on the heels of a series of revealing reports in the *Mail* from his old boss, George Ham, along with some notably strong editorials. *Grip*'s follow-up comments endorsed Ham's reportage but implied that the *Mail*, as a government organ, could not be expected to tell the whole story:

The truth – the whole truth – is known to a few, from private sources of information. If the whole story of how horrible disease, introduced by white wretches in and out of government service, is consuming the unhappy aborigines; how their native virtue and morality have been undermined and well nigh destroyed by the drunkenness, lying and abominable wickedness of these same representatives of 'civilization,' the generous heart of Canada would swell with indignation.[21]

The following year Bengough quoted approvingly some lines from Charles Mair's drama *Tecumseh* ('Our sacred treaties are infringed and torn / Laughed out of sanctity and spurned away') and said the shameful record persisted in both the United States and Canada. But his tone echoed the paternalism of the day: 'Civilization, to say nothing of Christianity, demands a radical change in our dealings with the wards of the nation.'[22] He offered a similar image and a similar message in 1888 when he condemned the 'rascally officials' who had either neglected their duties or deliberately swindled Indians out of supplies of food and clothing. 'Under all circumstances the moderation and forbearance of the suffering redman are remarkable. On many a reservation they have seen their women and children die of starvation, and no deed of vengeance has in a single case followed. Where are the white men who would exhibit such patience? And why is it that they are called upon to endure such tortures?'[23]

At the time, this kind of support for the Aboriginal people was probably too strong for the views of most *Grip* readers. Certainly, Bengough was far more sympathetic than Sam Hunter of the 'people's' newspaper, the *News*. A Hunter cartoon in 1885 showed the prime minister as a policeman leading a march of immigrants, who were pushing a group of Indians off a cliff into the Pacific while telling them, 'Here, you copper colored gentlemen, no loafing allowed, you must either work or jump.' Similarly, *Grip*'s views were never in line with the typical *News* attitude expressed in such comments as: 'The ordinary Indians on our reservations are not only idle and dissolute, but are ignorant and entirely devoid of ambition. What he [*sic*] wants is something to live upon, with tobacco and whisky as luxuries ... His highest ambition is to do nothing, and to have a squaw that will do a great deal.'[24] Yet *Grip* was not entirely immune from the general attitude of contempt. In the late eighties the magazine ran a 'funny' poem about an Indian chief named Skilly-go-lee who, with some companions, had stolen and tried to toast a stick of dynamite:

> Old Skilly-go-lee, and the young bucks three
>   Were blown into chicken feed;
> There were pieces of Crees all over the trees,
>   And here and there a glass bead ...[25]

The Aboriginal people were not, of course, the only minority of the day to suffer the ridicule of the press – or of other elite institutions. The contemporary values were reflected in the popularity of one of Bengough's favorite chalk-talk items, a skit called 'Winnipeg Station' that lampooned various immigrant groups arriving there.[26] *Grip* satires of the same type often made French Canadians the target, as in an 1887 poem about Johnny Baptiste, who had come to Ottawa to 'make lots of boodle' and to do for his minister 'many things kept in the dark':

> How ze people would talk, and ze Grits zey would squall,
> Did zey know of my errands down in Montreal,
> But not even one word do I tell to my priest.
>   Sing hey, sing ho, sing Johnny Baptiste ...[27]

In similar vein, *Grip* occasionally portrayed criticism of French Canada as 'prodding the frog.' Or, with the same kind of humour but a different target, it gave an 'amusing' sketch of a Jewish rag picker harassed by street urchins:

His coat was rusty-black and long,
Long was his nose and slightly pendant;
Across his arm was thrown a sack,
And in its wake a cart attendant ...[28]

In some cases the humour targeted more than one race, as in a poem, illustrated with appropriate sketches, about a lonely Irishman on the prairies who was looking for a '"fittin" companion for me and my mule.' The Irishman proposed to a 'beautiful squaw' and lent her the mule, only to find later that her relatives had eaten it.[29] Similarly, what passed for harmless punning has a brutish quality to modern eyes – for instance, a throwaway line in 1873 asking, 'What colour is a nigger's ghost?' Or this, in 1875: 'Our Irish editor says that if he ever turns cannibal he would like to eat a coloured man and his children, because it would be *Ham an' nigs*.' As late as 1882, *Grip* could offer as a bit of fun a picture of a lynched black, illustrating a satirical 'lecture' by Professor Julius Caesar Hannibal on 'The Abolition of Punishment': 'Ladies and Gen'lemen, – I'se gwine to expostilate faw a few momints dis eb'nin on de subjick ob de ablushun ob punishmint.'[30] The same values showed in some serious items, such as this 1883 comment:

MAKE AN EXAMPLE OF HIM

The sleeping car nigger who attempted to assault a lady while occupying a berth in his car, was tried at Guelph the other day and committed for trial [*sic*]. If he is ultimately convicted – and it is most likely he will be – we sincerely hope the judge will give him the full penalty of the law. If Mr. Grip were on the bench, the rascal might think himself fortunate if he got off with twenty years at Kingston. This new outgrowth of crime must be crushed in its inception.[31]

Grip, 30 Aug. 1884 (Massa, Don' You ..., *opposite*), 21 Feb. 1891 (A Cruel, Unjust Suspicion, p. 206), and 23 July 1887 (Very Much Alike, p. 207). Many *Grip* sketches of blacks were no more enlightened than the standard images of the day, but Bengough made the occasional attempt at a more positive image, as when he equated slavery and labour exploitation in 'Very Much Alike.' The point of 'Massa' is that suggestions had been made to include Jamaica in Confederation. The point of 'Cruel Unjust' is that Macdonald had come up with a policy of 'partial reciprocity' – the label on the stolen hen – in trade with the United States in order to combat the Liberals' platform of unrestricted reciprocity.

MASSA, DON' YOU WANT TO 'DOPT A
:CULLED CHILE?

A CRUEL, UNJUST SUSPICION.

THE DARKEY—"Stole dat pullet? No, sah! Dat ain't never be'n in de Lib'rul coop, sah; dat's a bird wot I raised myself. De Lib'rul breed ob pullet ain't got dar wings clipped laik dis here!"

VERY MUCH ALIKE.

Henry George—I DON'T SEE ANY DIFFERENCE BETWEEN SLAVERY AND—SLAVERY.

Similarly, in 1884, when there was discussion about the possibility of Jamaica entering Confederation, *Grip* represented the island as a 'culled chile' with a rum bottle in her hand ('Massa, Don' You Want to 'Dopt a Culled Chile?' p. 205). And in 1888 a rumour that Macdonald had experienced a religious conversion caused the magazine to say that leaving him in Ottawa would be 'like putting a newly-converted darkey into a well-stocked hen-coop' ('A Cruel, Unjust Suspicion,' p. 206).[32]

This racism, however, must be set against serious comment that often was supportive of Native people and sometimes of blacks, Jews, and orientals. Bengough specifically condemned the anti-Chinese agitation that erupted in the western United States in the late seventies and feared it would spread into Canada. However, by the mid-1880s, *Grip* had come to share some of the anti-Chinese feeling fomented by the *News* and other newspapers, but its language was notably more restrained. In 1885, for instance, it marked the visit of a Chinese giant named Chang with a comment that the 'real Chinese giant' would be felt if Chinese immigrants 'get a thorough foothold in Canada,'[33] but this was moderate compared with the 'democratic' *News*, which said the Chinese were 'swooping down upon British Columbia like a yellow-skinned, almond-eyed, long-tailed swarm of Kansas grasshoppers'; and that Chinese with leprosy – members of a 'filthy, degraded and alien race' – were allowed, because of the greed of a few monopolists, to 'mingle freely with the white population' in Victoria.[34]

On another occasion, *Grip* was patronizing but supportive in the extradition case of a 'respectable colored gentleman' who had been charged in Georgia with striking a white man who had seriously assaulted his son: 'The southern officers of "justice" merely want to put the refugee in the chain gang for life, or perhaps lynch him,' *Grip* said. 'Of course, they won't get him. Col. Denison has got his Union Jack wound around the poor fellow, and any southerner who takes him has got to walk over the Colonel's dead body.'[35] Such positive if patronizing images emerged sporadically, despite the general tone of racist humour. The latter was typical of the age, and it was much less extreme than that of many contemporaries ('Very Much Alike,' p. 207).

Grip's anti-Semitism also was less extreme, especially when compared with the *News*, which stated in 1884 that the persecution of the Jews in Russia was 'mainly due to their own avarice and extortion as moneylenders and traders.'[36] *Grip*'s anti-Semitism was notably more pronounced during the year of Bengough's absence. It showed up most strikingly in cheap imported cartoons and also in the verses of G.C., the magazine's most prolific writer of this period:

THE LOST TEN TRIBES

When I think of the ten lost tribes of Jews;
  Do I wish they were found again?
No, sir; but I wish the remaining two
  Had been lost with the blooming ten.[37]

Although Bengough's cartoon image of Jews was certainly negative, it was not notably more cruel than his stereotypes of other groups – snobbish British 'dudes,' for instance, quarrelsome Irish, and shrewd Yankees. (If any group escaped cruel comment, it was probably the Scots; their kilted and bonneted figures seem to have rated more kindly treatment.) From a later perspective, even a cartoon deploring Jewish pogroms in Russia used a very negative image ('Hep! Hep! Sic Him, Towser!' p. 210). The vocabulary of recognizable images in Bengough's mind, and in the minds of his readers, seems to have been too limited to permit anything else.

Despite its later reputation as a reformer, *Grip* was by no means a soft-hearted liberal in the areas of law and order or welfare nets, especially in its first decade. An 1875 comment on corporal punishment for hooligans had the same tone as the comment on the sleeping-car rapist, seeming to relish every swish of the whip:

The cat o' nine tails is an indispensable portion of the machinery of the law, in a city so disgraced with brutal violence as Toronto. By all means let such wretches as Irvine, the murderer of Mr. Burke, be tied to the triangle and lashed, if the jury can't do us the favour of hanging them. If *Grip* were czar of this city for a day he would larrup the flesh from the coward back of every rowdy who insulted a lady, or jostled a gentleman. Nothing but the cat, administered with a strong and willing arm, will teach the peg-top, swaggering roughs of this city good manners. There are plenty of willing arms to be had; scarcely a respectable citizen amongst us would not gladly and enthusiastically swing the whip.[38]

On another occasion, *Grip* (without the slightest hint of humour) called for formation of a 'vigilance committee' to extirpate the 'large and despicable class of ragamuffins who infest the street corners and insult young women.' It ran a small cartoon depicting one of these street gangs, a sketch that was totally lacking in sympathy that the young people might be unemployed and destitute. It was strong as well in support of capital punishment, as shown by the 1876 satire on wife murder. In the same

HEP! HEP! SIC HIM, TOWSER!

(Dedicated to the Czar of Russia, with assurances of GRIP's profound contempt.)

Grip, 30 Aug. 1890. Racial stereotypes were a standard feature of cartoons and humorous poetry at this time, but Bengough's work reveals some interesting patterns. For instance, even a cartoon attacking pogroms in Russia used a very negative Jewish image, as though none other existed that could convey the message to readers.

---

period, it reported that a series of commutations had led to four murders in one district in a week, and it predicted a brisk sale in revolvers, 'for if the authorities won't protect them, those people who are so old-fashioned as to object to being murdered will get ready to protect themselves.'[39]

While thus encouraging lynch law, the magazine also favoured the execution of the criminally insane. In the case of a murderer named McConnell, it said the argument that the man was insane was no reason to refrain from hanging him. 'A species of insanity like that, which allows a man to manage his business, pursue his affairs, scold, beat and abuse his wife, and finally transfix his landlord repeatedly with a butcher knife, is just the sort of insanity best suspended by suspension.' In the same period, *Grip* sniped at the justice minister, Edward Blake, for dragging his feet in approving executions. It ran a cartoon and a poem entitled 'The Hangman to Mr. Blake' with the message: 'Wot ever's the good o' me hangin' around / With never no hangin' to do?'[40]

A year later, the magazine showed a glimmer of interest in the abolition of hanging: 'Human justice awakes, takes off the bandage from its eyes, and beholds itself in its true form of mercy and infinite respect for the life of even a murderer.' This sympathetic attitude quickly disappeared, but it re-emerged in the late eighties. When eighteen-year-old Robert Neil was condemned to be hanged for the murder of a jail guard, *Grip* endorsed the efforts to save the youth. However, its main concern seems to have been the practice of hiring professional hangmen rather than entrusting executions to the elected sheriffs. 'Poor young Neil was "worked off" on Tuesday morning by a cold-blooded wretch who took the job for $50 and evidently relished it,' the magazine complained. It went on to say that hangmen 'generally possess all the qualifications of a murderer' and concluded: 'If hanging is to be continued, let the sheriff do the business.'[41] Again, this tentative interest in abolition was quickly abandoned.

In its early stages, the magazine also showed little of the democratic touch that it would later develop. There was a distinctly high-Tory sound to an 1874 colomn, very much in the Goldwin Smith idiom, which complained that Canadian newspapers were sinking to the depths of their American counterparts:

The American press, influenced by the democratic idea of the exclusive rights of the majority, has long treated the private life of public men as public property. A total disregard for individual rights has produced the vilest press the world has ever seen, saturated with vulgarity, teeming with slanderous items, peering impudently into the family circle, pandering to the lowest appetites of a half-educated mob, and leaving the public men no moment of privacy.[42]

As well, *Grip* in its early years showed little patience for the downtrodden. There was probably no intended irony in the poem entitled 'The Terrible Tramp':

> The Terrible Tramp is infesting the land,
> And his number is more than the country can stand ...
> But *Grip* thinks the thing is now almost played out;
> That from country and town we the nuisance shall rout,

And that workhouse and prison should crushingly stamp
Out this terrible torment, the Terrible Tramp.'[43]

Similarly, in these early years the magazine showed little sympathy for labour rights. It satirized workers who were not prudent enough to save and buy property yet still felt they were entitled to vote. And after noting the efforts to organize protection for the 'laboring masses' in the United States, it suggested that any similar Canadian code should include rules such as 'Eight hours, at present, to constitute a normal working day; but if the employee does not feel like working, or wants to smoke, or read a new novel, or take a walk, a lesser number of hours at his discretion, should answer.'[44]

Such items are clearly out of keeping with *Grip*'s progressive tone in its later stages, but they may to some extent have been accidental. They may reflect no more than the editor's pressure as he worked to fill his sheet with the contributions of various 'paragraphers' who arrived at the editorial office to offer their gems. They may also reflect Bengough's immaturity; he was only in his twenties during the 1870s, and he could have felt insecure in dealing with such journalistic elders as Phillips Thompson and R.W. Phipps. Of course, another explantion is that attitudes changed.

By the late 1870s, the magazine was showing signs of the radicalism that would develop further in the 1880s. In 'Sitting on the Poor Man' (19 Jan. 1878), Bengough condemned the tax exemptions of officials and clergy. In the early 1880s his discovery of the philosophy of Henry George was clearly a watershed, provoking not just his fascination for tax reform but a much broader concern for the labouring classes. It was the beginning of a period in which *Grip* would become something of a bore in its attacks on monopolists and capitalist exploiters ('The Tournament of To-day'; 'The Workingman's Delicate Position'; 'The Government "Investigating" Monopoly').[45] Like the American populists, the magazine became preoccupied with talk of equal rights and special privileges, and of the evils arising from economic and political institutions aligned against the people.[46]

Grip's class-consciousness showed in various ways. When in 1886 the *Globe*'s 'Women's World' praised Upper Canada College as a good place

---

Grip, 19 Jan. 1878 (*opposite*). Bengough's class-consciousness was not very noticeable in his early work, but it began to show up strongly in the late seventies and early eighties in cartoons like this one.

SITTING ON THE POOR MAN; OR, THE INJUSTICE OF EXEMPTION.

THE TOURNAMENT OF TO-DAY.
A SET-TO BETWEEN MONOPOLY AND LABOR.   [FROM *Puck*.

Grip, 11 Aug. 1883. The American influence on *Grip*'s social views is evident in this copy of a cartoon from *Puck* magazine. While the idea of labour confronting the giants of monopoly may seem commonplace now, it was relatively new at the time.

---

for a boy because it meant he did not have to come in contact with 'the rabble of the earth,' *Grip* replied with:

> Blessed are the boys of Upper Canada College!
> For they mingle not with the rabble of the earth.
> Praise to the powers that be for such an institution!
> Success and honor and glory to Upper Canada College![47]

Similarly, Bengough lampooned the social pretensions of the Methodist Church in 'A Hundred Years Later' (21 Mar. 1891; p. 218). By this point, though, *Grip* was caught up in a distinctly radical trend, one that was

THE WORKINGMAN'S DELICATE POSITION.

Grip, 19 July 1884. The rise of the Knights of Labor in the mid-1880s helped increase the hostility that Canadian workers felt towards immigrant labour, especially towards the Chinese workers brought in to build railways.

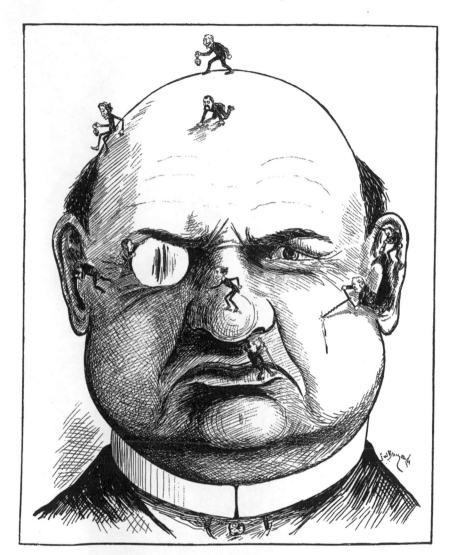

THE GOVERNMENT "INVESTIGATING" MONOPOLY.

Grip, 17 Mar. 1888. By the late eighties, Bengough had wholeheartedly adopted the populist conviction that capitalists and politicians were jointly exploiting 'the people.' In this cartoon, he painted the Canadian government as being too weak to curb the trusts.

more extreme than anything that would appear in Canada until the 1930s.[48]

Only in one area was Bengough entirely consistent throughout his career, and that was in his hostility to the liquor trade. In *Grip*'s early years he tried to engage both political parties in the cause, and in its mature years his talk of a third party was often linked to prohibition. In 1886, for instance, the magazine reported favourably on the development of electoral unions whose members pledged not to support any candidates from the old parties who were not supporters of prohibition: 'A straight-out third party on this question is one of the certainties of the near future.'[49] Throughout *Grip*'s life, this theme was continued without let-up – and without any touch of humour ('Stop the Death Factories!' p. 219; 'Miss Canada, Barmaid,' p. 220).

On many other issues of general morality, from lotteries and animal protection to prizefighting and smoking, Bengough comes across, especially in his later work, as an earnest and rather pedantic reformer. At times he combined favourite causes. When an American general distributed cigarettes to imprisoned Sioux warriors, *Grip* said the cigarettes would probably finish the work of extermination left undone by whisky and starvation, smallpox and bullets.[50]

On clean water, Bengough was ahead of his time, condemning Toronto's sewers, its water supply, and its harbour pollution. He wrote of the rushing torrents of sewage that each day would empty into 'the calm still bay / And return through the water-works pipes next day.' On another occasion, he offered a Boswellian satire in which Dr Johnson, on a visit to Toronto, condemned Toronto Bay as a 'putrescent and malodorous cesspool' and Torontonians as a contemptible people tamely allowing themselves to be taxed for the privilege of drinking a fluid that compared unfavourably with the contents of a Neapolitan sewer.[51] Bengough was outraged, too, by even the most respectable of lotteries. A Masonic draw in London, Ontario, provoked him to produce a cartoon that showed a spirit labelled 'chance' enticing a crowd of grasping people

---

Grip, 21 Mar. 1891 (A Hundred Years Later, p. 218). In his mature years Bengough became more class-conscious, under the indirect influence of Henry George and the direct influence of Phillips Thompson. One of his most effective cartoons on bourgeois hypocrisy visualized John Wesley returning to lament the pretensions that had crept into the Methodist Church.

A HUNDRED YEARS LATER.

SHADE OF WESLEY—"And this is Methodism! I should hardly have known it!"

STOP THE DEATH FACTORIES!

Grip, 30 Oct. 1886. Two of Bengough's anathemas, the Roman Catholic Church and the liquor interests, were combined in this sketch.

MISS CANADA, BARMAID.

WHEN WILL THE COUNTRY BE "RIPE" TO GET OUT OF THIS PARTNERSHIP?

Grip, 9 July 1887. Bengough's passion for prohibition brought out the worst of his tendency to melodrama. This is just one of the many humourless prohibition sketches that he drew during his half-century of cartoon production.

towards the abyss of ruin, and an editorial spoke of the shame and disgust of all patriotic Canadians over this spread of the virus of gambling.[52]

On prizefighting, which was illegal but was widely condoned, Bengough condemned newspapers that gave the sport extensive coverage and said they ought to be running their stories under the heading of 'criminal intelligence.' He also condemned the 'useless cruelty of snow bird shooting matches' and the popular style of using dead birds as hat decorations: 'Statistics show that 10,000,000 birds are butchered annually to decorate the headgear of – no, not the savages of the South Seas Islands – the Christian ladies of America! The girl who reads this paragraph and can go on countenancing the barbarous fashion has not the heart of a woman.'[53]

Bengough was also a passionate antivivisectionist. A poem for this cause left in his personal papers is one of the more effective in his collection. A covering note, presumably by Thomas Bengough, who assembled the papers, describes it as probably the last poem written by Bengough before his death in 1923. It begins:

> I am not brave, but if there be some ill
> Awaiting me, to rack me in its throes,
> Rather would I endure it than escape
> By safety purchased through the mortal pain
> Of poor, dumb creatures.[54]

While Bengough's earlier work was more likely to have a political or economic flavour, the emphasis on social issues shows up more in *Grip*'s second decade and even more strikingly in Bengough's post-*Grip* career. His poetry from that period has a strongly Christian flavour, offering inspiring stories of redemption or compassion – of the criminal who is reformed in an instant by the kiss of an innocent child, or of the hardened newsboys who rally to protect their lame comrade. The tone of these stories and poems may seem ingenuous to modern readers, but the sincerity is inescapable. It gives some clue to the orientation or motivation of the *Grip* cartoonist.

11

Conclusion: 'A Lesser Craft'

John Bengough rarely achieved true depth in his drawing. One exception is the cartoon called 'The Last of the Paragraphers,' which was published in 1890, near the end of *Grip*'s most interesting period. This drawing is distinctive partly because it taps into Bengough's personal experience in dealing with the freelancers who shuffled or blustered their way into his office to offer their satirical poems, jokes, and sketches. It is also unusual in the way it penetrates surface appearances to suggest the subject's feelings. Indeed, it may well reflect Bengough's own emotions as he adapted to a changing world. From a later perspective, it seems that Bengough's career after the collapse of *Grip* was of little relevance – except, perhaps, in illuminating the *Grip* years. Like the paragrapher, he was soon passed over by a fickle and unforgiving audience. The pain shows in the paragrapher's face. The eager smile and the crossed, supplicating hands speak compellingly of the burnt-out artist, the clown who no longer commands attention.

The ferment of the nineties, marked by swift social and technological change combined with economic depression, left Bengough facing this kind of fate, and it is hard to think he could have looked back on this 'Last of the Paragraphers' sketch without seeing something of himself and his times. In this period, Bengough could see a proliferation of good-quality photographs in the weekend newspapers and in such magazines as *Saturday Night*, and also the much-improved colour production in the American satirical magazines that were coming into Canada. He could also see profound changes in taste, style, and values. For instance, on the May night in 1897 when he found himself projecting his cartoons on a big canvas screen at Massey Hall as part of a campaign against Sunday streetcars, he may well have glimpsed the future both in the technology and in the losing cause.

These social and technological changes were paralleled by changes in

THE LAST OF THE PARAGRAPHERS.

Grip, 1 Nov. 1890. Bengough often sketched from the stereotypes in his mind rather than from observation, but there is an authentic quality to his poignant portrait of the 'paragrapher.' This was the type of freelancer who was described by Bengough as stumbling down the cement steps to the *Grip* office with contributions of recycled jokes, poems, and satires.

the political world – changes that introduced not only new actors but also new codes of perception governing the way politics was seen. Veterans of the Macdonald era, especially the prime minister himself, had seemed peculiarly susceptible to caricature. Their faces were craggy, mobile, and interesting, their dress and figures distinctive. They seemed Dickensian. Whether this was because they actually were or because Bengough drew from Dickensian images in his mind is an open question. It is at least possible that the increasing availability of photographic images impinged on and limited the internal pictures that guided his hand. In any event, the political characters who took the stage in the new era had a less interesting look. Their clothes and grooming became uniform and anonymous. W.L. Mackenzie King, as plump and anonymous as an undertaker's assistant, was perhaps the prototype for the new style – and if so, all cartoonists must have despaired.

In time, Bengough came to be called 'Canada's first great political cartoonist,'[1] but in the 1890s, after twice losing his magazine, he must have wondered what he had to do to achieve stature in his native country. While there was still a demand for his work at such papers as the *Montreal Star* and the *Toronto Star*, he was under much more pressure to conform to an uncongenial (sometimes anti-Laurier) editorial policy.[2] The *Globe* was a more congenial employer, at least in the sense that he sympathized personally with most of its Liberal propaganda. For several years in the late nineties his cartoons ran daily in the *Globe*, often on the front page, and were reprinted in other Liberal dailies. They showed no decline in technique, though they lacked some of the originality and verve – and most of the independence – of his *Grip* work. It is understandable that Bengough often turned to serious writing, politics, and lecturing in an always energetic effort to make his mark. He seems to have lost faith in his special craft.

If in fact he did so, it may partly have been because of the public attitude. While the world around Bengough saw him as a clever cartoonist and platform performer, sketching rapidly as he mingled songs, sketches, and sermons, it had no great regard for his type of work. It saw him as a sort of harlequin – an amusing fellow, very able in his way, of course, and astonishingly deft with his pencil – but hardly the equal of great literary, political, or ecclesiastical figures. There were no gurus of pop culture to deconstruct his cartoons or elevate them into cultural icons.

Nor were his social messages taken with much seriousness. His campaigns for prohibition or tax reform or quiet sabbaths had earned him mostly the reputation of a scold. Contemporaries who praised his reform efforts did so in a tone of surprise, as though it were somewhat quaint to see a cartoonist join in the good work. Even Principal George M. Grant of

Queen's University, an admirer, was slightly patronizing in a preface to Bengough's cartoon collection. After praising *Grip* as patriotic, truly Canadian, impartial, and scrupulously clean, Grant stated, 'You may think him at times Utopian. You may not agree with the means he proposes, but you must always sympathize with the end he has in view.'[3]

Fellow journalists also tended to patronize Bengough. In an 1890 article listing those who deserved more credit than they were given, *Saturday Night* managed to include Bengough while still belittling him: 'Johnny Bengough is doing well; his cartoons are as good and often better than those in *Puck* and *Judge*, though not displayed in colors, but who booms him, as white a man and kindly a little gentleman as there is on earth. In election times the papers quote his cartoons when they suit party purposes and abuse him when they don't.'[4] This lofty line was written two years before Bengough was first ousted from the magazine, at a time when (if Joseph Clark is a trustworthy witness) Torontonians were getting fed up with *Grip*'s 'fads.'[5] Bengough seems to have accepted the verdict of the crowd and to have looked to literary achievement as a more fitting field than caricature. He lost his devotion to his métier and tried to become a Tennyson, a Longfellow, a Wilde – or at least an echo of the immensely popular Gilbert and Sullivan. In all these efforts he failed.

Whether he considered going abroad, as his younger brother William did in the hard times, is uncertain. Thomas Bengough later wrote that J.W. 'showed his love for Canada and his patriotism by refusing to go to the United States, where he could have earned many times his earnings here.'[6] But this evaluation is questionable. Undoubtedly Bengough could have gone to New York at the peak of his *Grip* stature in the eighties, but he would have had to abandon his magazine and whatever reputation he had built in his homeland. In the harder days of the nineties, a relocation to New York would have been difficult. His contacts and his reputation were in Canada. Whatever his main motivation, it appears in retrospect that the decision to stay in Canada was at every stage a practical one. Although Bengough cartooned frequently for American publications (often repeating ideas of the old *Grip* days), his feel for American issues never matched his understanding of Canadian undercurrents. He did a good deal of work for the radical *Public* of Chicago, for instance, but his harsh treatment of Theodore Roosevelt had none of the subtlety of his Macdonald or Mowat sketches. His efforts to draw for British publications are similarly unmemorable.

Undoubtedly, Bengough's reputation as a radical shut off many avenues for him. There is a bitter note to this effect in his 1909 memoirs, where he complained of the rejection of his work by leading journals. In the old days, he said, few had objected to his controversial cartoons, whereas 'the present-day conductors of leading journals ... are manifestly afraid to speak out plainly on certain questions for fear that ruin should suddenly descend upon their counting houses.'[7] Yet some of his work for the *Public*, which took a strong progressive line on race and monopoly issues, shows clearly why conservative editors were reluctant to use him.[8]

There is a distinct sense of disillusionment as well in Bengough's abortive attempt to get into politics. The idea may have been in his mind just before or after *Grip*'s death, at a time when fellow journalists such as Sheppard, Thompson, and Maclean were running for office. Just a few months after *Grip* folded, Bengough wrote to Laurier declaring full support for the Liberals and appearing to ask for reciprocal benefits. 'I hope to be able to help the Liberal cause quite frankly now, as the principal medium of my cartoon work is the *Globe*,' he said, 'and I trust the result of the campaign will be at long last a change of Government.' In the wake of Laurier's victory in 1896, his enthusiasm was unrestrained. He hailed the new leader as 'the embodiment of the New Era for which we have long looked, the era of brotherhood, peace, unity and honest administration.'[9] In the *Globe* he offered a cartoon on the election result that stands as one of his least edifying efforts. It shows Miss Canada on her knees, murmuring, 'Thank God!' If he was angling for a public appointment, though, it was not forthcoming.

Whether his closer ties to the party led him to consider running for Parliament is not known. Thomas Bengough recalled that in the 1896 campaign his brother had declined an offer to run as a Liberal in North Bruce, but his reasons are obscure.[10] At the time, Bengough's stature as an artist was still high, and from the party's point of view it would have been foolish to use his skills in any other way. His cartoons, especially in their harsh depiction of Sir Charles Tupper, were considered a significant factor in Laurier's victories in both 1896 and 1900, and to a lesser extent in later elections ('He Has Struck It Precisely').[11]

Globe, 20 Oct. 1900 (*opposite*). In the federal elections of 1896 and 1900, Bengough's propaganda cartoons were considered a factor in Laurier's success – and Tupper's failure. The figures on the right in this sketch are the former finance minister George Foster and Hugh John Macdonald, son of Sir John A. The latter is shown failing to fill his father's large hat – a technique that American cartoonists had used on President Benjamin Harrison, grandson of President William Henry Harrison. (Reprinted courtesy of the *Globe and Mail*)

HE HAS STRUCK IT PRECISELY.

SIR CHARLES—(Suddenly starting out of a long reverie)—Foster! Macdonald! I have it—I have thought it out—now I know what is the matter. It is this: The People of Canada DO NOT TAKE US SERIOUSLY!!!

At the same time, Bengough was deeply engaged in the public affairs of Toronto, as in the 1897 campaign against Sunday streetcars, when he not only prepared cartoons for the cause but provided literature and a campaign song.[12] His engagement in such issues prompted him to run for local office, despite his earlier preference for national affairs. After one unsuccessful attempt, he was elected a Toronto alderman in 1907 and re-elected in each of the following two years. Stanley Kutcher, who has examined Bengough's political performance, shows that Bengough devoted himself to vigorous (but apparently not always practical) efforts at social reform, sometimes in areas more relevant to higher levels of government. He worked to curb the liquor interests, to force landlords to live up to their responsibilities – and, of course, to reform the tax system. He sought to improve the sewer and water system, to set up supervised playgrounds, and to bring hydroelectric power under public control. He campaigned for free school texts and for abolition of the Toronto coal trust. But despite all this fervour, Bengough left the city council in the middle of a term. In 1909 he received a leave of absence from the council to make an extended tour of Australia and New Zealand, and when he returned he abandoned his council post. 'Although he had fought hard for his social programs he had enjoyed only a modicum of success, and his real interest did not lie in the daily round of pedantic administrative activity. His was the self-asserted duty of judge and prophet.'[13]

Although Bengough had given up politics, he remained enormously prolific in other ways. He continued his chalk talks, campaigned for an array of causes, lectured on elocution, held office in a number of associations, and produced a stream of plays and comic operas. One of the latter, entitled *Bardwell vs. Pickwick*, was produced by the Dickens Fellowship of Toronto. A note in Bengough's papers says that it earned $1,200 in a week and that the proceeds were used to finance a Bengough cot at Toronto's Hospital for Sick Children. Bengough illustrated a number of books, most of them tracts of one kind or another. Typical is *The Up-to-Date Primer*, an illustrated homily on social righteousness written laboriously in words of one syllable. At the same time, Bengough contributed cartoons to a score of publications, among them the *Square Deal* (organ of the Tax Reform League of Eastern Canada), the *Canadian Courier*, the *Canadian Graphic, Canadian Single Taxer, Citizen and Country, Weekly Templar*, the *Moon*, and the *Industrial Banner*.

An indication that he aspired to more serious illustration work appears in an article by D.R. Keys analysing a 'rare ... indeed a wholly unique'

SARTOR RESARTUS

In his mature years, Bengough experimented with a variety of techniques, as these three sketches show ('Sartor Resartus' [*above*], from Keys, 'Bengough and Carlyle'; portrait of Louis F. Post [p. 230], from *Public* [Chicago], undated; 'The Grand Old Tactician' [p. 231], from *Grip*, 25 Jan. 1890).

THE GRAND OLD TACTICIAN.

Miss Canada—"Let me congratulate you, Sir John, on your seventy-fifth birth-day. You must be weary of public life by this time, and anxious to give way for younger men."

Sir John—"Not a bit of it, my dear. I'm good for quite a lot of mischief yet!"

edition of Thomas Carlyle's *Sartor Resartus* illustrated by Bengough (see p. 229). The sketches, which are reproduced in Keys's article, are simple line drawings, astonishingly different from the cluttered sketches of *Grip*.[14] Also striking is a caricature, much bolder and more forceful than his usual work, of the *Public* editor Louis F. Post (p. 230). In a sense, this change of style had been predicted by some of his work in *Grip*'s last years, including the simple drawings that were signed L. Côté and also those that were in a more solid style, evidently exploiting the magazine's new zinc etching process ('The Grand Old Tactician,' p. 231). Clearly, Bengough was capable of growth as an artist, even though much of his later work showed banal and repetitive themes. In any event, his later drawing stands up better than his poetry, which suited the age but seems melodramatic today. His later satirical writings also fail to travel well over time. Some of his sketches, produced in a country patois under the pseudonym Caleb Jinkins, echo Thompson's work as Jimuel Briggs, but they are much less comprehensible to a later generation.[15]

All of this effort encouraged Bengough to expect a higher level of public recognition than he was getting, as is shown by the slightly pathetic tone in his 1911 letter to Laurier asking for a senatorship:

I think my qualifications for the position, in my long experience of journalism and public life, will be admitted, and I believe the appointment, if made, would meet with favor throughout the country. I would certainly appreciate the honor myself.

I may add that since the occasion on which you expressed the view that my work was deserving of recognition (a kindness I well remember) precedents have been set in the honoring of Cartoonists who are regarded as having 'done the state some service.' In the United States W. Thomas Nast of *Harper's Weekly* was appointed to a South American consulate and more recently in Great Britain W. John Tenniel, of Punch, and Mr. F.C. Gould, of the *Westminster Gazette*, were given knighthoods.[16]

Thirty years earlier Bengough, or one of his writers, had offered a rather different view of Senate appointments, greeting an unpopular arrival in the Upper House with the ditty:

> Never mind the why or wherefore
> I'm a senator and therefore ...
> Set the merry bells a-ringing
> Fill the air with warbling wild ...[17]

No congratulatory bells were set ringing for Bengough, possibly because Laurier sometimes found him a nag, as in the Saskatchewan land issue. Yet Bengough maintained his support for Laurier until the late days of the First World War. In the early years of the war he regularly and faithfully cartooned for the *Canadian Liberal Monthly*, blending patriotism with anti-Tory bile. An example is 'Treason without Reason' (p. 234), which crossed the bounds of good taste by portraying Prime Minister Robert Borden as the Kaiser, and his minister Bob Rogers as the Turkish sidekick. Laurier's refusal to back conscription was the rock that forced Bengough to part with his leader. The pain he felt in doing so was expressed in an awkward poem in which he said he had revered Laurier for many a year but could not support his faith in voluntary enlistment.[18]

After the war, Bengough pursued a close and loyal relationship with Laurier's successor, Mackenzie King. Towards the young leader he was sometimes patronizing – the old campaigner addressing a novice – but his admiration for King seems to have been genuine. The two shared many radical and arcane views about labour and capital which sustained the relationship. On occasion, Bengough lectured the new leader as he had lectured the old one, and he even broke into sketches to illustrate yet again the Henry George credo that unearned increases in land value should go to the community, not to the capitalist.[19] This lecture – to a recognized international expert on capital and labour – has a presumptuous ring to it. But there is a genuinely admiring note to the poem Bengough published when King assumed the leadership in 1919.[20] He sent King a copy of this poem, along with a letter offering practical support (as well as a typical bad pun): 'I believe you have come to the King-dom for a great purpose, and none of your friends will watch your course with a more sympathetic eye (and hand) than yours truly.' King replied in similarly high-flown terms, while making it clear that he understood the drift of Bengough's promise: 'I am glad you are willing to lend your pen – and pencil – in the cause, and also your heart and mind.' But if Bengough hoped for some more tangible recognition, again it was not forthcoming.

In his last years, Bengough maintained a strenuous schedule of touring and lecturing – often to audiences that included those who had seen and loved his *Grip* cartoons as children, a half-century earlier. At the same time, he probed in a dozen artistic directions: towards operetta, towards literature on social reform, towards screenplays, and especially towards serious poetry. An inventory of the minor writings in his personal papers at McMaster University is remarkable for its diversity – and for the seeming absence of anything of lasting value. While the titles of his screenplays

TREASON WITHOUT REASON

GERMANY—Who Goes There?   BORDEN—A Friend.
"Assistance rendered to the Enemy in any way whatever is Treason."—THE LAW.

Canadian Liberal Monthly, May 1915. In the First World War Bengough drew Liberal propaganda sketches, condemning not only the Kaiser and war profiteers but also the Tories. Portraying Conservative Prime Minister Robert Borden in a German uniform (and his colleague Bob Rogers as a Turk) was a gross insult. In the last year of the war, Bengough broke with Laurier on the conscription issue, as did many other Anglo-Canadian Liberals.

have a dated quality (*The Farmhand, The Lover's Ruse, The Tramp's Triumph*), it should be remembered that they were very much in keeping with the Keaton/Chaplin era of filmmaking and that Bengough, as a man well into his sixties, was making a strong effort to stay with the times. He was doing so while keeping up with a punishing schedule of road shows and while continuing to do cartoon work for a score of publications.

Whether Bengough ever considered that he was spending his late years in the energetic pursuit of mediocrity is unclear. In his carefully constructed persona he seems to have permitted no sign of doubts, and his brother's account reinforces the 'Never say die!' credo that was the most attractive quality of the *Grip* raven. Undoubtedly he was sustained, as Ramsay Cook has noted, by a simple and confident Christian faith. He kept a stiff upper lip, seldom revealing the tensions that most affected him. Of the darkest point in his life, his removal from *Grip*, all he said in his memoirs was that his departure had occurred 'through no consideration of failing health.'[21] If he felt bitter about losing his magazine just before the arrival of the Laurier era, which could have sustained and strengthened it, he gave no sign. Bengough thus emerges as a quintessential Victorian, with all that this implies of outward virtue and hard work – and, possible, inward repression. It would be useful to know what early or late formative influences made him what he was. Since the clues are so limited, we are left with no choice but to study his work, assuming that the work defined the man.

The same could be said of Phillips Thompson, though the definition there is easier, less ambiguous. If the tragedy of Bengough's life was the failure to concentrate on his métier, the tragedy of Thompson's came with the bitterness of disappointed idealism. A man of great energy, talent, and imagination, he had failed in his repeated attempts to become a journalistic or political advocate of the workers. He had failed, perhaps nobly, in trying to make the *News* a distinctive radical voice in the land. He had also apparently failed, or become disillusioned, during his attempts to establish himself in England and the United States. Late in life he was reduced to writing government reports[22] and angry letters to the editor – tilting at windmills. He was clearly too radical to maintain a place in the mainline press.

The difference between the two men is symbolically illustrated by their contrasting attitudes to the First World War. Thompson, listening only to his own inner voices, took the lonely road of pacifism.[23] Bengough faithfully reflected the agonizing shifts of his community, in sketches and rhymes that supported enlistment or condemned 'slackers' while becoming increasingly aggressive on the conscription issue. Thompson thus earns respect for individuality – but Bengough better reflects the tensions of his times.

Bengough's strenuous efforts, and his long record, earned him in his own time many superlatives, most of them overstated. Typical was a biographical sketch that included a number of laudatory quotations: from the British editor W.T. Stead, who called him 'one of the ablest cartoonists in the world'; from the *Canadian Gazette*, which called him 'the Tenniel of Canada'; and from the *Christian Guardian*, which called him a 'genial companion, a brilliant conversationist [*sic*], a peerless cartoonist.'[24] Similarly effusive was a lengthy article by the editor of the *Methodist Magazine and Review*, which praised his versatility, geniality, and morality ('He is always on the right side of every moral question') and, more surprisingly, his impartiality ('He sent his wit-tipped arrows indiscriminantly into each camp').[25]

The praise for his energy was certainly fully earned. It was typical of Bengough that when he died in 1923 at the age of seventy-two, it was with pencil in hand, drawing a cartoon for an anti-tobacco campaign. It was typical as well that his heart problem had caught up with him the previous year after a tour in which, according to one obituary, he had 'taken ill while in Moncton in the course of a tour, as a result of overwork on a Western trip, when he gave 60 lectures beyond his regular schedule.'[26] Thomas recalled the death in more emotional terms: 'On October 2, 1923, my gifted and much-loved brother ... fell from his chair while drawing a series of cartoons on moral reform. He died as he had lived, working for the uplift of humanity.'[27] A plaque erected at one of his homes, 66 Charles Street East, justly paid tribute to his 'remarkable diversity of talent.'

The accolades that followed Bengough's death were mostly of the fulsome kind. Editor A.E.S. Smythe, editor of the Hamilton *Herald*, was quoted as calling him 'Canada's Dickens' and one of Walt Whitman's 'great companions' with an instinct for human brotherhood and a friendship for the world. Professor D.R. Keys, who recorded Smythe's words, added his own tribute: 'No man with a greater genius for friendship has ever been known to the present writer.'[28] Curiously, though, Smythe's editorial page at the *Herald* blended personal praise with censure in a critique that was probably informed by political slant, since it objected even to the exaggeration of caricature:

As a cartoonist, Mr. Bengough was fertile in ideas and had a real comic gift. But he was not a real draughtsman, and even his best work was crude in execution.

Moreover, he was too intensely partisan to be generally popular, In all his views he was an extremist – an extreme Liberal, an extreme Single Taxer, an extreme pro-hibitionist – and was usually less fair and tactful than zealous in his advocacy of his principles. Even in his cartoons he was an extremist. His portraits of public men were always caricatures, any prominent features being enormously exaggerated; and he always made sure Tories got the worst of it.

The comment went on to say that Bengough was personally a charming man: 'His satirical vein, which occasionally led to what seemed like malevolence, was from the heart, not the head.'[29]

Later assessments of Bengough's art would be kinder, though not effusive. Doug Fetherling has saluted him as the kind of all-round journalist and communicator who is sadly lacking in modern life: 'He was a reporter, lecturer, poet, artist, campaigner and general thorn in the side of the established order.' But Fetherling added that few people listened to Bengough's ideas.[30] He might also have said that Bengough's diffusion of effort eroded his best talent.

Hector Charlesworth, who shared few of Bengough's passionate convictions, was less kind. He regretted that over the years Bengough had become 'more of a propagandist and less of a cartoonist.'[31]

Desbarats and Mosher were equally restrained: 'Bengough's prose, like his cartoons, was constructed according to the conventions of his time ... Bengough was a crude artist whose inventive political imagination and passionate convictions eventually would triumph over his artistic awkwardness to make him the greatest political cartoonist of his age in Canada.'[32]

A century later, a good deal of ambiguity remains about the durability and significance of Bengough's art and the impact of his social campaigns. A case can be made, though, that his long-term importance lies not in his Christian dogma, or his Grit propaganda, or his radicalism but in the way he absorbed and reflected the views of at least one part of Canadian society. Even when he adopted attitudes that now seem disreputable (as in the race and creed wars) he is wonderfully authentic in showing what was going on in the minds of Ontario's Christian, liberal, reformist, Anglo-Protestant dominant class. If Phillips Thompson was remarkable for his single-minded individuality, Bengough was remarkable for his capacity to assimilate and reflect, to be a true manifestation of the conventional wisdom of his group. Even when he was inconsistent – as on women's rights or imperialism – his sketches say much about the tensions of his day.

In defining those tensions, Bengough successfully gave imaginative form to at least some of the vague concerns of the bourgeois Protestants. He created for them the ogres that would personalize and make targets for their resentments: the capitalist exploiter, the Catholic prelate, the liquor manufacturer, the CPR magnate, the grasping Tory politician. If he was effective in doing this, it was because he was sensitive to his community, matching much of its reformist Protestant outlook in a way that Phillips Thompson never would. If his own ideas were sometimes faddish or derivative, if he at times allowed others to shape *Grip*'s text, these weaknesses were perhaps less important in the political process than the vitality of his connection with his audience. While Thompson's more extreme socialist rhetoric is now little more than a historical curiosity, Bengough's sketches are still a strong and continuing force in making sense of his times.

Notes

AO Archives of Ontario
MUA McMaster University Archives
NA National Archives of Canada

Preface

1 Waite, 'Reflections on an Un-Victorian Society,' 28–9.

1: The Texture of the Times

1 E.W. Thomson reminiscence, Toronto *Globe*, 2 July 1904.
2 For some other Confederation-era images, see Brown, *The Illustrated History of Canada*, Hall et al., *The World of William Notman*, and Cavell, *Sometimes a Great Nation*.
3 *Grip*, 11 Sept. 1875. The indication that the poem was about abortion victims comes in these later lines: 'Whose is the guilt – the wretch who holds the knife, / Or he who finds the victim – maid betrayed, or wife.' The poem was apparently related to the sensational case of 'Dr' Arthur Davis and his wife Olive, who were sentenced to be hanged because of an abortion death but were later reprieved (Toronto *Mail*, 3–4 Sept. 1885; Toronto *Globe*, 30 Nov. 1875).
4 Waite, 'Sir Oliver Mowat's Canada,' 23.
5 Feaver, *Masters of Caricature*, 96. The assessment probably derives from Terry Mosher, a contributor to the book.
6 Press, *The Political Cartoon*, 358.
7 The stereotypical Jewish caricature goes back at least seven hundred years

(Parton, *Cariicature and Other Comic Art*, 63). The Irish stereotypes are brilliantly defined in Curtis, *Apes and Angels*.

8 Compare, for instance, 'Mammon's Rents' (*Punch*, 10 Nov. 1883) with 'Who's Entitled to Compensation?' (*Grip*, 7 Mar. 1885).

9 This point was shown vividly by a study done during a 1960s crisis in China that found no less than six U.S. cartoons featuring a dragon biting its tail (*Editor & Publisher*, 28 Jan. 1966, cited in Press, *The Political Cartoon*, 20).

10 For a comparative view, see Desbarats and Mosher, *The Hecklers*.

11 Quoted in Batten, 'Penciling the Purveyors of Power.'

12 Woodcock, *Faces from History*, 74.

13 Stewart, 'Political Cartoons,' 58.

14 AO, Alexander Campbell Papers, Macdonald to Campbell, 23 Mar. 1885.

15 Laurier to Blake, 29 Dec. 1891, cited in Underhill, *The Image of Confederation*, 27.

16 Bengough, 'Recollections of a Cartoonist,' 250–1.

17 Cook, *The Regenerators*, 127.

18 Cleaver, *Life's Great Adventure*, 16–17.

2: Bengough, Thompson, and *Grip*

1 For a fuller sketch of Thompson's life, see Jay Atherton's introduction to Thompson, *The Politics of Labor*. Thompson's performance as chief editorial writer of the *News* under E.E. Sheppard is explored in Hann, 'Brainworkers and the Knights of Labor.' His record as a labour writer is covered in Kealey and Palmer, *Dreaming of What Might Be*, and Verzuh, *Radical Rag*. Thompson's religious and ideological orientation is discussed in Cook, *The Regenerators*, chap. 9. For further biographical information, see Blackburn Harte, 'Canadian Journalists and Journalism.'

2 *Saturday Night*, 2 Aug. 1890.

3 Blackburn Harte, 'Canadian Journalists and Journalism,' 425; Kealey and Palmer, *Dreaming of What Might Be*, 302–5.

4 Berton, *Starting Out*, 59–60.

5 The biographical information on Bengough is drawn principally from the following sources: (1) memoirs by Bengough in his book *Bengough's Chalk Talks*, largely duplicated in a series in the *Westminster* magazine; (2) a paper by Thomas Bengough entitled 'Life and Work of J.W. Bengough, Canada's Cartoonist' (MUA, John Wilson Bengough Papers, box 3, file 4, Bell Club address, 20 January 1937); (3) theses by Dennis Edward Blake, Stanley Paul Kutcher, and Dugald E. Stewart; (4) a family genealogy by Larry Driffield of Toronto, which gives the following details:

J.W.'s grandfather, also named John, was born Aug. 1792 in a family whose name was originally spelled Bingay or Bingo. He married Johanna Jackson in St Andrews, Scotland, on 11 July 1812 and died 5 Apr. 1867 in Whitby, Ont. They were living in a one-storey log house on division 2 of Whitby Township at the time of the 1851 census.

Their oldest child, also John, was born on 23 May 1819; he married Margaret Wilson on 22 May 1845 in Toronto and died 30 Oct. 1899 in Toronto. A story in the Whitby *Free Press* of 27 Sept. 1978 identifies her as Margaret Wilson of Bailieboro (presumably Bailieborough), County Cavan, Ireland. She died in Toronto 11 Feb. 1900.

Their children were George (b. 1846, d. 9 Aug. 1900 in Toronto); Joanna (b. 1848); John Wilson (b. 5 Apr. 1851, d. 2 Oct. 1923 in Toronto; m. Helena Siddall, 1 June 1880; m. Mrs Annie Robertson Matteson, June 1908); Thomas (b. 1853, d. 5 Jan. 1945); Mary (May) (b. 1857, d. 31 Dec. 1928 in Toronto); and James (b. 17 Jan. 1862, d. 14 Dec. 1930 in Niagara Falls, N.Y.).

The Driffield material and other sources offer further information on the siblings:

Thomas, a shorthand reporter and journalist, eventually became a Senate clerk; he was survived by two sons, E.J. Bengough, registrar of McMaster University, and William J. Bengough of Grimsby Beach, Ont.

William, who occasionally sketched for *Grip* and other Toronto publications, became a portrait painter in New York (Keys, 'Bengough and Carlyle,' 65; Stewart, 'Political Cartoons,' 70–2). His obituary in the Toronto *Telegram*, 27 Sept. 1932, said he had a distinguished career 'and was a war correspondent for the American press during the Philippine and Cuban wars and for a few years lived in Paris and London.' When his father died in 1899, William was said to be working in the Philippines for the New York *Morning Journal*, presumably as a war artist in the Spanish-American War (*Globe*, 31 Oct. 1899).

George was attached to the family printing business for a time.

James, an American businessman, had four children. The youngest, Bernard Oliver, born in Niagara Falls, N.Y., was a catcher for the New York Yankees, 1919–29, the era of Babe Ruth and Lou Gehrig, and was a roommate of Gehrig.

Mary (May) worked for the provincial government in Toronto.

6 Whitby Archives, Whitby, Ont., typescript of Whitby *Chronicle* obituary, dated only 1899 and attributed to 'Farewell Scrapbooks,' Oshawa Public Library.
7 While earlier census records list all of the family as 'Free C' or 'Church of Scotland,' the 1871 and 1881 records list Captain John as Unitarian.
8 Stewart, 'Political Cartoons,' 58–9; Driffield genealogical information; Brian Winter, 'Historical Whitby,' *Whitby Free Press*, 20 Sept. 1978.

9 For an interesting discussion of the social, religious, and political attitudes of Scots settlers, see Murison, 'Scottish Emigration and Political Attitudes.'

10 Hamilton *Herald*, 3 Oct. 1923.

11 *Globe*, 4 Oct. 1823.

12 Driffield genealogy. The *Toronto Star* (24 Mar. 1908) said that Mrs Matteson was born in Whitby and attended the same school as Bengough but that her parents had left Whitby for the United States when she was quite young. She had visited her old home about three years earlier and there met Bengough: 'Old friendships and affections were revived and the announcement of the engagement is the outcome of the meeting.' The story also said Mrs Matteson was 'greatly interested in settlement work in Chicago.'

13 Bengough, *Chalk Talks*, 4; MUA, John Wilson Bengough Papers, box 3, file 4, Thomas Bengough, 'Life and Work,' 1–3.

14 *Globe*, 4 Oct. 1923.

15 *Saturday Night*, 2 Aug. 1890. The writer was given only as 'T,' which indicates that it was neither the editor, E.E. Sheppard (Don), nor his associate Joseph T. Clark (Mack).

16 Bengough, *Chalk Talks*, 8.

17 See, for instance, the recollections of Alexander Maclean in the *Globe*, 2 July 1904, and the accompanying letter from Brown to Maclean, 8 Nov. 1872.

18 Whitby Archives, Whitby, Ont., typescript of Whitby *Chronicle* obituary, dated only 1899 and attributed to 'Farewell Scrapbooks,' Oshawa Public Library.

19 On one occasion, John Bengough backed Thomas's request for appointment as trade commissioner to the West Indies and reminded Laurier that 'no member of the family has yet received anything at the hands of the government over which you preside, though all have been ardent Liberals' (NA, Laurier Papers, 98832, Bengough to Laurier, 21 June 1905). On another occasion, Thomas, in a letter to Sen. J.K. Kerr (NA, Laurier Papers, 98835, 21 June 1905) said that Sir Wilfrid and other ministers had thanked J.W. for his great work in their interests, especially in the 1896 election. 'Mr. Jaffray [*Globe* publisher Robert Jaffray] was good enough to tell my brother at the time that anything the members of our family should ask from the Laurier government would be granted. My deceased brother George applied for a position in the customs department four years ago but for some reason unknown to us the appointment was not made.'

Thomas Bengough continued to have close links with the party long after J.W.'s death. In 1930 he apparently published a Liberal propaganda sheet that revived the *Grip* title (NA, King Papers, 156748–53, Jessie M. Bengough to King, 12 Jan. 1931, and King's reply, 13 Jan. 1931). In 1930 Thomas and King also exchanged letters on the possibility of taking over the *Globe* to enforce Liberal party control (ibid., 145732–4, Thomas Bengough to King, 14 Oct. 1930, and King's reply, 20 Oct. 1930).

20 Bengough, *Chalk Talks*, 12. In his *Westminster* memoirs ('Recollections of a Cartoonist,' 186–8), Bengough explained that in *Grip*'s early years the cartoons were lithographed on a separate sheet: 'The drawing was done with lithographic ink upon "transfer" paper coated with a surface of composition which enabled the work to be transferred to the lithographic stone, under severe pressure in a press operated by hand.' Because this produced faulty reproduction, he reverted to wood engraving, getting a professional engraver to transfer his drawings to boxwood blocks. This also proved unsatisfactory, so lithographing was resumed. In the late 1880s, one William Stewart sold him on a new method of etching on zinc, a technique soon replaced by photoengraving.

21 Bengough, 'Recollections of a Cartoonist,' 77.

22 Blackburn Harte, 'Canadian Journalists and Journalism,' 431.

23 Bengough, *Chalk Talks*, 9.

24 Paine (*Th. Nast: His Period and His Pictures*, 529–30) quotes Bernhard Gillam as saying (perhaps facetiously), 'I never bother to think up subjects. I just look up Nast's things in the old numbers of Harper's and get what I want. Nast has done about everything.'

25 For a discussion of this point, see Press, *The Political Cartoon*, 83–106.

26 Bengough, 'Recollections of a Cartoonist,' 186–8.

27 The review of 21 Mar. 1874 is quoted in Bengough's *Chalk Talks*, 18–19.

3: Politics: The Seventies

1 Waite, *Macdonald: His Life and World*, 209.

2 The *Jester*'s Tory leanings are shown by, for instance, its account on 13 Sept. 1878 of a Macdonald election rally which, despite disruption by rowdies, turned into 'a great Conservative triumph.'

3 Reprinted in *Grip*, 11 June 1892.

4 Bengough, *Chalk Talks*, 13.

5 *Grip*, 6 Sept. 1873 and 15 May 1880.

6 *Grip*, 27 Sept. 1873.

7 *Grip*, 3 Jan. 1874.

8 *Grip*, 24 Jan. 1874.

9 *Grip*, 7 Feb. 1874. Cook (*The Regenerators*, 126) quotes another version of this poem, from the *National*, 22 Jan. 1874, which suggests that it may have been Thompson's work. The *National* version starts out: 'Sing a song of scandal, the Premier fond of rye / With half-a-hundred Tories knotted in a pie.'

10 *Grip*, 6 Mar. 1875. These anti-Brown diatribes were similar to attacks being

published about this time by the *Nation*, presumably coming from Goldwin Smith's pen. See, for instance, the articles of 15 Jan. and 22 Oct. 1875.

11 *Grip*, 13 Mar. 1875.

12 *Grip*, 29 July 1876.

13 See, for instance, 'Perfect Freedom!' (*Grip*, 24 July 1875), 'The Political Samson' (25 Mar. 1876), 'Master of the Situation' (15 July 1876), and 'The New Cabinet Minister' (27 Oct. 1876).

14 *Grip*, 20 May and 14 Oct. 1876.

15 Bengough, 'Recollections of a Cartoonist,' 189.

16 See, for instance, comments on the Toronto *Liberal* and London *Advertiser* in *Grip*, 20, 27 Feb. and 6 Mar. 1875.

17 'The Political Giant-Killer' (*Grip*, 13 Dec. 1873).

18 *Grip*, 20 Dec. 1873.

19 *Grip*, 21 Feb. 1874.

20 *National*, 22 Jan. 1874; Kealey and Palmer, *Dreaming of What Might Be*, 303; Cook, *The Regenerators*, 156–7.

21 *Grip*, 6 Mar. 1875, 24 Oct. and 14 Nov. 1874.

22 The changes in Canada First are traced in Berger, *The Sense of Power*, chap. 2.

23 *Grip*, 14 Feb. 1874.

24 *Grip*, 29 Aug. 1874.

25 'The Unpatronized Nostrum Vendor' (*Grip*, 7 Aug. 1874).

26 *Grip*, 10 Oct. 1874.

27 *Grip*, 29 May 1875 and 30 Sept. 1876. Curiously, Denison later claimed that the movement had been killed by a speech of Howland's condemning 'toadyism' to English aristocratic usages (*The Struggle for Imperial Unity*, 60, cited in Berger, *The Sense of Power*, 76).

28 *Grip*, 7 Oct. 1876.

29 *Grip*, 30 Jan. 1875.

30 *Grip*, 12 June 1875.

31 *Grip*, 9 Sept. 1876.

32 Bengough, *Caricature History*, 1:356.

33 See 'Running before the Protection Wind' (*Grip*, 18 Mar. 1876) and 'The Blue Glass Cure' (17 Mar. 1877).

34 In 1879 Phipps showed his venom in the following letter to Macdonald (NA, Macdonald Papers, 166298, 30 June 1879):

> I think Sir John, you must now be convinced of the soundness of my advice to keep me with you. Had you offered me an honorable position ... you would have retained me. But you would not.
>
> Had I been with you ... your tariff would have proved beneficial – and I defy you to fix it without me ...

I think you know whether my advice or that of your particularly 'sane' friend [Christopher] Bunting was worth having. He runs Ontario nicely for you, doesn't he? Very powerful man! ...

I regret it all – with the aid of your pliant majority I might have done much. But destiny rules.

R.W. Phipps

35 *Grip*, 5 May 1877.

36 *Grip*, 1 July 1876.

37 *Grip*, 20 May 1876 and 2 Feb. 1878.

38 *Grip*, 11 Nov. 1876.

39 See, for instance, 'The Retiring Minister' (*Grip*, 2 Mar. 1878).

40 Bengough, *Caricature History*, 1:306.

41 Cook (The Regenerators, 128–9) notes that this cartoon is very similar to Nast's 1872 sketch entitled 'Anything to Get In.'

42 *Grip*, 21 and 28 Sept. 1878.

43 They included 'Running before the Protection Wind' (*Grip*, 18 Mar. 1876), 'Ancient Tory Tactics' (6 July 1878), 'The Great Political Conjurer' (3 Aug. 1878), and 'All at Sea' (17 Aug. 1878).

44 See also 'In the Ring at Last' (*Grip*, 22 Mar. 1879).

45 *Grip*, 5 Oct. 1878.

46 The new format appeared on 29 Mar. 1879. *Jester*'s last issue was apparently on 14 Mar. 1879.

47 Kutcher, 'John Wilson Bengough, Artist of Righteousness,' 40; Stewart, 'Political Cartoons,' 64. On 5 May 1883 the magazine said that a newspaper directory's report giving a circulation of 2,000 had been 'furnished two years earlier' and that the figure had since increased to 7,000–10,000, while 50,000 readers perused the paper weekly.

48 *Grip*, 28 Sept., 9 Nov., and 21 Dec. 1878; 14 June 1879.

49 *Grip*, 7 Dec. 1878.

50 *Grip*, 27 Mar, 1880.

51 *Grip*, 10 Apr. 1880. At the time of Mackenzie's death in 1892, Bengough eulogized him as a 'sternly upright' man who gave the lie to the idea that there was no such thing as an honest politician (*Grip*, 23 and 30 Apr. 1892).

52 *Grip*, 3 Apr. and 15 May 1880.

53 Bengough, *Motley: Verses Grave and Gay*, 83.

54 *Grip*, 15 May 1880.

4: Politics: The Eighties

1 *Grip*, 21 Feb. 1891.

2 *Grip*, 28 Feb. 1891.

3 *Grip*, 4 June, 1892.

4 The cartoons the Tories objected to presumably included 'Gulliver Gerryman-
   dered' (*Grip*, 6 May 1882)], 'What Are You Going to Do About It?' (13 May
   1882), 'The Grit Nursery' (20 May 1882), and 'We've Hived the Grits' (17 June
   1882).

5 NA, Macdonald Papers, 138748–50, cited in Stewart, 'Political Cartoons,' 65.

6 *Grip*, 13 July 1878.

7 *Grip*, 2 Apr. 1881.

8 'Ribstabber Ridivivus' (*Grip*, 18 June 1881).

9 *Mail*, 23 and 27 June 1881; *Grip*, 23 July 1881.

10 *Gazette*, 29 June, 6, 8, and 10 July 1881.

11 *Mail*, 12 July 1881.

12 *Grip*, 21 Dec. 1878.

13 It may be significant that Plumb in a letter to Macdonald on 1 July 1883
   referred to 'that hopeless *Crank* Phipps' (NA, Macdonald Papers, 189240).

14 NA, Macdonald Papers, 175281, 25 July 1881. A letter from Macpherson to
   Macdonald dated 26 Aug. 1881 (ibid., 111966) also contains what appears to be
   a fragment of a Plumb letter on the issue. In it Plumb says, 'Bunting dined with
   me quietly last night. We had a good laugh over the Grip business in respect to
   which I have had several congratulatory letters. I think I have taught him a
   lesson but I know he is at heart a thoroughly [unclear] Grit with prejudices that
   prevent him from dealing with public questions fairly and impartially.'

15 Macpherson's letter to Macdonald dated 12 July 1881 (NA, Macdonald Papers,
   111902) said it seemed to him that 'JBP in his letter to the Mail missed Blake
   and fired over Grip.' He added, 'I tried to knock their [Blake and *Grip*'s]
   heads together. I expect the article is in this morning's Mail.'

16 *Nation*, 10 Dec. 1874.

17 See, for instance, the discussion of Conservative efforts to influence labour
   journals, in Verzuh *Radical Rag*, 21, 63, 130–1.

18 In 1894 Sanford told Prime Minister John Thompson that the *Globe* was in a
   very demoralized condition and two people had approached him with a pro-
   posal for taking it over. He added, 'I am almost inclined to think this can be
   done without its being known to be under the control of Conservative interests[,] the articles being liberal, at the same time of a mild type' (NA, Sir John
   Thompson Papers, 25506, Sanford to Thompson, 19 Mar. 1894).

19 NA, Macdonald Papers, 260261, W.P. Atkinson to Macdonald, 2 Aug. 1882;
   ibid., 260283, Atkinson to Macdonald, 13 Mar. 1888; ibid., 223684, J.H. Beaty
   to Macdonald, 16 Nov. 1887; and ibid., 260287, Atkinson to Joseph Pope,
   10 Sept. 1891.

Over the years the Grip company went through several permutations of partnership and limited company, for reasons that were not always clear but seem to have been related to the expanding printing operation. A memo in Bengough's papers by his brother Thomas gives a bare-bones account of the business history of the paper. It says that after *Grip* became firmly established at 2 Toronto Street, a firm called Bengough Brothers was set up with George, the eldest of the five brothers, in partnership with J.W. 'Later on the firm was changed by George's retirement and the business was taken over by Bengough, Moore and Bengough, with S.J. Moore as manager, I having introduced Mr. Moore, who was my partner in the firm of Bengough, Moore and Co. Later on the Grip Printing and Publishing Company was carried on for some years'(MUA, John Wilson Bengough Papers, Thomas Bengough memo, 9 Mar. 1939).

This change apparently came about in 1881–82: On 30 Aug. 1881, John Wilson Bengough, Samuel John Moore, and Thomas Bengough gave notice of a partnership to be known as Bengough, Moore & Bengough (AO, RG31, MS2052, subseries RG-55-17-60, CP 2396 and 2459, Provincial Partnership Registration). Early in 1882 the Grip Printing and Publishing Company was incorporated, with capital of $50,000 in 5,000 shares at $10 each, by John Wilson Bengough, Samuel John Moore, Thomas Bengough, George Clarke and James Leckie Morrison. The capitalization was expanded to $100,000 in 1884 (*Ontario Gazette*, 4 Feb. 1882, 95; also 15 Jan. 1884, 7). Moore, a onetime printer's devil in Barrie, went on to become one of Canada's leading industrialists.

20 NA, Macdonald Papers, 183344, Plumb to Macdonald, 20 Sept. 1882, and 22511, Plumb to Macdonald, 12 Jan. 1888. The first letter acknowledges receipt of Macdonald's cheque for $500 and says Plumb had tried without success to interview Bengough and Atkinson. Plumb added, 'I intend to see them the next time I go to Toronto and to insist that Bengough shall take the stock off our hands. I don't think there is any public sale for it.'

21 *Grip*, 7 June 1882.

22 Bengough, 'Recollections of a Cartoonist,' 252.

23 *Mail*, 7 Aug. 1885. Similarly, the Halifax *Herald* (19 Dec. 1885) said that *Grip* had been 'getting some "fat takes" in the way of printing from the Mowat government' and that some of its anti-Macdonald cartoons apparently were purchased by the Grits. It also suggested (4 Jan. 1886) that *Grip*'s printing contract was in effect a transfer of the *Globe* job printing department to *Grip*: 'The change in the name is simply a blind that the Globe may do Ontario government printing and at the same time slander the concerns that do Dominion Government printing at half the cost the Globe charges.'

24 *Grip*, 8 Aug. 1885; MUA, John Wilson Bengough Papers, Thomas Bengough

memo, 9 Mar. 1939; AO, Aemilius Irving Papers. The $5,000 deal was made openly with the original contractor, Frank Wilson, covering a five-year period starting 1 Jan. 1884, but it gave weight to Tory criticism that the contract rates were above normal market levels. For instance, the *Mail* (7 Aug. 1885), complained that the provincial departments were paying 44 to 68 cents per thousand ems, compared with the *Mail*'s 'fair commercial rate' of 35 cents for Ottawa's printing.

25 *Grip*, 16 Jan. 1886.

26 AO, Sir Alexander Campbell Papers, Allen to Campbell, 6 Jan. 1886, cited in Stewart, 'Political Cartoons,' 69–72. The *Mirror* prospectus accompanying this letter is dated 31 Dec. 1885. It lists 'Capt. C.W. Allen, late of the Department of the Interior' as a provisional director, along with artists William D. Blatchly and John Kelly.

27 William had earlier tried to start his own publication, an amateurish advertising and almanac-type monthly called *Bengough's Illustrated Monthly*. The project evidently tried to cash in on the Bengough name and fully deserved its quick death. William Colgate (*Canadian Art*, 47) says that William was 'a much more competent draughtsman than was his brother,' but this ability apparently developed later.

28 Stewart, 'Political Cartoons,' 69–72.

29 MUA, John Wilson Bengough Papers, Thomas Bengough memo, 9 Mar. 1939. The main lines of this memo were borne out in an 1887 letter from Tory J.H. Beaty to Macdonald concerning Macdonald's fifty shares: 'Re "Grip" I have made inquiries into the matter as you requested. The company has a capital of $100,000 all paid up. Two years ago they took the printing contract for the local government, and bought a lot of new machines, etc., but they lost money. They gave it up some months ago. The stock is in the hands of very few and the large owners want to get all the stock and freeze the small ones out' (NA, Macdonald Papers, 223684, 16 Nov. 1887).

30 AO, Aemilius Irving Papers, MU1494, reel MS1925, contains an extensive but inconclusive file on the dispute. These documents suggest that a bank failure played a part in the company's downfall. A letter of 15 Feb. 1888 from Grip general manager J.V. Wright to Oliver Mowat (as attorney general) said the Grip company had been injured by 'loss of accommodation by the liquidation of the Federal Bank in which we kept our account.'

31 Bengough, 'Recollections of a Cartoonist,' 250–1.

32 *Grip*, 18 July 1885.

33 *Grip*, 20 June 1885.

34 *Grip*, 25 July and 1 Aug. 1885.

35 *Grip*, 8 Aug. 1885. In his *Westminster* memoirs Bengough wrote: 'On another

occasion a protest came ... from a great and notable party leader who went so far as to order his paper stopped. In this case, too, the hon. gentleman was himself responsible for the facts, upon which *Grip* had commented in a way that was, I still think, only fair and legitimate' ('Recollections of a Cartoonist,' 252–3).

36 *Grip*, 23 Jan. and 10 Apr. 1886.
37 'Forward to the Flag' (*Grip*, 31 July 1886).
38 *Grip*, 5 June and 14 Aug. 1886.
39 See 'A Want of Confidence' (*Grip*, 29 Jan. 1887), 'The Marriage of Convenience' (5 Feb. 1887), and 'The Protected Manufacturer' (12 Feb. 1887).
40 *Grip*, 18 June 1887, 18 Apr. 1891, 25 June and 2 July 1892.
41 See also 'The Same Old Diet' (*Grip*, 27 Aug. 1887).
42 *Grip*, 7 July 1888 and 19 July 1890.
43 *Grip*, no. 1089 [1894].
44 *Grip*, 6 Sept. 1879.
45 *Grip*, 16 Jan. 1886 and 14 May 1887.
46 *Grip*, 12 July 1890, 31 Jan. 1891, 21 Jan. 1893, and 8 Apr. 1893.
47 *Grip*, Aug. 13, 1887.
48 *Grip*, 19 June 1886. For a discussion of M'Lachlan's work, see D.M.R. Bentley's introduction to his McLachlan, *The Immigrant*. (The poet's name was spelled both M'Lachlan and McLachlan.)
49 See, for instance, *Grip*, 28 Feb. 1880 and 23 Apr. 1881.
50 *Grip*, 28 May 1892.
51 *Grip*, 13 June 1891.
52 *Grip*, 13 June 1891.

5: *Grip* and the Press Wars

1 *Grip*, 14 Feb. and 13 Nov. 1880, 8 Jan. 1881.
2 *Grip*, 13, 20 Aug. 1881, 13 Jan. 1883, 26 Apr. and 10 May 1884.
3 *Grip*, 7 Jan. 1888; *Debates*, House of Commons, 7 May 1883, 1028–30; *Grip*, 12 May 1883. For the rat cartoons, see 'Caught at Last' (*Grip*, 22 Mar. 1884), 'The Great Cur-tailer' (22 Mar. 1884), 'Will She Drown Them?' (29 Mar. 1884), 'The Cat on Trial' (11 Oct. 1884), and 'Escaped' (18 Apr. 1885).
4 *Grip*, 30 Dec. 1882.
5 Baker, *Timothy Warren Anglin*, 235–42; *Grip*, 16 June 1883.
6 *Grip*, 2 Apr. 1892. The poem was signed T.W., B.
7 MUA, John Wilson Bengough Papers, box 3, file 4, Thomas Bengough, 'Life and Work,' 15–16.
8 Charlesworth, *Candid Chronicles*, 197.

9 The 'Ontario' poem was printed in the *Mail*, 6 Feb. 1886. Its tune apparently was the version of 'Maryland!' based on the music of 'O Tannenbaum.'

10 Charlesworth, *Candid Chronicles*, 196–7.

11 *Mail*, 11, 18, and 19 Jan. 1886; *Globe*, 16 Jan. 1886; *Grip*, 30 Jan. 1886.

12 The note in Bengough's papers by W.H. Withrow, dated 14 Dec. 1898, praises material for Bengough's poetry book *Motley* but expresses reservations about a poem entitled 'British Free Trade' that is listed as 'a Liberal campaign song' (MUA, John Wilson Bengough Papers, box 1, file 1).

13 Hann, 'Brainworkers and the Knights of Labor,' 37; *Grip*, 7 June 1884; *News*, 5 and 11 July 1884.

14 See 'Disgraceful Case of Child-Desertion' (*Grip*, 28 Sept. 1889).

15 The *Mail*'s independent phase is described more fully in Cumming, *Secret Craft*.

16 In a signed article in the *Week*, 2 Aug. 1889, Thompson wrote: 'No one who has closely followed the course of the *Mail*, the parent of the present anti-Catholic agitation, can doubt that this able and astute journal is actuated by the well-defined and deliberate purpose of bringing about a political union between Canada and the United States. The unthinking and fanatical masses of the Orange body are its dupes.'

17 Blackburn Harte, 'Canadian Journalists and Journalism,' 431.

18 Bengough, 'Recollections of a Cartoonist,' 249. *Grip* started out in a small basement on Front Street but soon moved to 2 Toronto Street, 'one door from King.' However, the 'sanctum' was at 30 Adelaide Street, 'just west of the Post Office,' where *Grip* was located through much of the seventies and into the eighties. Thomas's memo says the Grip office was later at 26–29 Front Street West, but moved to 203 Yonge Street when his brother was ousted on 6 Aug. 1892.

19 Bengough, 'Recollections of a Cartoonist,' 189, 250; MUA, John Wilson Bengough Papers, box 3, file 4, Thomas Bengough, 'Life and Work,' 14–17. Other correspondents included 'Mr. Fielding, of the Evening Sun,' Highlander Gordon, Rev. C.P. Mulvany, Mrs J.K. Lawson (who 'combined in an unusual degree the deep moral fervor of the reformer with the rollicking spirit of the born humorist' and invented the character Hugh Airlie), and Mrs Curzon ('a petite embodiment of sweetness and culture' who was 'one of the early pioneers of women suffrage in Canada, and became editor of "The Citizen"'). Other contributors were George Orran, Norman Bethune, Fred Swire, and 'a host of others.'

6: Race and Creed

1 The Syllabus was a catalogue of errors issued by Pope Pius IX in 1864, reject-

ing liberty of conscience and asserting the primacy of the church in culture and education. For a discussion of Nast's hostility to Catholicism, see Keller, *The Art and Politics of Thomas Nast*, 159–62.

2 *Grip*, 5 Dec. 1874.

3 *Grip*, 18 Sept. 1875.

4 *Grip*, 9 Oct. 1875.

5 *Grip*, 29 Jan. 1876.

6 *Grip*, 20 July 1878.

7 'The Archbishop and the Monster' (*Grip*, 22 May 1880).

8 *Grip*, 23 May 1885.

9 'Too Late!' (*Grip*, 11 Apr. 1885). Both Crowfoot and Poundmaker have also been credited with creating the Old Tomorrow title.

10 'What Will He Do With Him?' (*Grip*, 23 May 1885). See also *Grip*, 1 Aug. and 5 Sept. 1885.

11 *Globe*, 17 Oct. 1885. In another editorial (5 Nov. 1885), the *Globe* said that Macdonald had a choice of hanging Riel 'to satisfy his Orange supporters' or finding 'a reason or pretext for satisfying Quebec supporters.'

12 *Globe*, 5 Dec. 1885.

13 *Grip*, 21 Nov. 1885.

14 *Mail*, 23 Nov. 1885, cited in Schull, *Laurier*, 178–9.

15 *Grip*, 9 Jan. 1886.

16 *Grip*, 31 Aug. 1889.

17 *Grip*, 3 Oct. 1885.

18 'The New Martin Luther' (*Grip*, 23 Feb. 1889). See also *Grip*, 15 Jan. 1887 and 21 Jan. 1888.

19 'The Mail-ed Warrior' (*Grip*, 23 Mar. 1889).

20 See also 'Our "Shining" Leaders' (*Grip*, 6 Apr. 1889) and 'On to Ottawa!!' (21 June 1890).

21 *Grip*, 2 Mar. and 22 June 1889.

22 *Grip*, 17 Aug. 1889 and 8 Feb. 1890.

23 Other cartoons reflecting this line include 'Signor Johnna, the Lion King' (*Grip*, 25 Jan. 1890), 'Mr. Blake's Brilliant Idea' (1 Mar. 1890), and 'The Babes in the Wood' (18 Apr. 1891).

24 *Grip*, 1 Mar. 1890.

7: Opening of the West

1 Bengough town administrator Arleen A. Reitenbach in a letter to Bengough genealogist Larry Driffield, 6 Nov. 1979, gave these circumstances: 'Bengough was a friend of the chief surveyor's father for the C.N.R. This chief surveyor

chose the name Bengough for the town. The railroad was completed in the fall of 1911.'

2 *Grip*, 2 Apr. 1881.

3 NA, Laurier Papers, 105985, Bengough to Laurier, 14 Jan. 1906; ibid., 105990–1, Laurier to Bengough 30 Jan. 1906, and 146199, 28 Oct. 1908.

4 'Their Ingenuity Exhausted' (*Grip*, 8 Dec. 1883).

5 *Grip*, 17 Nov. 1883.

6 'I Stand for Justice' (*Grip*, 7 Nov. 1883), 'Blowing Out the Gas' (26 Jan. 1884), and 'Sir Hector Fails to See Any Grievances' (27 Sept. 1884).

7 *Grip*, 29 Jan. 1876 and 24 May 1879.

8 *Grip*, 7 Apr. 1888.

9 *Grip*, 8 Mar. 1884.

10 'At "Cross" Purposes' (*Grip*, 3 Nov. 1888); Creighton, *The Old Chieftain*, 485.

11 'The Contract Swallowed' (*Grip*, 19 Feb. 1881), 'The Prodigal Sons' (9 Feb. 1884), and 'Crushed!' (8 Mar. 1884).

12 *Grip*, 18 Mar. 1882.

13 'The Political Bad Boy and His Pa' (*Grip*, 14 Apr. 1883), and 'Dewdney's Certificate of Character' (9 June 1888).

14 'The New Manitoba Retriever' (*Grip*, 3 Feb. 1883).

15 'The Manitoba Barons' (*Grip*, 14 May 1887).

16 *Grip*, 12 July 1890.

17 *Grip*, no. 1057, 1894. Bengough pressed the same ideas on Laurier in private correspondence (NA, Laurier Papers, 24339–40 and 3808–11, Bengough to Laurier, 14 and 13 July 1895).

18 'But Not a Word' (*Grip*, no. 1085, 15 Sept. 1894).

8: The Radical Times

1 *Grip*, 11 May 1889.

2 *Grip*, no. 1049, 4 Jan. 1894. The dating of issues in Grip's final year is sometimes difficult because the date was included only in the covering advertising matter, not in the magazine proper.

3 Russell Hann concludes: 'Phillips Thompson was Sheppard's strongest ally in guiding the *News* along a course of independent democracy. Often he would come into conflict with Sheppard, whose later career as a Tory politician, a society editor, and a jingoistic editor of the Toronto *Star* suggests the mercurial nature of Sheppard's personality' ('Brainworkers and the Knights of Labor,' 40). Certainly, the *News* writer from the days of Sheppard's control showed a distinct similarity to the bite of the later unsigned *Grip* material. For instance, while Phillips Thompson was at the *News* he had savaged Martin

Griffin, calling him a 'Uriah Heep who uses the Mail editorial columns as a long and slimy tongue to lick the dust from the shoes of Tory officials.' He had ridiculed George Taylor Denison's family for holding office from generation to generation until its mouth had 'fairly grown fast to the udder of the official cow.' The same kind of harsh rhetoric showed up in Thompson's labour columns and appeared as well in the late years of *Grip*.

4 *Grip*, 5 Nov. 1892. Cook (*The Regenerators*, 130–2) attributes the comment to Bengough, but by this point Bengough had left the magazine.

5 *Grip*, no. 1049, 4 Jan. 1894; Mack (Joseph T. Clark), *Saturday Night*, 20 Jan. 1894.

6 *Grip*, no. 1052, 27 Jan. 1894.

7 *Grip*, 4 Aug. 1883.

8 *Grip*, 17 Dec. 1887.

9 *Grip*, 17 Mar., 11 Aug., and 7 Oct. 1888.

10 *Grip*, 7 Mar. 1891, 1 Nov. 1890, and 11 Apr. 1891.

11 *Grip*, 25 Apr. 1891.

12 *Grip*, 9 and 16 May 1891.

13 *Grip*, 6 Aug. 1892.

14 *Grip*, 27 Aug. 1892.

15 *Grip*, 24 Sept. 1892.

16 *Grip*, 22 Oct. 1892 and 12 Dec. 1891.

17 *Grip*, 24 Sept. 1892.

18 *Labor Advocate*, 2 Oct. 1891, cited in Verzuh, *Radical Rag*, 79.

19 *Grip*, 4 Feb. 1893.

20 *Grip*, 28 May and 1 Oct. 1892, 11 Feb. 1893, and 29 Oct. 1892. The first of these comments came before Bengough's departure, but it has the tone of Thompson's work.

21 *Grip*, 3 June, 1 July, and 22 Apr. 1893. However, Kealey and Palmer say that Thompson was among a number of former Knights of Labor who tried to create a farm-labour alliance (*Dreaming of What Might Be*, 358).

22 *Grip*, 29 Oct. 1892.

23 *Grip*, 15 Oct. 1892.

24 *Grip*, 12 Nov. 1892.

25 'Uncle Sam and the Snake' (*Grip*, 26 Nov. 1887).

26 *Grip*, 18 Feb. 1893.

27 *Grip*, 22 Oct. 1892 and 11 Feb. 1893.

28 *Grip*, 29 Oct. 1892.

29 *Grip*, 27 Aug. 1892.

30 See, for instance, 'Too Big a Contract' (*Grip*, 3 June 1893).

31 MUA, John Wilson Bengough Papers, Thomas Bengough memo, 9 Mar. 1939.

32 See also 'A Delicate Situation' (*Grip*, no. 1051 [20 Jan. 1894]).

33 *Grip*, no. 1099 [22 Dec. 1894].

34 One exception was a poem in *Grip*, no. 1051 [20 Jan. 1894] that deplored Cecil Rhodes's rampaging imperialism in Africa and questioned whether 'it was heaven's will / That Chartered Companies should rob and kill / The native tribes who would their homes defend, / That our own glorious empire might extend!'

9: Imperialism and Independence

1 *Grip*, 6 May 1893.
2 Atherton's introduction to Thompson, *The Politics of Labor*, xiv–xv.
3 'Christian England Enlightening Africa' (*Grip*, 22 Oct. 1888).
4 *Grip*, 28 May 1892.
5 *Grip*, 14 Feb. 1874.
6 *Grip*, 12 Sept. 1874.
7 *Grip*, 1 Jan. 1876.
8 *Grip*, 13 June 1891; Farrer, 'Canada and the New Imperialism,' 773.
9 Winnipeg *Times*, 11 Apr. 1883.
10 *Grip*, 7 Apr. 1888.
11 *Grip*, 21 Oct. 1876. The same sentiments were expressed in a poem of 19 March 1892 predicting:

> ... William of Prussia
> And Aleck of Russia
> Will play war's mad game
> And set Europe aflame.
>
> And massacre millions
> And war-debt by billions
> Will tell the old story
> Of National Glory.

12 *Grip*, 4 Apr. 1891. McGill was also a frequent contributor of both prose and poetry to the *Week* from 1888 to 1896. Much of this work was nonpolitical, but occasionally he attacked the monarchy or aristocracy, as in 'Canadian Loyalty,' 30 Aug. 1889, and 'London Dockmen,' 18 Oct. 1889.
13 'Our Own Tail-Twister!' (*Grip*, 7 Apr. 1888).
14 *Grip*, 14 Jan. 1888.
15 *Grip*, 1 Nov. 1890, signed by Body Guard.
16 *Grip*, 1 Nov. 1890.
17 *Grip*, 18 Feb. 1888, 11 June 1887, and 1 Nov. 1884.
18 See also '"Bait" as Usual' (*Grip*, 3 Mar. 1888).

19 *Grip*, 14 Apr. 1888.

20 *Grip*, 26 Nov. 1887. See also 'Salisbury's Plan for Securing "Peace" in Ireland' (*Grip*, 16 Apr. 1887).

21 *Grip*, 19 Jan. 1889.

22 'Gush' (*Grip*, 8 Feb. 1890).

23 *Grip*, 24 May 1990.

24 *Grip*, 9 Aug. 1990.

25 *Grip*, 3 Jan. and 28 Mar. 1891.

26 *Grip*, 6 Aug. 1892.

27 Bengough, *In Many Keys*, 68.

28 Bengough, *Motley: Verses Grave and Gay*, 69.

29 MUA, John Wilson Bengough Papers, box 4, file 1, 57.

10: *Grip*'s Social Conscience

1 Variations on this aphorism are attributed to several authors, including L.P. Hartley.

2 'The Parliamentary Grosvenor' (*Grip*, 21 Apr. 1883).

3 *Grip*, 17 Feb. 1877.

4 *Grip*, 4 May 1878.

5 See, for instance, the *Nation* article of 19 Feb. 1875, apparently by Smith, deploring the extension of the franchise in Britain and fearing 'the inevitable extension of the vote to the peasantry'; also an article of 5 Mar. 1875 on the harmful effects of exposing women to vivisection in biology classes: 'History has shown us ... how quickly unsexed women can be turned in Harpies and Furies.' See also the discussion of capital punishment on 19 Nov. 1875.

6 *Grip*, 11 Oct. 1884 and 8 Feb 1890.

7 *Grip*, 1 Oct. 1892.

8 *Grip*, 10 May 1890.

9 *Grip*, 15 July 1876.

10 'The Unfortunate Husband' (*Grip*, 31 Dec. 1881).

11 *Grip*, 14 June 1884.

12 *News*, 5 May 1881 and 18 Apr. 1882.

13 *Grip*, 20 May 1893 and 3 Dec. 1892.

14 Kirk Makin, 'Image of First Woman Lawyer Tainted by Anti-Semitic Letters,' *Globe and Mail*, 19 July 1990. For an account of the legislative background of the case, see Evans, *Sir Oliver Mowat*, 212–13.

15 *Grip*, 24 Sept. 1892.

16 Ibid. Cook (*The Regenerators*, 137) attributes this poem to Bengough, but it was printed after Bengough had left the magazine.

17 *Grip*, 7 July 1876.

18 'The Cat's-Paw of Rome' (*Grip*, 6 Oct. 1890).

19 Press (*The Political Cartoon*, 209) notes that in Europe the 'Indian Princess' was long a popular representation of America, and it is interesting that Bengough transferred it to the Canadian West.

20 *Grip*, 26 Oct. 1889.

21 'Lo! The Poor Indian' (*Grip*, 13 Feb. 1886) *Grip*, 20 Feb. 1886.

22 'A Timely Quotation' (*Grip*, 29 Jan. 1887).

23 'Christian Statesmanship' (*Grip*, 14 April 1888).

24 *News*, 20 June 1885, cited in Beal and Macleod, *Prairie Fire*, 69; *Grip*, 17 Sept. 1886.

25 *Grip*, 17 Apr. 1886.

26 Thomas recalled that his brother was adept at various dialects: 'He could imitate the voice of a child in reciting Whitcomb Riley's "Little Orphan Annie," and the feeble old man in "Gettin' On, I Guess," but the pièce de résistance was his own production, "Winnipeg Station," in which he imitated the speeches of New Canadians' (MUA, John Wilson Bengough Papers, box 3, file 4, Thomas Bengough, 'Life and Work').

27 *Grip*, 1 Oct. 1887.

28 *Grip*, 28 May 1887.

29 *Grip*, 16 July 1892. The poem was bylined L. St Leger McGinn.

30 *Grip*, 27 Dec. 1873, 13 Mar. 1875, and 2 Dec. 1882.

31 *Grip*, 22 Dec. 1883.

32 See also *Grip*, 17 Mar. 1888.

33 '*Goods* Prohibited but *Evils* Admitted' (*Grip*, 26 Apr. 1879), 'The Real Chinese Giant' (*Grip*, 12 Sept. 1885).

34 Toronto *News*, 15 May 1882 and 17 Oct. 1885.

35 *Grip*, 19 May 1888.

36 *News*, 15 Aug. 1884.

37 *Grip*, 22 Apr. 1893. For a more blatant instance of anti-Semitism, see the cartoon 'A Keen Eye for a Bargain' by Sam Jones (3 Dec. 1892).

38 *Grip*, 18 Sept. 1875.

39 'The Gauntlet' (*Grip*, 2 May 1874); *Grip*, 29 July 1876. See also the poem of 13 May 1876 condemning abolitionists who 'raise the quavering cry, / That the slayer shall not be slain.'

40 *Grip*, 5 Aug. and 25 Nov. 1876. In this instance, *Grip* intervened on the *Globe*'s side in an intraparty dispute between the paper and Blake. See Thomson, *Alexander Mackenzie*, 275.

41 *Grip*, 8 Dec. 1877, 3 and 10 Mar. 1888.

42 *Grip*, 15 Aug. 1874.

43 *Grip*, 3 Nov. 1877.

44 *Grip,* 3 Feb. and 18 Aug. 1877.

45 See also 'King Landlordism' (*Grip,* 28 Dec. 1889).

46 For a good discussion of the American populist movement, see McMath, *American Populism.*

47 *Globe,* 23 Oct. 1886; *Grip,* 13 Nov. 1886.

48 For a discussion of this pattern, see Watt, 'The National Policy.'

49 *Grip,* 17 July 1886. For an early example of *Grip*'s prohibition cartoons, see 'The Curse of Canada' (8 Feb. 1874).

50 *Grip,* 13 Mar. 1886, 9 July 1892, and 21 Feb. 1891.

51 *Grip,* 29 May 1885, cited in Kutcher, 'J.W. Bengough and the Millennium in Hogtown,' 48; *Grip,* 21 Feb. 1885. See also *Grip,* 2 Aug. 1885, which describes Toronto Bay as a cholera puddle.

52 'The Chase after Chance' (*Grip,* 17 Feb. 1883).

53 *Grip,* 9 July 1892, 27 Mar. 1875, and 3 Apr. 1886.

54 MUA, John Wilson Bengough Papers, box. 2.

11: Conclusion: 'A Lesser Craft'

1 Desbarats and Mosher, *The Hecklers,* 31.

2 See, for instance, 'Stop this Grovelling!' and 'Laurier's Statesmanlike Attitude on the Prohibition Question,' undated *Toronto Star* cartoons (MUA, John Wilson Bengough Papers, box 8, file 7).

3 Preface to Bengough, *A Caricature History of Canadian Politics,* vol. 1.

4 *Saturday Night,* 2 Aug. 1890. The writer was given only as 'T,' which suggests that he was neither the editor, E.E. Sheppard (Don), nor his associate Joseph T. Clark (Mack).

5 *Saturday Night,* 20 Jan. 1894.

6 MUA, John Wilson Bengough Papers, box 3, file 4, Thomas Bengough, 'Life and Work,' 24.

7 Bengough, 'Recollections of a Cartoonist,' 253.

8 A considerable number of the *Public* sketches are included in the John Wilson Bengough Papers at McMaster University Archives. For his image of Theodore Roosevelt and his views on race relations, for instance, see 'A Noble Motive,' box 6, file 7.

9 NA, Laurier Papers, 3808–11, John Bengough to Laurier, 23 July 1895, and 4568–70, Bengough to Laurier, 27 June 1896.

10 *A Standard Dictionary of Canadian Biography,* 45–6, says the offer was made by 'the Prohibitionists.'

11 Bengough's cartoons ran regularly in the *Globe* from 1895 to early 1899, reappearing thereafter in election campaigns.

12 *Mail and Empire*, 13 and 14 May 1897. For more on Bengough's part in this movement, see Armstrong and Nelles, *The Revenge of the Methodist Bicycle Company*, 116–17, 163.

13 Kutcher, 'John Wilson Bengough, Artist of Righteousness,' 121–5. See also Kutcher, 'J.W. Bengough and the Millennium in Hogtown,' 30–49.

14 Keys, 'Bengough and Carlyle,' 54. The edition was later described as 'one of the Routledge edition, London, 1888' (ibid., 56).

15 These columns appeared, for instance, in *The Farmers Advocate* between Nov. 1902 and Aug. 1904. They also showed up at various times in the Toronto *Globe*, *Saturday Night*, the *Pioneer* (organ of the Prohibitory Alliance for the Suppression of the Liquor Traffic), and the *Canadian American* of Chicago. See *Globe* columns of July–Sept. 1908, from 'The Old Kentry,' and May–Sept. 1909, from Australia. Both Thompson and Bengough may have modelled the columns on the work of David R. Locke, who under the pseudonym Petroleum V. Nasby wrote this kind of material in Ohio newspapers (Paine, *Th. Nast: His Period and His Pictures*, 114).

16 NA, Laurier Papers, 185760–2, Bengough to Laurier, 4 May 1911, and Laurier to Bengough 8 May 1911. One of the ironies of this letter is that Nast had received his consular appointment to Ecuador only in dire necessity – and would soon die there of yellow fever. Like Bengough, he had watched his magazine fail and had sought political favour.

17 *Grip*, 21 Feb. 1880 (regarding the Senate appointment of John Boyd).

18 MUA, John Wilson Bengough Papers, box 3, file 1. The poem is entitled 'Apologia of an Old Liberal.' It begins:

> A've lo'ed Sir Wilfrid mony a year,
> An' gloried in his graun' career,
> But when tae me it's unco clear
> That he's astray
> Believin' troops wull volunteer,
> What wull A' dae?

19 NA, King Papers, 37399/J1/V43, Bengough to King, 21 March 1919. The rough sketches are labelled 'As It Is ... As It Ought to Be.'

20 NA, King Papers, 37404–6, Bengough to King, 4 Sept. 1919, and King to Bengough, 9 Sept. 1919. The poem recalled King's descent from the rebel of 1837, William Lyon Mackenzie:

THE SPIRIT OF WILLIAM LYON MACKENZIE TO HIS GRANDSON

'In helping to shape the destiny of the Liberal party in this country I cannot forget the part that my grandfather played.'   W.L. Mackenzie King at Ottawa

Wullie ma laddie, ye'll na' doot
Ma speerit's hoverin' aboot
To speak congratulations oot
An' greetin's bring
On yon immense convention vote.
Fit for a King!

Nae higher honor could there be
Than to be chosen, fair an' free,
To lead yon graun' democracy,
   The Leeberal Party;
Ma blessin's on ye'r head the day,
   An' wishes hearty! ...

An' ye'll in time see Preevilege slain
   As sure as heaven.

21 Bengough, 'Recollections of a Cartoonist,' 183.
22 Atherton notes that from 1900 to 1911 he served as a correspondent for the *Labour Gazette*, published by the federal labour department, and that on at least one occasion his work was praised by Mackenzie King, who was then deputy minister (Atherton's introduction to Thompson, *The Politics of Labor*, xiv).
23 Ibid., xiv, xv.
24 Morgan, *Canadian Men and Women of the Time*, 90–1.
25 Withrow, 'An Artist of Righteousness,' 204–16.
26 *Globe*, 3 Oct. 1923.
27 MUA, John Wilson Bengough Papers, box 3, file 4, Thomas Bengough, 'Life and Work,' 24.
28 Keys, 'Bengough and Carlyle,' 49–73.
29 Hamilton *Herald*, 3 Oct. 1923.
30 Bengough, *The Up-to-Date Primer*, introduction to 1975 facsimile edition, i.
31 *Saturday Night*, 13 Oct. 1923.
32 Desbarats and Mosher, *The Hecklers*, 61.

A Note on Sources

This study is based mainly on the examination of *Grip* magazine itself over its two decades of operation. A second major level of research lay in *Grip*'s Toronto contemporaries, especially the *Mail*, the *Globe*, the *News*, and the *Nation*.

Some archival resources have also provided limited help, especially the John Wilson Bengough Papers at McMaster University, which include notes and memoranda by Bengough's brother Thomas. The papers of Sir Aemilius Irving at the Archives of Ontario were consulted for extensive though not especially helpful material on *Grip*'s dispute with the Ontario government over printing matters. The papers of Sir Alexander Campbell at the same archives yielded limited information on *Grip*'s short-lived rival, the *Mirror*. The small collections of T. Phillips Thompson's papers at the National Archives of Canada and the Archives of Ontario were not of use concerning *Grip*. Material on the Bengough family was obtained from genealogist Larry Driffield of Toronto and from Bengough family memorabilia at the Whitby, Ontario, archives. Some correspondence regarding Bengough and *Grip* was obtained at the National Archives from the papers of Prime Ministers Macdonald, Laurier, and King.

Secondary sources of particular value include Ramsay Cook's chapters on Bengough and Thompson in *The Regenerators*; Jay Atherton's introduction to Thompson's *Politics of Labor*, and Russell Hann's article on Thompson's role at the Toronto *News*. Also of value were the theses on Bengough by Dennis Edward Blake, Stanley Paul Kutcher, and Dugald E. Stewart. The comparative study of Canadian cartooning by Peter Desbarats and Terry Mosher was useful in putting Bengough's work in context. Bengough's own memoirs, printed in *Westminster* magazine and repeated in his book *Bengough's Chalk Talks* were an important source, although the author clearly avoided dealing with most of the major controversies of his career.

Bibliography

ARCHIVAL SOURCES

ARCHIVES OF ONTARIO
Sir Alexander Campbell Papers
Sir Aemilius Irving Papers
T. Phillips Thompson Papers

MCMASTER UNIVERSITY ARCHIVES
John Wilson Bengough Papers

NATIONAL ARCHIVES OF CANADA
William Lyon Mackenzie King Papers, MG24, B18
Sir Wilfrid Laurier Papers, MG26, G
Sir John Alexander Macdonald Papers, MG26, A
Sir John Sparrow David Thompson Papers, MG26, D
T. Phillips Thompson Papers, MG29, D71

WHITBY TOWN ARCHIVES
John Wilson Bengough memorabilia.

OTHER SOURCES

Armstrong, Christopher, and H.V. Nelles. *The Revenge of the Methodist Bicycle Company: Sunday Street Cars and Municipal Reform in Toronto, 1888–1897*. Toronto: Peter Martin Associates, 1977
Baker, William. *Timothy Warren Anglin*. Toronto: University of Toronto Press, 1977

Batten, Jack. 'Penciling the Purveyors of Power.' *Review* (Toronto: Imperial Oil Ltd.), 68, no. 4 (1984)

Beal, Bob, and Rod Macleod. *Prairie Fire: The 1885 North-West Rebellion.* Edmonton: Hurtig, 1984

Becker, Stephen. *Comic Art in America.* New York: Simon and Schuster, 1959

Bengough, John Wilson. *Bengough's Chalk Talks.* Toronto: Musson Book Company, 1922

– *A Caricature History of Canadian Politics.* 2 vols. Toronto: Grip Publishing Company, 1886

– *Cartoons of the Campaign.* Toronto: Poole Publishing Company, 1900

– *In Many Keys: A Book of Verse.* Toronto: William Briggs, 1902

– *Motley: Verses Grave and Gay.* Toronto: William Briggs, 1895

– 'Recollections of a Cartoonist.' *Westminster* 14, no. 2 (Feb. 1909), 73–9; (Mar. 1909), 183–9; (Apr. 1909), 249–55

– *The Up-to-Date Primer.* London: Funk and Wagnalls, 1895. Facsimile reprint, Toronto: Peter Martin, 1975

Berger, Carl. *The Sense of Power.* Toronto: University of Toronto Press, 1970

Berton, Pierre. *Starting Out: The Days of My Youth.* Toronto: McClelland Stewart, 1987

Blackburn Harte, Walter. 'Canadian Journalists and Journalism.' *New England Magazine* 5 (Dec. 1891), 411–41

Blake, Dennis Edward. 'J.W. Bengough and *Grip:* The Canadian Editorial Cartoon Comes of Age.' MA thesis, Sir Wilfrid Laurier University, 1985

Briggs, Jimuel [T. Phillips Thompson]. *The Political Experiences of Jimuel Briggs, DB.* Toronto: Flint, Morton, 1873

Briggs, Susan, and Asa Briggs, eds. *Cap and Bell: Punch's Chronicle of History in the Making, 1841–1861.* London: Macdonald, 1972

Brown, Craig, ed. *The Illustrated History of Canada.* Toronto: Lester & Orpen Dennys, 1987

Brown, R.C. *Canada's National Policy 1883–1900.* Princeton, NJ: Princeton University Press, 1964

Careless, J.M.S. *Brown of the Globe.* 2 vols. Toronto: Macmillan, 1959

Cartoons from Punch. Vol. 3. London: Bradbury & Agnew, 1906

Cavell, Edward. *Sometimes a Great Nation.* Banff, Alta: Altitude Publishing, 1984

Charlesworth, Hector. *Candid Chronicles.* Toronto: Macmillan, 1925

– 'J.W. Bengough, Pioneer Cartoonist.' *Saturday Night,* 13 Oct. 1923

– *More Candid Chronicles.* Toronto: Macmillan, 1928

Cleaver, Solomon. *Life's Great Adventure – Prayer.* Toronto: Ryerson, 1931

Colgate, William. *Canadian Art: Its Origin and Development.* Toronto: Ryerson, 1943

Cook, Ramsay. 'The Professor and the Prophet of Unrest.' *Transactions of the Royal Society of Canada* (1975), 227–50
– *The Regenerators: Social Criticism in Late Victorian Canada*. Toronto: University of Toronto Press, 1985
Cooper, Frederick Taylor, and Arthur Bartlett Maurice. *The History of the Nineteenth Century in Caricature*. New York: Dodd Mead, 1904. Reprint, Detroit: Tower Books, 1971
Creighton, Donald. *John A. Macdonald, The Old Chieftain*. Toronto: Macmillan, 1955
Cumming, Carman. *Secret Craft: The Journalism of Edward Farrer*. Toronto: University of Toronto Press, 1992
Curtis, L. Percy, Jr. *Apes and Angels: The Irishman in Victorian Caricature*. Washington, DC: Smithsonian Institution Press, 1954
Denison, George Taylor. *The Struggle for Imperial Unity*. London, Toronto, New York: Macmillan, 1909
Desbarats, Peter, and Terry Mosher. *The Hecklers: A History of Political Cartooning and a Cartoonist's History of Canada*. Toronto: McClelland & Stewart / National Film Board of Canada, 1979
Evans, A. Margaret. *Sir Oliver Mowat*. Toronto: University of Toronto Press, 1992
Farrer, Edward. 'Canada and the New Imperialism.' *Contemporary Review* 84, pt. 2 (Dec. 1903), 761–74
Feaver, William. *Masters of Caricature*, ed. Ann Gould. New York: Knopf, 1981
Geipel, John. *The Cartoon: A Short History of Graphic Comedy and Satire*. New York: A.S. Barnes, 1973
George, M. Dorothy. *English Political Caricature*. Vol. 2. Oxford University Press, 1959
Hall, Roger, et al. *The World of William Notman*. Toronto: McClelland & Stewart, 1993
Hann, Russell. 'Brainworkers and the Knights of Labor: E.E. Sheppard, Phillips Thompson and the Toronto News, 1883–1887.' In *Essays in Canadian Working Class History*, ed. Gregory S. Kealey and Peter Warrian. Toronto: McClelland & Stewart, 1976
Hess, Stephen, and Milton Kaplan. *The Ungentlemanly Art: A History of American Political Cartoons*. New York: Macmillan, 1968
Kealey, Gregory S., and Bryan D. Palmer. *Dreaming of What Might Be: the Knights of Labor in Ontario, 1880–1900*. Toronto: New Hogtown Press, 1987
Kealey, Gregory S., and Peter Warrian, eds. *Essays in Canadian Working-Class History*. Toronto: McClelland & Stewart, 1976
Keller, Morton. *The Art and Politics of Thomas Nast*. New York: Oxford University Press, 1968

Kesterton, W.H. *A History of Journalism in Canada.* Toronto: McClelland & Stewart, 1967

Keys, D.R. 'Bengough and Carlyle.' *University of Toronto Quarterly* 2, no. 1 (Oct. 1932)

Kutcher, Stanley Paul. 'John Wilson Bengough, Artist of Righteousness.' MA thesis, McMaster University, 1975

– 'J.W. Bengough and the Millennium in Hogtown: A Study of Motivation in Urban Reform.' *Urban History Review* 2 (1976), 30–49

McLachlan, Alexander. *The Immigrant,* ed. D.M.R. Bentley. London, Ont.: Canadian Poetry Press, 1991

McMath, Robert C., Jr. *American Populism: A Social History 1877–1898.* New York: Hill and Wang, 1993

Masters, D.C. *The Rise of Toronto 1850–1890.* Toronto: University of Toronto Press, 1947

Maurice, Arthur Bartlett, and Frederic Taber Cooper. *The History of the Nineteenth Century in Caricature.* New York: Cooper Square Publishers, 1970

Miller, J.R. *Equal Rights: The Jesuits' Estates Controversy.* Montreal: McGill-Queen's University Press, 1979

Morgan, Henry James. *The Canadian Men and Women of the Time.* 2nd ed. Toronto: William Briggs, 1912

Morris, Raymond N. *Behind the Jester's Mask: Canadian Editorial Cartoons about Dominant and Minority Groups 1960–79.* Toronto: University of Toronto Press, 1989

Morton, Desmond. *Mayor Howland: The Citizen's Candidate.* Toronto: Hakkert, 1973

Murison, Barbara. 'Scottish Emigration and Political Attitudes: Old Wine in New Bottles.' In *Boswell's Children: The Art of the Biographer,* ed. R.B. Fleming. Toronto and Oxford: Dundurn Press, 1992

Nevins, Allan, and Frank Weitenkampf. *A Century of Political Cartoons: Caricature in the United States from 1800 to 1900.* New York: Scribner's, 1944

Paine, Albert Bigelow. *Th. Nast: His Period and His Pictures.* New York: Macmillan, 1904

Parton, James. *Caricature and Other Comic Art.* 1878. Rev. ed., New York: Harper & Row, 1969

Press, Charles. *The Political Cartoon.* East Brunswick, NJ: Associated University Presses, 1981

Price, R.G.G. *A History of Punch.* London: Collins, 1957

Rutherford, Paul. *The Making of the Canadian Media.* Toronto: McGraw-Hill Ryerson, 1978

– *A Victorian Authority: The Daily Press in Late Nineteenth-Century Canada.* Toronto: University of Toronto Press, 1982

St Hill, Thomas Nast. *Thomas Nast: Cartoons and Illustrations.* New York: Dover Publications, 1974

Schull, Joseph. *Edward Blake.* 2 vols. Toronto: Macmillan, 1975, 1976

– *Laurier.* Toronto: Macmillan, 1966

Shikes, Ralph E. *The Indignant Eye.* Boston: Beacon Press, 1969

Spencer, David Ralph. 'The Alternative Vision: A History of Educational Ideas in Canada's Working Class Press, 1870–1910.' PhD thesis, University of Toronto, 1990

Stewart, Dugald E. 'Political Cartoons in the Canadas and Then Ontario 1849–1889.' MA thesis, University of Toronto, 1977

Sutherland, Fraser. *The Monthly Epic: A History of Canadian Magazines 1789–1989.* Markham, Ont.: Fitzhenry & Whiteside, 1989

Swainson, Donald, ed. *Oliver Mowat's Ontario.* Toronto: Macmillan, 1972

Thompson, T. Phillips. *The Politics of Labor.* New York 1887. Rev. ed., with introduction by Jay Atherton, Toronto: University of Toronto Press, 1975

Thomson, Dale C. *Alexander Mackenzie, Clear Grit.* Toronto: Macmillan, 1960

Underhill, Frank. *The Image of Confederation* (Massey Lectures, 1963). CBC Publications, 1964

Verzuh, Ron. *Radical Rag: The Pioneering Labour Press in Canada.* Ottawa: Steel Rail Publishing, 1988

Vinson, J. Chalmers. *Thomas Nast, Political Cartoonist.* Athens: University of Georgia Press, 1967

Waite, P.B. *Canada 1874–1896: Arduous Destiny.* Toronto: McClelland & Stewart, 1971

– *Macdonald: His Life and World.* Toronto: McGraw-Hill Ryerson, 1975

– *The Man from Halifax: Sir John Thompson, Prime Minister.* Toronto: University of Toronto Press, 1985

– 'Reflections on an Un-Victorian Society' and 'Sir Oliver Mowat's Canada.' In *Oliver Mowat's Ontario,* ed. Donald Swainson. Toronto: Macmillan, 1972

Walkom, Thomas L. 'The Daily Newspaper Industry in Ontario's Developing Capitalist Economy: Toronto and Ottawa, 1871–1891.' PhD thesis, University of Toronto, 1983

Wallace, Elisabeth. *Goldwin Smith: Victorian Liberal.* Toronto: University of Toronto Press, 1957

Wallace, W.S. 'Journalists in Canadian Politics.' *The Canadian Historical Review,* Mar. 1941, 14–24

Watt, F.W. 'The Growth of Proletarian Literature in Canada, 1872–1920.' In

Twentieth Century Essays in Canadian Literature, ed. F. Lorraine McMullen.
Ottawa: Tecumseh Press, 1976
– 'The National Policy, the Workingman, and Proletarian Ideas in Victorian
Canada.' *Canadian Historical Review* 40 (1959), 1–26
Werthman, William C. *Canada in Cartoon.* Fredericton: Brunswick Press, 1967
Willison, Sir John. *Reminiscences Political and Personal.*Toronto: McClelland & Stewart, 1919
Withrow, W.H. 'An Artist of Righteousness.' *Methodist Magazine and Review*, Sept.
1897
Woodcock, George. *Faces from History.* Edmonton: Hurtig, 1978
Wynn Jones, Michael. *The Cartoon History of Britain.* New York: Macmillan, 1971

Index